Television Cities

A production of the Console-ing Passions book series
Edited by Lynn Spigel

Television Cities

Paris, London, Baltimore

CHARLOTTE BRUNSDON

DUKE UNIVERSITY PRESS *Durham and London* 2018

© 2018 Duke University Press

All rights reserved

The moral right of the author has been asserted

Printed in the United States of America

on acid-free paper ∞

Designed by Amy Ruth Buchanan

Typeset in Warnock Pro

by Westchester Publishing Services

Cataloging-in-Publication Data is available

from the Library of Congress.

ISBN 978-0-8223-6894-6 (hardcover : alk. paper)

ISBN 978-0-8223-6920-2 (pbk. : alk. paper)

ISBN 978-0-8223-7251-6 (ebook)

Cover art: Rupert Davies as Maigret. Moviestore
Collection Ltd/Alamy.

Contents

Acknowledgments

The BBC Written Archives Centre at Caversham is a wonderful place to research television, and I am grateful to archivist Jess Hogg for her assistance with the *Maigret* files, and to Hannah Ratford for her help with gaining permission to quote from these files. Acknowledgment is hereby made to the BBC for this permission. Kathleen Dixon and Steve Tollervey at the British Film Institute were, as usual, helpful far beyond the call of duty in enabling me to watch episodes of the BBC *Maigret* in a full range of sometimes fragmentary formats. I hope that one day these episodes will be available to a wider public. Ginette Vincendeau lent DVDs from her extensive *Maigret* collection and advised on various aspects of French culture. She also, with Irene Bessière, Laurent Creton, and Alastair Phillips, invited me to contribute to the 2012 conference, Paris au cinéma: Au delà du flâneur, at Paris 3. Aspects of this work have been presented in a range of other contexts, and I am grateful to all who have invited me, and for the subsequent discussions, particularly Michael Curtin and Dick Hebdige at the University of California, Santa Barbara; Ellen Seiter at the University of Southern California; Lynn Spigel at Northwestern; and François Penz and Richard Koeck at the Cinematic Urban Geographies conference, Cambridge, 2013.

I met Deborah Rowan when she was crewing a water taxi in Baltimore; she has been a faithful informant about changes to the city's waterfront, and I've loved getting her photographs. I also learned much from the students who took my graduate course "Modernity and Innovation in the Audio-Visual Media" on the MA in film and television studies at the University of Warwick, 2009–11, and from my colleague

Michael Pigott, who helped with *The Wire* installations. Nic Pillai has shared many *Maigret* enthusiasms, and Richard Perkins, film and TV librarian at the University of Warwick, has once again offered invaluable assistance characteristically inconspicuously. I have been helped in research and manuscript preparation by Patrick Pilkington, Paul Cuff, and James Taylor, and in many different ways by the administrative team in the Department of Film and Television Studies at Warwick, led by Tracey McVey: Anne Birchall, Adam Gallimore, and Lynsey Willmore. The Midlands Television Research Group has continued to help me make sense of television in transition, while the Projection Project team has been understanding when I have had to concentrate on the newer medium. I'm also very grateful for contributions of different kinds from Karen Alexander, Jon Burrows, Daniel Callaghan, Christine Geraghty, Ann Gray, Jostein Gripsrud, David Morley, Rachel Moseley, Alastair Phillips, Karl Schoonover, Bill Schwarz, Ellen Seiter, Stephen Shapiro, Lynn Spigel, Rick Wallace, Helen Wheatley, and James Zborowski. Ken Wissoker, Elizabeth Ault, and Liz Smith have been a great team to work with at Duke: patient, supportive, and attentive to detail.

The in-house reading service has maintained its excellent record, and this time also contributed quite a bit of viewing company down some very dark streets. The book would not have been completed without this support—and distraction.

Thanks to all: and the errors are all mine.

Introduction

Peckham, in southeast London, was the setting for the popular twentieth-century British television sitcom *Only Fools and Horses* (BBC, 1981–91).[1] The action was mainly studio filmed using a domestic and a public interior: the Trotter family's council flat and their local pub. These television rooms, reappearing weekly on the TV screens in the audience's homes, became very familiar to British, and then worldwide audiences.[2] Peckham, through the Trotter family, was established as a recognized location within London as a television city. The exterior location shots of the Trotter's high-rise home were actually filmed in Bristol, more than a hundred miles to the west of London, while the title sequence used stills of a London street market to establish a milieu in which "only fools and horses work." This mélange of elements—studio-shot interiors, limited location-shot exteriors, and place-identifying title sequence— are the characteristic components of the twentieth-century television city. Although the glamorous heroines of *Sex and the City* (HBO, 1998–2004) seem so very different to the Trotter family, and the show used location shooting in Manhattan for its title sequence, exterior, and some interior scenes, this television city too was created out of a mixture of similar elements—as was the now-unmentionable *Cosby Show* (1984–92).[3] The precise articulation of these constituent elements— location, studio, and title sequences—in the creation of television cities to which audiences return week after week, becoming familiar with places they have never visited, is one of the topics of this book.

In the early twenty-first century, in which "television" seems increasingly to connote a type of content (not films, not YouTube videos) that can be watched on a range of screens, rather than a particular domestic apparatus on which programs might be viewed, this book inquires into the relationship between television and the city. It is concerned with locations produced by television, at a point at which, as Graeme Turner has argued, it is more important than ever to specify actual location when speaking of television at a general level.[4] The traveler in the contemporary city can be surrounded by people intently watching television drama on phone screens, perhaps interspersing narrative fiction with quick bursts of e-mail or Twitter. Television is in the city—outside, in the streets, in people's hands—in ways it has never been before, just as the city itself is increasingly populated by giant screens, reflecting citizens back to themselves or bringing news from afar.[5] This twenty-first-century mobile television, slipped into a handbag or a back pocket on a phone, is an undocumented mixture of old and new. If you peer over someone's shoulder at what they are watching, it seems as often to be old familiar programs as new serial drama.[6] New technologies have made past television available just as they have transformed production practices for contemporary television. This book explores the prehistory of this mobile moment, this glut of content. It seeks to intervene in developed debates and histories of cinematic and media cities by asking whether there is more to be said about the television city as a place and dramatic location, rather than simply noting the dispersal of television across multiple screens and hence the current ubiquity of television in the city.

In this inquiry, my concern throughout is to attend to both the specificity of particular television cities, including Maigret's Paris in the 1960s, the London of *Call the Midwife* in the twenty-first century, and the Baltimore of *Homicide*, and to untangle some more general threads that might characterize the television city across different contexts. Are there particular ways in which television presents, and has presented, the city to viewers? How does the familiarity of television affect our understanding of the cities we find there? How have ideas about the medium of television affected attitudes to the cities shown thereon? How do television cities relate to cinematic and literary cities?

This book combines analysis of the cities produced in a variety of television programs with attention to the changing historical forms of television as a medium. Its core case studies are selected from different historical periods to permit consideration not only of changing production regimes and modes of distribution, but also of the changing nature of the television text as an object of study. The television city on the TV set in the twentieth-century living room is contrasted with the portable TV city of the twenty-first-century DVD box set as it in turn gives way to a contemporary multiscreen environment. This is a book about television versions of Paris, London, and Baltimore. It is a book about BBC cities and HBO cities; about studio-shot cities, location-shot cities, and cities shot in other cities. But it is also a book about changing attitudes to television and the different ways in which television contributes to senses of the urban.

The Place of Television 1: Television, Cinema, and Modernity

The place of television seemed fairly obvious in the second half of the twentieth century, certainly within the U.K.-U.S. axis that generated much of the serious study of television. Television sets were in the home, where they were watched by families.[7] On these sets, in the period of nationally regulated terrestrial television—roughly the 1950s to the 1990s—could be found a world of other places. Hospital wards, living rooms, panel game studios, the American Wild West, football stadia, the galaxy, variety halls, the exotic habitats of wildlife, and the live wherever of breaking news. Television sets began in the living room, and then started spreading over the rest of the house so that children—and their parents—could watch in their bedrooms and opt out of shared national familial scheduling, particularly when videotape made time-shifted viewing possible for the first time. Early scholarly attention to television considered the manner in which it brought the outside into the home. The hybrid classical etymology of the medium's name (from the ancient Greek *tèle*, far, and Latin *visio*, sight) was invoked as paradigmatic of one of its functions, and it was much referenced in discussions of privatization and the retreat into the home from public space. Along with the refrigerator and the automobile, television was one of the holy trinity emblematic of twentieth-century domestic modernity.[8] And this modernity, particularly in the United States, was characterized as a dispersed suburban modernity.[9] With this characterization of the place of television came an image of its audience as predominantly female. The television viewer was sitting at home in her living room, watching the world go by and credulous about the promises made by those who appeared on the screen.

This characterization of television and its role in domestic, suburban modernity contrasts strongly with the way in which cinema has been envisaged. Cinema is the medium of the city. Cinema has been seen both to express and to be symptomatic of city life. In cinema, one can sit anonymously in a crowd, participating in a cultural form that, through its editing process, its visual shocks, its disparities of scale, and its uncontrollable pace, has been seen to embody the experience of city life. Cinema–modernity–the city has been an enormously productive trilogy in the investigation of the first half of the twentieth century, and many scholars of both modernity and the city have turned to cinema as the art form of the new century and developing urban conurbations.[10] And within this scholarship, so much of which is indebted to the meditations on Paris of Charles Baudelaire and Walter Benjamin, the figure of the flâneur is pivotal. The flâneur, detached and observant, aristocratic and bohemian in origin, haunts scholarship on the city, providing an ideal image for many fascinated by the anonymous crowd, the bright lights, and the dark alleys of the modern metropolis.[11] His relationship to the city, both perfectly at ease but not compelled by its rhythms of labor and travel, able to pause and consider the urban spectacle around him, embodies a leisured and contemplative, but nonetheless modern, lifestyle. The flâneur is glamorous in what has been seen as a modern urban manner, and has inspired psychogeographers, situationists, poets, painters, and scholars. His attractions can be detected in cinema ranging from film noir to work as various as Wim Wenders's drama of angels come to earth, *Himmel über Berlin* (*Wings of Desire*, 1987), and Patrick Keiller's celebrated city essay film, *London* (1994). The flâneur's mobility and his loitering, his very presence in the street, assumes the privilege of masculinity—and particular types of masculinity at that.

The elision of women from this imagination of the city, except most notably as prostitutes, has been challenged in debates about the invisible flâneuse, while films such as Agnes Varda's *Cléo de 5 à 7* (1962) and Susan Seidelman's *Desperately Seeking Susan* (1985) can be seen as serious attempts to render female characters as autonomously mobile within the city.[12] Scholars such as Rachel Bowlby and Anne Friedberg have demonstrated the significance of the nineteenth-century birth of the department store in legitimating the presence of women on city streets, and there is consequently now a greater self-consciousness about the romantic masculinity and privilege of the figure of the flâneur.[13] In terms of television, these debates were suddenly animated at the end of the century with the enormous success of *Sex and the City*, which followed four single white women friends in Manhattan as they pursued and discussed available feminine destinies of romance, sex, marriage, career, and maternity.[14] The title sequence of the show, in particular, has been read convincingly as enacting the constraints on the flâneuse, as the central heroine, Carrie Bradshaw (Sarah Jessica Parker) is shown as both in love with Manhattan (in an alternating montage of New York landmarks and her blissed-out face), and impeded by it (when her stroll is halted by the gutter water splashed on her dress by a bus that has an advertising image of her own face emblazoned on it). Deborah Jermyn notes that "the implication that flânerie continues to pose a 'problem' for women is still present in SATC, embedded from the start in the opening credits. In the ambiguous moment where Carrie is splashed by the bus, it seems as if she is humiliated by her own image, knocked back or belittled for having mistakenly thought that these streets were hers for the taking."[15] This knowing opening to the series inscribes its self-consciousness about the difficulty of the position of the woman in the city. While individual flâneuses may be discernible (if only for moments, before getting splashed by buses) in an increasing number of texts, the discursive construction and history of the figure of the flâneur remains masculine.

My concern is not so much with whether or not Carrie Bradshaw— or Stella Gibson, as I discuss below—is an embodied flâneuse, but with disturbing the relations between the patterns of assumption in which television and the city are produced as objects of study. For I want to bring together questions of television, with its attendant associations of the suburb, the armchair, the female viewer, and the city (modernity, cinema, the flâneur). These are distinct bodies of scholarship that are constructed almost against each other in a manner which impoverishes our understanding of each. While much of what follows is devoted to the analysis of particular television programs, one of my motivating concerns has been with television as a medium. My project seeks to consider the city as constituted by homes as well as streets, and its difficulty can be summarized in the question used as the title of this introduction, "Does the Flâneur Watch Television?"

This book proceeds from the argument that the paradigms of the cinematic city, which emphasize the relationships between the city, the cinema, and modernity, tend to ignore the banal, the mundane, the repetitious, and the complicated relation between home and the street.[16] As Matthew Taunton has observed, in a work that also challenges the dominance of the flâneur, "city dwellers are not usually freewheeling nomads lost in a maze of streets. They are often powerfully attached to certain locations."[17] It is on this terrain of domestic repetition and everyday life—with all its banality—that the televisual city is constructed, and its cultural invisibility has much to do with attitudes to television and the domestic sphere more generally. The television city, like the television set, was just there, in the corner. The emergency siren might indicate an urban setting, just as a filmed title sequence might locate the ensuing drama in a city. But the city, and the look and sounds of the city, were often subordinated, formally, to the studio-shot conversations between characters so important to much television drama. However, what if these unspectacular invocations of cities, and the stories set therein, become the topic of analysis? What can be learned? What histories can be found?

The Place of Television 2: In Transition

Within television studies, it is a commonplace of the field that the medium has low cultural status, and that is not an argument to rehearse here.[18] However, the place of television, and the study of television, has in the twenty-first century become rather more complicated. On the one hand, so long the cultural form against which cultural value has been asserted, television is now disregarded as old-fashioned, so twentieth century, and the domestic apparatus itself, as a habitual site of viewing, is being dislodged. On the other, the new television associated with the U.S. premium cable channels, and particularly the dramas of masculinity such as *The Sopranos* and *The Wire*, have been hailed as constituting a new golden age of "quality television."[19] These two attitudes were explicitly combined in the editorial of a 2014 special issue of *Cineaste* on television that declared, "For most of *Cineaste*'s existence . . . TV has been looked down upon as an inferior art form."[20] This sentence marks the first move in the reluctant recognition, for these cinephiles, that television too can host good writing, sophisticated plotting, and compelling drama. However, it is a very particular type of television—the not-television of subscription services such as HBO.[21] Even *Cineaste* will pay attention, and this new television is beginning to appear in accounts of the audiovisual city.

Studies of the Western cinematic city have developed a recognizable chronology and set of nodal points—which starts with the early twentieth-century city symphonies, and then moves through attention to, for example, film noir, the location shooting of the 1960s and 1970s, new black cinemas, essay films, and the cities of migration.[22] Alongside and sometimes imbricated with the cinematic city, as exemplified in Scott McQuire's *The Media City*, has developed a body of scholarship on mediated and media cities, its own nodal points including the rise of closed-circuit television (CCTV), the expansion of public screens, the networked citizen, and the digital home.[23] The city symphony is reinvented as a participatory city of bits. New digital technologies, and particularly the mapping possibilities afforded by GPS systems and the digital layering of historical maps, have been employed in a flourishing of new scholarship on the cinematic and the digital city. Patterns of cinema going can be mapped, long-vanished picture palaces inserted in redeveloped neighborhoods, intricate websites that link each of a film's locations to a city's architecture constructed.[24] Into these evolving genealogies of the audiovisual city, the cinematic television associated with U.S. prestige cable television, represented in this context most notably by shows like *The Wire* (2002–8) and *Treme* (2010–13), have been heralded as the creative front line for audiovisual work, bringing new, more complex, understandings of the city.[25] The disappearing element in these histories, as cable television becomes affectively assimilated to cinema, is twentieth-century network television.

This book seeks to challenge this chronology. The expansive serial cities of twenty-first-century television, which finally made cinema scholars such as the editors of *Cineaste* turn their reluctant attention to the small screen, did not spring fully formed to the screen. While their storytelling certainly owes something to the novel, their look something to cinema, television too has been formative. *The Wire* owes greater debts to *Hill Street Blues* (1981–87) than to Dickens. *Cagney and Lacey* (1982–88), as Horace Newcomb points out, provided exemplary instances of cumulative narratives, a form that he argues to be specific to television.[26] There has been a great deal of Dickens's London on British television, as I explore in chapter 2, much of it exported worldwide, while series such as *Holding On* (BBC, 1997) provide compelling witness to the ravages of the neoliberal city. The tendency toward the erasure of network television in the history of the audiovisual city has complex causes, some of which have been addressed in the skeptical eye with which some television scholars have regarded the new telephilia.[27] These are matters to which I return in the final chapter of the book, when I consider the Baltimore of *The Wire*, a program that I argue has both made the television city visible and sought to erase its history.[28]

Television may not have been culturally prestigious in the twentieth century, but that does not mean that it is without significance in the making and imagining of cities, particularly in the period of mass viewing on mainly national channels, which is roughly the 1950s to the 1980s. The importance of the imagined city to the felt, lived, and known city is uncontested if the imagined city is embodied in the writings of, say, Virginia Woolf or Honoré de Balzac, or in the films of Robert Siodmak or Jacques Rivette. However, the historically low cultural prestige of television works against recognition of its power in contributing to our understanding of cities, and this book seeks to rectify this by analyzing some of the cities that are brought into the living room through television. In doing this, the book will also challenge prevalent assumptions in the field such as the contrast between cinema as the medium of urban modernity and television as quintessentially suburban, as well as demonstrating the complexity of some of television's city stories.

Making Place on Television

Television has always been a hybrid medium, drawing on traditions from journalism, radio, cinema, music hall, theater, and the novel. This hybridity of origin and influence is matched in the mixture of spaces and places found on television. These were traditionally divided between studio space and the spaces of outside broadcast, with the latter bringing sporting, ceremonial, and news events into the viewer's home, often using the more expensive medium of film, while studio work was live or taped. In this book I am not concerned much with these spaces of news and reportage, concentrating instead on the fictional places of television, which are themselves often constructed through mixtures of studio and location filming. Here though, I want to draw attention to an often-neglected television space, the space of continuity announcements and channel idents, what could be called the home space of television channels, the place where television programs come from.[29]

In the twentieth century, this place would be identified with familiar faces, bringing news, weather forecasting, and program updates. With multichannel, digital programming, much of this has gone, apart from the main national channels, which still provide a sense of a "we" of CBS, or ITV, or France 3. And this television place is both internationally variable and internationally recognizable. The studio will have a decor with local and sometimes seasonal inflections. The announcers will provide the focus of the image within a relatively stripped-down (and cheap) studio, although there may well be the appearance of a window or a screen on a back wall, apparently locating the studio in a particular city, or providing access to film or video. The channel or program logo will either be incorporated into the studio design, or feature through onscreen graphics. This is a place not unrelated to the "non-places," such as airports and hypermarkets, described by Marc Augé.[30] It is generic and without specificity or particularity. And yet, at the same time,

I.1–I.3. The curious place of the television studio: different but the same. I.1: *Good Morning Britain* (breakfast show, ITV, UK; 27 August 2016). I.2: *CBS This Morning* (4 April 2016). I.3: *Channel 4 News* (UK; 4 September 2016).

it produces a rhetoric of location and belonging, a "we" who will be watching later, who will be affected by traffic jams and sudden downpours, who may later be celebrating, for example, the New Year. This location effect is most marked in relation to the local segments of programming, when weather and traffic news has real pertinence for the audience, but it is present in all national news with its assumptions of a national audience who are interested in the outcome of an election, or care about the number of their fellow nationals held at gunpoint in a hijack, or victorious in a sporting event, or increasingly using food banks. As Benedict Anderson pointed out in relation to the daily press, television is one of the sites on which nationhood and locality are made and remade, and one of the sites of this remaking is this apparently unimportant television place.[31] It is a nonplace that is engaged in constant place making.

Detectives and Cities: Selecting the Case Studies

This is a short book written with the aim of opening up discussion about television cities, and countering a widespread assumption that television did not contribute significant representations of cities before exceptional programs like *The Wire*. Its research focus is principally on television cities as they appear on the screen, and thus its project is quite different to Michael Curtin's pioneering work on what he calls, in a suggestive phrase, "media capitals."[32] My focus is textual, rather than industrial. I have had to be extremely selective in constructing the case studies, and have encouraged ruthlessness by telling myself that it will be productive if readers find themselves thinking of counterexamples and arguments. Each chapter takes a different city—Paris, London, and Baltimore—and draws on different types of material, and programs made in different periods and regimes of television production, in order to illuminate both something about that particular television city, and about the historical and critical analysis of television, itself a technology in transition.

Many of the programs discussed feature detectives or police, and the long connection between the detective and the city makes the police-detective genre my preferred choice for case studies for two reasons. First, television production is generic. Programs are initiated and produced as instances of recognizable types—as sitcoms or game shows or hospital dramas. One of the arts of television production is to innovate within, and increasingly across, genres, so that, for example, the structure of the investigation within an episodic format might remain the same, but the type of person doing the investigating changes. Genres have rules, and within their constant dance of repetition and renewal, these conventions are revealed and negotiated. The manner in which genres change, the ways in which their popularity waxes and wanes, can be identified as one of the sites on which the historicity of television production is inscribed. Changes within genres, and the differential prominence of different genres at different periods, can often be best understood in relation to wider sociohistorical factors. This is often, at the production end, experienced instinctively. Certain kinds of innovations, or castings, or attempted genre combinations prove difficult to countenance (at the production stage) or, in practice, often only on broadcast, prove not to "work." In British television, for example, until the second decade of the twenty-first century, it has proved impossible to sustain a police series with a black lead.[33] Idris Elba's success in *The Wire* made him castable as John Luther in *Luther* (2010–15), and Lennie James starred in the first season of *Line of Duty* (2012), although he is dead by the end, while Ashley Walters, after a series of drug and inner-city roles, finally made it over the line to play a sergeant in the Brighton-set *Cuffs* (2015).[34] Within the invisible rules of the police series—the genre most explicitly concerned with the enforcement of the law, and one that often aspires to realism with plot lines taken from contemporary news stories—black policemen, as leads, just weren't plausible on British television in the twentieth century. Instead, as I discuss in chapter 2, it was the sitcom (and the social documentary) in which the limited visibility of Caribbean migrants to Britain was first manifest.

The detective is recognized as a privileged investigator of the city, and there is long history to the relationship between the detective and the urban in literature, film, and television.[35] The man who walks alone (and it is usually a man), observing, noticing, and following up clues has proved an attractive guide to dark places of the city for readers and viewers over many years. Weighting my case studies toward the detective-police generic grouping enables me both to consider the conventions of a genre, and thus make comparisons across programs, while also attending to some of the possible historical reasons for changes within the genre. Analysis of detection and investigation on television also points to some of the aspects of storytelling that may be specific to the medium. What can be shown in an image, or conveyed through an off-screen sound, can contribute to a version of the city that may exceed the strict requirements of narrative progression. As I discuss particularly in chapter 1, filming in the city for contemporary television production—particularly for a genre that requires close attention to everyday surroundings—may inadvertently generate an archive for the future.

This has been notable in the Belfast-set five-part detective series *The Fall* (BBC, 2013), which was made in Northern Ireland, where the post-peace-process city, since securing the production of *Game of Thrones*, is busy reinventing itself as a media capital in Michael Curtin's sense. The long, contested history of the British imperial presence in Ireland and the associated military and political turbulence has meant that there is very little Northern Ireland–originated detective fiction. Dramas about murders, informants, and men with guns have had a more direct and overtly political provenance, and so *The Fall* was an interesting arrival, concerned as it was to bring Detective Superintendent Stella Gibson (Gillian Anderson) to Northern Ireland to investigate a series of sexual murders. The Belfast setting, manifest in location shooting in insignificant residential streets as well as the regenerated Titanic quarter and waterside, spoke of other narratives in its glimpses of territorial murals on house gable ends and the familiarity of all characters, apart from Gibson, with banal militarized procedures. A city shown to be both small—everyone knows everyone, or where they live—and sectarian keeps threatening to usurp the narrative, to take it away from the entertainment of sexual murder and return it to the continuing anxiety, hostility, and murderous horse-trading of peace-process Northern Ireland. In this context, the drama enacts the complicated relation between detection, femininity, and dark city streets with a splitting and doubling between the female detective and the male serial killer. The narrative innovation is that the killer's identity is known from the opening, and his character, Paul Spector (Jamie Dornan) is depicted across the roles of loving father, bereavement counselor, and sadistic murderer. As the killer, dressed in black, he is inconspicuous as he crosses the city with an urban mobility that extends from the streets to his silent penetration of his victims' homes. In contrast, his pursuer Gibson, while explicitly linked through match cuts or twinned shots, such as close-ups on each of their faces in cars, or the intercutting, in the second episode, between her having sex and his sexual murder rituals, has almost no autonomous mobility in the city streets. She is repeatedly filmed in cars being escorted through the city, arriving at crime scenes in high heels, or against the tableau of the city seen through her hotel windows. The much-commented-on cream silky blouses she wears serve throughout to accentuate her separateness from the city she is investigating, providing a focus for the image while her antagonist's indistinguishable dark clothing permits him to merge with the city.[36] However, within the circumscription of her actual movement, Gibson is shown to be both resourceful and decisive, as well as agent of her own desires. Being driven past a nighttime police operation, she instructs her police escort to introduce her to the officer in charge after he catches her eye and, when introduced, proceeds to tell him her hotel room number.[37] Gibson is also shown to be mobile across the city in a different way, roaming crime scene photographs on her computer, zooming in onto images of dead young women. The trope of the senior policewoman surrounded by images of murdered female victims has recurred in police series since the framing of Jane Tennison (Helen Mirren) in *Prime Suspect* (1991), serving to contextualize and admonish the exceptional woman, and here, too, although Gibson is demonstrably able to render these images legible in a manner that can forward the investigation and link together previously isolated killings, she is also linked to the victims. Their fate could become her fate.[38] So although empowered by status and profession, and evidently an exceptional detective, Gibson's mobility through the city is constrained, threatened, and mediated. It is with the killer, Paul Spector, that the city streets are explored. Stella Gibson, like Carrie Bradshaw, understands something of the city, but is not autonomous within it. Belfast, though, appears on the television screen in a way that is fresh for Belfast but generically familiar for the television city: as a place where women get murdered. This is a complicated benefit of the peace process.

The most successful television detectives and police shows have been series or serials.[39] The crime may vary, but the investigators stay the same, returning week after week to deal with chaos and reassure the viewer. There are different modes and balances to these returns and relationships: some programs have tight, forty- to fifty-minute episodes with crimes that are solved within the episode. Some borrow more from the continuous unfolding time of soap opera; some series have long story arcs that evolve over seasons as team relationships change and actors come and go. But it is the repetition and familiarity that is important in securing the location of the fictional world, and a key aspect of these narrative conventions that I explore below is the way in which the television city is a city of repetition. The city of the television crime series reappears in living rooms and on screens elsewhere, but its fearsomeness is mediated by the returning familiarity of its detectives and police. The television city of crime may be alarming, but—usually—its investigators will guide the viewer through the dark streets, returning the viewer safely home at the end of an episode. This is a city of a double repetition, returning to the screen as an enigma to be solved, and repeatedly supplying the onscreen expertise to do this.

The Nationalness of Television

In addition to matters of genre, the selection of case studies has also been determined by the peculiar relation of television to the nation. Television was an enormously significant constituent of, in Homi Bhabha's phrase, the "narration of nations" in the second half of the twentieth century.[40] John Ellis called television "the private life of the nation state," and as anyone who has moved countries will testify, there is something peculiarly impenetrable about the television of another nation. Television seems simultaneously the key to, and to epitomize the inaccessibility of, cultural life in the new country.[41] Television, developing from national radio broadcasting, has historically been more national than cinema, and has lacked the commodity form in which it can circulate internationally. While film cans are shipped internationally, the live broadcasts of television, particularly before the invention of videotape, were transmitted to the nation and then lost. Television is also a primarily domestic medium, and, from the 1950s on, many generations have grown up with television. This too imparts a peculiar nationalness to television in the form of shared television heritages that may not be discussed explicitly but can easily be referenced. In Britain, for example, the character of Del Trotter, from the 1980s London-set sitcom *Only Fools and Horses* (1981–91) with which I started this introduction, has long escaped from the confines of the television screen. Del Boy (David Jason) is the economically active member of an all-male household consisting of himself, his younger brother, and Grandad (later, his uncle). An entrepreneur of the everyday, Del Boy spends his life ducking and diving, trying to make the fantasy deal that would bring him riches, but his schemes always come to grief, often through a ridiculous oversight or fantastic misjudgment on his part. While the sitcom, which attracted huge audiences in its day, is long gone, the character of Del Boy has been incorporated into British cultural life to such an extent that economic commentary in the public sphere can refer, with ridicule, to a particular scheme exemplifying "Del Boy economics."[42] Which visitor to Britain will fully understand this reference, even if the tone and ridicule are clear? Similarly, I had never heard of *Leave It to Beaver* (1957–63) before I first went to the United States, but it soon became clear that this was significant shorthand for explaining something about U.S. family life in the 1950s and 1960s.

This nationalness of television has had, and continues to have, significant consequences for television scholarship, as Graeme Turner has been arguing for some time and as perhaps will be evident from the number of sentences I needed in the paragraph above to make the Del Boy point.[43] For the history and analysis of television cities, it leads to the privileging of native informants. I can write confidently about British television because I have watched it—off and on—for most of my life. But I am a tourist in relation to other national televisions, and much as I watch and study, I can never achieve that familiar inwardness with another national broadcasting system. I will never know what *Leave It to Beaver* meant, although I can get the idea. It is in this context that the most wide-ranging and generically diverse chapter of the book deals with television London, which is framed by chapters on Paris and Baltimore. Why this combination of cities?

Only Fools and Horses employs a famous prop that can helpfully illuminate the structure and balance of this book. This is Del's commercial vehicle, his yellow van, with Trotters Independent Trading Co. embla-

I.4–I.5. *Only Fools and Horses*: Del's Reliant Robin, "New York, Paris, Peckham."

zoned on its side. The vehicle, although it fills a van-shaped space in the narrative and identity of an independent businessman, as Del thinks of himself, is not actually a van. It is a Reliant Robin, a little, rather unstable three wheeler vehicle that was much cheaper to run as it was taxed at the rate of a motorcycle. In some ways more like a scooter, the much-ridiculed Reliant Robin was a vehicle for those who aspired to a car but couldn't in fact afford to run one. So the proud proclamation of Trotters Independent Trading (no apostrophe) on the side of the yellow Reliant Robin hints at a precariousness that rather undermines the claim. This is a characteristic *Fools and Horses* joke. It involves precise observation, sensitivity to aspiration, and an eye for the way in which overreaching can easily become preposterous. At the same time, it is

Does the Flâneur Watch Television?   17

not unkind. The absolute precision of the observation: knowing about the motor tax benefits of the three-wheeler, the use of the color yellow, the traces of previous encounters, and the rust on the bodywork— all of these ground Del's ambition and self-image. The coup de grâce, though, is the list of territories through which Trotters Independent Trading operates: "New York, Paris, Peckham."

The substitution of the local particularity of Peckham for what would be the expected, final global city in a list that would run "New York, Paris, London" is a move similar to the Reliant Robin joke. Del is shown again to understand the structure of his aspirations (businesses have vans; company slogans list territories in which the company operates), without quite seeing that the content which realizes these structures also has meaning. Peckham, while self-evidently the home of Trotters Independent Trading, is neither a rhetorical nor an actual equivalent to the internationally recognized cities of New York and Paris.[44] For those familiar with the cultural geography of London, Peckham, like neighboring Deptford, is one of the poorer southeastern London boroughs.[45] For those who don't know London, the point about Peckham is that it will be unfamiliar. Peckham, unlike Mayfair, or Knightsbridge, or—now—Notting Hill, is a local place, not part of the international residential geography of the wealthy. The slogan on Del's van juxtaposes international glamour with prosaic, local particularity.

While it might not be to my advantage to observe it, there is something of Del's van to this book. This is most immediately evident in my choice of cities: London, Paris, and Baltimore. Baltimore, like Peckham, comes limping in third: not a world city, not a global presence, although, unlike Peckham, it is actually a city, not just a borough. Furthermore, it is a city that too has become familiar to a much wider audience, and one of my interests lies in the way the local of Baltimore has been taken as metaphorical in a broader context.

However, the humor of the slogan on Del's van comes also from its absurd combination of ambition and absolute locatedness. Despite the gestures toward New York and Paris, it is Peckham that grounds the drama. And this is true of this book too. While the book does indeed discuss Paris and Baltimore, it does so from what could be called the point of view of British television, which, for reasons I discuss in my second chapter, is mainly the point of view of London. Like Del, I am based in a particular place, the place of British television, and from this starting point developed the project to investigate the television city. It is London on television, which I know to have been neglected in the enormous literature on London as a literary and, increasingly, as a cinematic city.[46] Also, London, because of the BBC, because of Charles Dickens, because of Sherlock Holmes, because of Britain's nineteenth-century imperial preeminence, has a very particular place in world television cities.[47] London is—iconographically—an old city. Paris, in contrast, the city of light, is the capital of modernity. Paris presents itself as a necessary case study because of its enormous significance in the literature of the cinematic city and modernity.[48] In chapter 1 on the French capital, by concentrating on Paris made mainly in London by the BBC, and only partly in Paris, I move immediately to some of the theoretical issues inherent in the consideration of audiovisual place. My interest here lies in considering a particular, mid-twentieth-century television city and demonstrating the significance of historical constraints and conventions of television production to the production and circulation of this city. This is matched, in chapter 3, by a discussion of Baltimore and its rapid ascent from a local to an internationally recognized television city. For the United States, many other possible case studies have presented themselves, and, certainly, the beauty of the archive of location shot New York in *Naked City*, along with its rich sitcom heritage, made New York particularly tempting, while the pioneering *Cagney and Lacey* (1982–88) marked out a city policed by women.[49] The Baltimore of HBO, however, is more precisely identifiable as marking a change in the mode of television production, distribution, and critical respect. The critical response to *The Wire*, while it is something with which I take issue, in some ways also made this book possible, and in this final chapter I deal more explicitly with the forms and modes of television criticism. New York, Los Angeles, Miami, and New Orleans are projects for other scholars, those with the long-term, domestic viewing of U.S. television that I lack, and which I consider essential to rigorous scholarship on this topic.

For Paris, I have organized my discussion through one of its emblematic characters, Commissaire Jules Maigret. Immediately, this choice points to one of the arguments of the book, which is that place is often embodied and signified through particular characters, such as Sherlock Holmes with his well-known residence in 221B Baker Street or, wearing his big coat in an often-rainy Paris, Jules Maigret. Georges Simenon's *Inspector Maigret* series, which has spawned two long-running French-language series, has had more international television adaptations than any other detective series.[50] Inspector Maigret's Paris has been made in Japan and Italy, just as Sherlock Holmes's London has been fabricated in Berlin and Los Angeles. The Paris chapter analyzes the first *Maigret* television adaptation, the BBC's extremely successful 1960–63 series, made, with Georges Simenon's enthusiastic approval, with Rupert Davies as the commissaire. This expensive, prestige production, which, unusually for the time, had substantial location shooting in Paris, was itself widely exported. There are extensive BBC files on this production, which are illuminating about production processes in this period, the international television market, and the understanding of Paris. This chapter considers a particular Paris, the 1960s BBC Paris, to introduce some of the complexities of making place on television and to analyze these in relation to particular production aims and constraints. This is a study of the production of television Paris from London. My findings here challenge some taken-for-granted ideas about the BBC's priorities as a national rather than an international broadcaster, while also capturing the role of Paris and Frenchness in midcentury British modernities. I also discuss, rather more briefly, some of the other television *Maigret*s, including the 1992–93 British Granada television version, which was filmed in Budapest and, like the Franco-Belgian Bruno Cremer series, stages a more retro Paris. The two British series were filmed at the beginning and end of the period of television history dominated by nationally regulated terrestrial broadcasting, but each was made with a clear eye to the export market, constructing a Paris that would appeal internationally. In the earlier series, Paris signifies modernity—particularly through production design—while in the later, it is nostalgic. Thus this chapter analyzes the televisual construction, by British production teams, of the city that most identifies cinematic modernity, while also considering questions of authenticity, location shooting, and the televisual production of place for international markets.

For London, the second case study, I take a different approach, bringing together television Londons over a longer historical period, and produced in a range of different contexts, to consider the making and remaking of televisual London as a taken-for-granted origin for most British broadcasting. Through the history of British television Londons, I argue, can be traced Britain's complicated relation with its past, and the peculiar difficulties of modernity for this former imperial nation. My concern here is first with the way in which British television, organized through a commitment to public service broadcasting, engages with the literary heritage of London: the new medium and the old city. Analysis of the persistence of London the Victorian city—particularly Dickensian London—on British television is followed by an exploration of some of the ways in which television has engaged with contemporary realities, and particularly, postimperial Britain's changing self-image. Here I explore the interrelationship of two significant post–Second World War stories, the end of empire and the expansion of the television service, and consider the way in which the domesticity of the television medium contributed to decolonization as an intimate experience. London is a privileged site here, both nationally and internationally. In this history I explore the construction of late twentieth-century London as a multicultural capital and pay particular attention to the notion of new neighbors. The final part of the chapter marks a retreat from the multicultural moment and a sense of the future, considering the return of emblematic characters and places, such as Sherlock Holmes, Jack the Ripper, and the East End of London, particularly as television moves into the twenty-first century, and London's oldness becomes globally marketable in new ways.

The Baltimore of *The Wire* has alerted viewers (scholars of many different disciplines among them) to the dramatic and analytic potential of long-form drama. Chapter 3 addresses the new enthusiasm for the analysis of "not-television" television such as *The Wire*. Many viewers of *The Wire* have become deeply—and messianically—involved in extolling the serious virtues of the program and the real knowledge of Baltimore that it produces.[51] Rather than contributing further to the already extensive analyses of this program, this chapter takes a sideways step and contextualizes both this scholarship and this television city, in an attempt to delineate what is at stake in this enthusiasm.

Chapters 1 and 2 deal mainly with twentieth-century television—the television that was frequently watched by the majority of a nation at the same time. This final chapter considers some of the new forms of television, and particularly the fin-de-siècle form of the DVD, now disappearing in favor of downloadable and streamed viewing. I consider some of the metaphors of viewing this more individualized commodity form television, such as bingeing, and also explore changing critical evaluations of, and attitudes to, television as it moves away from network normality. Much of the rhetoric of *The Wire*, both inside and outside the production, has been about the reality of the stories it tells. I contextualize these claims by examining some of the ways in which the port city of Baltimore has come to the television screen, paying particular attention to the work of Vincent Peranio, who has worked on the production design of nearly all substantial audiovisual productions set in Baltimore. Just as *The Wire* owes debts to network television, so too does its Baltimore draw on previous Baltimores.

Each of my cities is in a sense a device through which to explore methodological, as well as substantive, issues in the imbrication of cities and television. While each television city is specific, there are also broader determinants in the production of these cities, bound up with both questions of television as a medium and wider cultural and historical issues. In chapter 1, the making of Paris is explored in the detail of a production study in order to challenge the assumption that audiovisual place is produced through location filming. This is complemented with discussion of the complex temporality of place and space in relation to old film of vanished places and new re-creations of those same places. Each version of *Maigret* produces a different television Paris, while there are nevertheless continuities and ruptures across the body of texts that can be fruitfully scrutinized. In contrast to this simple organization of the Paris case study through different versions of the same stories, the London chapter ranges over a much more diverse set of programming. However, in some ways the London chapter is the most straightforward, although it has the widest program and temporal span, as it is organized through an analysis of an imperial capital, the greatest city in the world in the nineteenth century, depicted on a new medium as Britain as a world power passes into history. Once again, the complex temporality of television comes to the fore: at some moments apparently managing modernity, at others contributing to the sense of London as capital, in Patrick Wright's phrase of "an old country."[52] The historical coincidence of the new medium with the end of empire, and the late twentieth-century rhetorics of multicultural London, are finally surpassed by the return to the Victorian and the past that characterizes so much twenty-first-century British television. In the final chapter, Baltimore is a different kind of device again, as the televisual rise to fame of the city is traced in relation to changing ideas about television spectatorship and criticism. Here, matching, but contrasting with, the different Maigrets of chapter 1, I explore the development of Baltimore across a limited body of television work, which has resulted in the recognition of the particular strengths of serial storytelling for the imagining of cities. In this chapter, Baltimore becomes the device through which shifts in television scholarship and attitudes to television can be addressed.

My study seeks to restore television to the imagination of the city, while also, across the movement of change and repetition, demonstrating something of how television has responded to changes in both the city and its own modes of delivery. My argument is that television has been central to the apprehension of cities and how they are inhabited since the mid-twentieth century—so central, and so taken for granted, that it has been almost invisible.

1 The Modernity of Maigret's Paris

Viewers liked the outdoor shots of Paris immensely. These
sequences were expertly blended with the studio scenes, it was
thought, and were also very pleasant in themselves.
—BBC Audience Research Report on "Murder in Montmartre,"
21 November 1960

So Maigret is perhaps a bad social historian in so far as social
history is the awareness of change as well as of continuity.
But he is a very good popular historian in so far as popular
history is the observation of habit, routine, assumption, banality,
everydayness, seasonability, popular conservatism.
—Richard Cobb, "Maigret's Paris"

Paris is the great European city of modernity: the city of light. The
Eiffel Tower, Notre Dame and the Seine, the Arc de Triomphe—these
are instantly recognizable landmarks. The very names of Parisian dis-
tricts (Pigalle, Montmartre, the Left Bank) and institutions (the Moulin Rouge, the Louvre) resonate within international imaginations of
the French capital. Paris is central to histories and debates about the
city and modern life, and the canonical writers on this topic, such
as Honoré de Balzac, Charles Baudelaire, and Walter Benjamin, have
taken Paris as their topic. The painting and photographing of modern
life has, through the treatment of Paris, shaped much broader understandings of the transformations of the nineteenth and twentieth
centuries. And in the 1895 exhibition by the Lumière brothers, Paris is

1.1–1.2. "Viewers liked the outdoor shots of Paris immensely." Views of the Pont de Bir-Hakeim and the bank of the Seine (*Maigret*, "Death in Mind").

assumed to be the birthplace of cinema. The coupling of Paris and cinema has formed our understanding of each, and the Paris that is familiar the world over is a Paris known through *Le quai des brumes* (1938), *Hôtel du Nord* (1938), *Gigi* (1958), *À bout de souffle* (1959), *Les Amants du Pont-Neuf* (1991), *La Haine* (1995), and *Amélie* (2001). Key terms used in scholarship on the cinematic city, most notably *flâneur*, but also *dérive* and *psychogeography*, have their origins in the contemplation of Paris.[1] However, televisual Paris has not been much discussed and is often assumed to be an inferior version of cinematic or literary Paris when it is considered at all. While twenty-first-century French television series such as *Engrenages* (*Spiral*, Son et Lumière, 2005–14) offer dynamic images of contemporary Paris that would reward further analysis, I want to return to the twentieth century to consider the Paris of Jules Maigret. In particular, I will discuss the very successful 1960s BBC dramatization of Georges Simenon's Maigret novels, which were partly filmed in Paris.[2]

My concerns are threefold. I want to analyze how the BBC imagined and staged Paris and its most famous detective in the early 1960s. What was BBC Paris like? How did the production demonstrate and manage the Frenchness of its setting? In seeking to answer this question, watching surviving archive copies of the programs and scrutinizing the extensive production files, I have encountered material which challenges certain assumptions that are commonly made about the BBC as a public service broadcaster, and so I want to use this production to reconsider certain emphases in BBC history and demonstrate the way in which each television city must be considered both as a representation (of a particular city) and as an institutional production (of a broadcaster or production company). Finally, I want to return to questions of modernity and the city. In the literature of modernity, Paris is celebrated not just for the birth of cinema, but also, in Edgar Allan Poe's M. Dupin, for one of the first detectives. The detective must, by profession, pay attention to his surroundings. Through his observation, details of banal everyday life are recorded. How is the detail of Paris preserved through these generic conventions? As the epigraph from Richard Cobb suggests, Maigret's manner of detection is characterized by a prodigious, but unaccented, analytic familiarity with the rhythms of Parisian life. His modes of attention to the everyday provide the understanding through which crime can be solved. The 1960s BBC series was set in the present, although it drew on novels that had been written over the previous thirty years.[3] To what extent is this televisual Jules Maigret a figure of modernity, and what kind of Paris does he inhabit, and bring into the homes of viewers in the 1960s?

Just as Paris is the most visited tourist destination on earth, so Jules Maigret—with the exception of Sherlock Holmes—is the most televised detective. The 1960s BBC *Maigret* was the first of many television adaptations of the detective, including, most notably, the long-running French-language series with Jean Richard (1967–90) and Bruno Cremer (1991–2005). There have also been television adaptations in Italy, Russia, Holland, and Japan, while French and British versions have circulated in dubbed and subtitled versions.[4] In the person of Commissaire

Maigret, Paris has been brought to homes all over the world. However, because of copyright issues, the BBC Maigrets have hardly been shown after their first broadcast, and so they are not discussed in Ginette Vincendeau's persuasive analysis of screen Maigrets, which ranges from the 1930s Jean Gabin films through to the later television versions.[5] Her account notes a move from cinema adaptation to television in the 1960s (when U.K., Italian, Dutch, and French versions first appeared), and, in commentary on these multiple Maigrets, she cites Pierre Beylot's judgment that Simenon is an "eminently televisual" writer "because his oeuvre perfectly combines variety and repetition."[6] While repetition with difference is characteristic of all generic fiction, I have already indicated the significance of repetition in the televisual production of place, and return to these questions at the end of this chapter, where I argue that the regular appearance of Paris in British living rooms in the 1960s had its own contextual significance. In Vincendeau's periodization, the two expensive coproductions of the 1990s, with Bruno Cremer (made in Prague), and with Michael Gambon (shot in Budapest), are heritage pieces, combining high production values with a certain thinness in their evocation of France, and demonstrating that the commissaire belongs to a fondly remembered past rather than the present. In contrast, she is attentive to the way in which the first French version with Jean Richard, with its documentary aesthetic, captures something of a France that was disappearing in the 1960s, in particular an intimacy with the everyday life of the Parisian quartiers.

Like the later Cremer and Gambon series, the 1960s BBC Davies series was mainly made outside France. However, unlike these, the BBC series shares with the Jean Richard series a contemporary setting and the use of location shooting in France, and particularly Paris. Whether this British-shot location Paris achieves the same intimacy as the Jean Richard version is one of my concerns in what follows. The BBC *Maigret* was enormously popular in Britain, seems to have pleased Georges Simenon, and was very widely exported. Its credit sequences establish signature tropes for the detective that recur in later versions, while its film footage of 1960s Paris, as the epigraph to this chapter suggests, was seen as one of the key attractions of the programs. Location shooting for television fiction was unusual in the period, and, relative to other television drama of the time, extremely expensive. So the BBC *Maigret* provides a case study of a particular rendition of Paris as a television city in the 1960s and, more abstractly, a record of what was considered the essential Paris for a British television production team, which can in turn be compared to some of the other television Maigrets, most notably the later Granada television version starring Michael Gambon.

The Business of Maigret

The BBC *Maigret* was planned as a prestige project with high production values, described at the time in a BBC press release as "the largest project the BBC have attempted to date."[7] Following the success of a single play adaptation by Giles Cooper of "Maigret and the Lost Life" (transmitted [tx.] 12 April 1959; not preserved), the series was envisaged from inception as involving at least three series of thirteen "plays" (as they are called), "the thirty nine." The BBC paid handsomely for the rights, engaging in arduous negotiation with Mme. Simenon, who first emerges in correspondence with the BBC in 1956 when there is a radio adaptation of a Maigret story, *Maigret and the Young Girl* (*Maigret et la jeune morte*, 1954). Mme. Simenon, at this stage, lays out principles that will guide her negotiations in the move to television. These include insisting that adaptations are made from the original French ("so that the minimum be lost in the transposition from one medium to the other"), a tendency to negotiate each territory separately (she always insists that the United States and Canada are excluded from English-language contracts), and the granting of rights for short periods and for one performance at a time.[8] Thus the first television adaptation, "Maigret and the Lost Life," had to be (made and) broadcast within two years of the contract signing, and rights were granted for only one performance.[9] One of the results of Mme. Simenon's indefatigable defense of her husband, which is always couched in terms of morality, not finance ("surely you will understand that ours is a position of principle and not dictated by strict mathematics"[10]), is that Simenon quickly enters the BBC's Special One-Sixth Category, which, in the words of the BBC's Heather Dean, who conducts many of the negotiations with Mme. Simenon, "is a small and very exclusive number of authors to whom we pay an additional one-sixth fee . . . in recognition of their world fame and literary merit."[11]

This expenditure by the BBC in the rights to the selected Maigret stories is matched by the exceptional technical resources allocated to the program and the generous rehearsal time and production work hours.[12] It is in this context that the further expense of filming in France must be understood.[13] The BBC was making a substantial investment in a product, for which, from the planning stage, it intended overseas sales. Ronald Waldman, the General Manager of Television Promotions, comments on these expectations in his prebroadcast discussion of the first four programs: "Because of the 'investment' money in 'Maigret,' however, it is necessary that the series should be produced *ab initio* for the world market while adhering to our own standards of quality and taste."[14] Waldman's invocation here of "our own standards of quality and taste" makes a straightforward assumption about recognized standards (presumably both BBC and British) shared between the writer and reader of the memo. The juxtaposition of "our own standards" and "the world market" points to an important element in the BBC's self-image, in which the market is seen as a potential corruptor of BBC standards, a danger that is perhaps the more pronounced when the programs concerned—as with *Maigret*—could be seen as genre fiction. It is clear from the production files that the BBC prided itself on having secured Georges Simenon's cooperation in the project, and saw its programs as being true to Simenon's vision. The recognition of Georges Simenon as an artistic origin was an important part of the legitimation of the BBC project (*Maigret* was not an anonymous committee-written TV series), particularly when it came to defending the production resources allocated to the programs. This can be seen clearly in the answer Michael Barry (Head of Drama, Television) circulated very widely to his superiors in response to pressure to reduce production time: "I have no doubt, for example, that an American organisation would have turned the concentrated effort of a Gunsmoke unit upon this series, and, disregarding any question of the Simenons' wishes regarding casting and quality would have turned out a glossy article in quicker time. The fact remains that Simenon firmly resisted the relinquishment of his rights for such an operation and, apart from our own satisfaction at the result we have obtained, declares that these have justified his reasons for resisting such an offer."[15] Barry here gives a content to the demands of the "world market": a quickly made "glossy article" that would not respect the integrity of the author. So on the one hand, the BBC is financially committed to success in the international market, and, on the other, it is determined that there will be no compromise with the lures of the glossy. This underlying attitude to, in particular, U.S. television, illuminates the *Maigret* project in a slightly different manner, one to which I return at the end of the chapter, which is to see the project as explicitly European. The Paris-set *Maigret* will, by implication, be contesting the terrain occupied by U.S. programs such as the popular Western serial *Gunsmoke*, but will have contrasting, BBC aesthetics and values.[16]

The image of the BBC in this period is very much a national public service broadcaster, but the calculations which surround *Maigret* demonstrate that, in fact, productions such as this were inaugurated with a clear international sales agenda from the beginning. Indeed, the insistence on the very high production values of the series, which are seen to constitute "our own standards of quality and taste," actually make international sales through the auspices of BBC Enterprises more necessary. The huge U.S. market, in particular, becomes even more desirable. As Jason Jacobs has demonstrated with a radio series from the 1950s, *The Third Man*, the BBC was both willing and practiced in the international marketing of its products.[17] For *Maigret*, an enticing press book was produced particularly for the U.S. market. This handsome, glossy ten-page publication puts its pitch on the cover alongside photographs of Georges Simenon and Rupert Davies (Maigret), pipe in hand, declaring breathlessly, "Georges Simenon the world's most successful writer of crime stories created Maigret the world's best known and best-loved detective in a series produced by the world's senior television broadcasting system."[18] This pitch indicates something of why the BBC thought its investment was merited, and the brochure also reports that the programs were available for purchase "on videotape, 35mm kinescope (combined optical or separate magnetic tape) or 16mm kinescope (combined track only)," which further indicates the seriousness of the BBC's engagement with the market.[19] From the beginning of the production, there was an exceptional decision—which caused enormous logistical problems for the BBC—to record the episodes in several formats as it was not known which formats international purchasers would want.[20] In terms of television production, therefore, *Maigret* marks a significant moment of transition between television drama series as a completely ephemeral live media form, and television as a recorded, and therefore saleable, commodity form.[21] There were, furthermore, aesthetic consequences of the orientation toward export. The "Notes for Directors" prepared by the series producer, Andrew Osborn, are explicit about the formal implications of this, insisting that episodes "must be capable of having six commercials and at the same time be shown on our screens without these breaks being obtrusive."[22] The double address that Osborn identifies here, in which each fifty-minute episode would be simultaneously seamless and perforated by advertising breaks, is another version of the contrast between "world" and "our own" standards. This double structure also emerges as a concern in relation to rates of pay, demonstrating that it was accepted that publicly funded television production would pay less than market rates. Vincent Tilsley, of the Script Department, writes to the H.S.D. Tel. (Head of Script Department, Television) in November 1960 identifying the problem thus: "I don't think the BBC, as a gentlemanly organisation, can really expect Contract Staff to undertake this kind of work which is intended for sale on world markets at considerable profits without payment outside their basic salary."[23] The "gentlemanly organisation," which had been held to hard terms by Mme. Simenon, invested heavily in advertising the availability of the series in the international market with considerable success. So when the Paris of these programs is analyzed, it should not be seen as a Paris produced for domestic consumption. It is not just a British Paris. It is a British Paris imagined within a world market. The internationally recognized attractions of Paris, in combination with a reassuring detective and a large number of stories, provided a package in which the BBC was eager to invest. What are the constituent elements of the BBC *Maigret*'s Paris, and how is this television city best analyzed?

Making Paris at the BBC

Most of the Maigret stories filmed by the BBC are set in Paris, and most episodes comprise a mixture of studio filming, French location filming, and some British location filming.[24] The structure of each episode provides an opening narrative setup, the titles, the body of the episode (with its unmarked commercial breaks), and the closing credits. The opening setups usually concern the crime or crime scene, with Maigret himself appearing only after the titles. The titles themselves, which use extreme close-up of a rough wall surface as background, offer no visual clues as to location, instead, just like the glossy press book, foregrounding author, star, and the identity and iconography of the pipe-smoking detective.[25] The literary provenance of the stories precedes any visual attention to location. The profile of the detective is illuminated by a flaring match as he lights his pipe. Location, though, is alluded to through the accordionesque soundtrack with its memorable tune, and it falls to the rest of the episode to establish what this Paris looks like.[26]

The Paris of these stories consists of a mixture of elements that need to be coherently combined to make its spaces believable. My interest lies in this work of combination, this production of a fictional story space, "Paris," using disparate materials that include film of Parisian streets and sights, models, props, West London studios, costume, music, writing, and language. This labor was noted in a contemporary BBC audience survey: "There was clearly a lot of admiration for the production, especially for the outdoor shots of Paris, for the smooth linking of film and studio scenes, and for the realism and 'Frenchness' of those 'dingy back rooms.'"[27] Although this BBC *Maigret* is particularly interesting because it does use location shooting of 1960s Paris, and this both is unusual for television drama of the period and provides footage that is fascinating in itself, I am not assuming or arguing that the significant Paris of this *Maigret* consists in the location shooting alone. This television city is precisely a production: it was made by the BBC in the 1960s and now provides evidence of ideas about Paris, of Maigret's milieu, and of the BBC's "standards of quality and taste" within an address to a world market.

1.3–1.5. Title sequence for the BBC *Maigret* used for all series.

How was this Paris made? What are the significant settings for the dramas? Which sequences were selected for location shooting, and how are these sequences related to other parts of the drama? What was understood to be necessarily shot in Paris? How, and to what extent, do these sequences signify Paris, and what else do they do? How significant are other factors in creating this television Paris?

Aiding this enquiry are the extensive production files retained by the BBC, which document the minutiae of the production, from pronunciation advice to detailed design photographs of the studio interiors.[28] Location shooting was not only expensive and unusual, it was also clearly quite taxing to organize. Most of the British cast and crew spoke no French, and if they had experience of overseas travel, it was likely to be as members of the armed forces. For each minute of location-shot screen time, there were many hours of arrangements and memos, enjoining employees, for example, to arrive at Heathrow in good time for their flights—allowing at least twenty minutes before takeoff. There was a complicated hierarchy of accommodation to organize, separating not only cast and crew, but also different cast members.[29] The exceptional opportunity to provide location footage in each episode put contradictory pressures on the program makers. On the one hand, they needed to demonstrate, every week, that they really had shot this in Paris. To use language that was not used by the "gentlemanly organisation," the money needed to be up there on the screen. For this, there must be landmarks, and the shooting scripts are very clear about this. For example, in "The Trap" (tx. 10 December 1962), which opens with location-shot footage of Maigret in Montmartre, the shooting script specifies that the first shot must include Rupert Davies in front of Sacré Coeur, while the second needs to put him in the same frame as the funicular railway shown in so many postcards of the cathedral.[30] On the other hand, Simenon's stories are detective fiction, which is generally set not in Parisian landmarks but in everyday, often banal, locations. This more ordinary Paris is much less clichéd, and therefore more attractive to program makers seeking to capture a sense of an authentic Paris, but may not always be immediately identifiable to viewers as Paris. And this is a problem for the production, because why spend all this money to go to France if the viewer cannot tell that you have been there?

These dilemmas of the production raise the more general question of how place is signified in audiovisual fiction. For although it may seem obvious to start with location filming, in fact the setting for audiovisual fiction is produced through a complex orchestration of elements. Accent, music, props, writing, costume—each of these can tell an audience where a scene is set, and often these methods are more important in confirming location than where something was actually filmed. Accordion music and the uniform of a gendarme are clichés, but, precisely because of this, they may identify a Paris location less ambiguously than a location-shot street, and clarity of setting was all important in constructing this Paris for domestic British and international consumption, as well as being an important prerequisite for the staging of the crime to be investigated. A character perceived as typically Parisian, such as a concierge, with an apron, keys, a crocheted shawl, and maybe a caged bird, can simultaneously identify setting and create atmosphere as in, for example, "Murder on Monday" (15 January 1962). The internationally recognizable iconography of Paris—landmarks, characters, and quotidian settings such as cafés and *tabacs* (tobacco kiosks)—can be invoked without expensively taking cast and crew over the Channel. This studio-created iconography is used extensively in these programs, partly and paradoxically, I suggest, because location shooting was also undertaken, and it was important that the ambiguities of the real should not confuse the viewer about where it was set.

Props were particularly important, and great effort was expended in trying to dress the British studio sets with French objects and décor, although sometimes, as in the order for "rubber cobblestones," compromises had to be made.[31] In this endeavor, the heroines of authenticity are two secretaries, Vanessa Virgo in Britain (secretary to the series producer, Andrew Osmond) and Maud Vidal in Paris, the BBC's Television Secretary. Vanessa must repeatedly contact Maud about details of arrangements but also to ask urgently, in June 1960, for a map of Paris to be rushed over, "as we cannot get one in this country with the writing in French."[32] More trying is the question of sourcing French cigarettes. The production is using empty Gitanes packets for set dressing, but the cleaners keep throwing them away and Vanessa must ask Maud to approach "the company Gauloises-Gitanes" to ensure a regular supply.[33] Alcoholic drink too is a constant challenge for the production, as bottle shapes and brands need to be authentic, but the BBC does not permit the use of real alcohol, and each proposed use requires approval. In the first of many such memos, Eric Tayler asks, during the preparation for the second episode, "Unscheduled Departure," "Could we please have a real bottle of Calvados for this production?"[34]

This concern for authenticity was particularly challenging in relation to the handling of French names. Language is a significant element in the evocation of place, and it was decided, early in the production, to retain French pronunciation of names and to use some French phrases and modes of address. Thus Maigret himself is addressed as "Patron," his colleague as "Monsieur le juge," and other characters as "Monsieur," "Madame," and "Mademoiselle." Characters, particularly the Maigrets, bid each other "au revoir," and there is a consistent effort to use French stress patterns in names. This decision had its travails, particularly for the British actors. As the producer, Andrew Osborn, observes during the shooting of the first series, "We are also in a bit of difficulty from time to time over the pronunciation of French words by people who can't speak French."[35] The BBC's pronunciation unit was used to provide detailed phonetic guidelines for difficult words and phrases in each episode, and the scale of the demands on the principal actors can be seen in the surviving list of fifty-seven pronunciations for "The Winning Ticket" (tx. 13 November 1961; see figs. 1.6–1.7).[36] The production decision to emphasize the Frenchness of the setting through the French pronunciation of words was, at the same time, judged likely to be confusing for a British audience, and there was some concern at "the difficulty of understanding some of the rather unusual names— both of characters and of places—that we are continually coming up against in these plays."[37] This translated directly into an instruction to the actors that elevates the comprehension of the English audience over the Frenchness of the pronunciation: "Would you please have a word with Rupert and Ewen . . . and ask them to take particular care that these difficult names are spoken slowly and clearly."[38] This contradictory demand on the actors, that they both perform Frenchness and speak "these difficult [foreign] names" "slowly and clearly" epitomizes the challenges of the production.

In none of the expensive filming trips to France for *Maigret* was money spent on filming interiors. Interiors, it was assumed, as is common in the production of both film and television, could be filmed in the studio. Or, if not there (which often meant the old Ealing Studios, which the BBC owned at this period), in London locations that were near the BBC headquarters in west London. Fulham, Hammersmith, and Shepherds Bush all provided locations for the series, and, on at least one occasion, the house of the producer, Andrew Osborn, was used for filming. The pattern of this distinction within the film and television industries, in which the money is used for "outside," echoes that of much scholarship on the city, in which the city is outside in the public spaces of streets, buildings, traffic, and crowds. However, the city also has an inside, which comes in forms both public and private: the places of labor, the sites of entertainment, and the private spaces of its citizens, the homes from which they venture forth and to which they return. In the BBC *Maigret* production, there were two regular interior sets that anchored the characters and narrative: Maigret's office in the police headquarters at 36 Quai d'Orfèvres and his home, the apartment he shared with his wife.

The *Maigret* office set, present, if only briefly, in nearly every episode, is a recognizably generic space: the detective's office. Many detectives, in many films and television programs, have offices with maps of their district on the wall. In Maigret's immediately generically familiar office, a map of France dominates the room, with the camera usually placed opposite, at a distance that reveals Maigret's desk and a window to the right. The production design signals location economically: the map, a photograph of President de Gaulle, a French calendar nearby on the wall (very difficult for the production secretary in London to source[39]), and a French-style casement window that opens to give a view of Paris. The arrangement of the map and the window, on walls at right angles to each other, means that there are a variety of possible setups through which to frame characters with France or Paris in the background. Doors on each side of the set permit some variation in the use of space, and one of them reveals (on occasion), a washroom that permits the commissaire to wash his hands after a particularly distasteful encounter (for example, in the opening of "The Old

PRONUNCIATIONS

Aux Caves de Beaujolais	ō kaáv dě bōzhōláy (-zh as 's' in 'measure')
Tabac de Sully	tăbaá dě sülee (-ü as in Fr. 'vu')
Ile St. Louis	eél sa(ng) lweé
Canon de la Bastille	kănō(ng) dě laa basteé
Place de la Concorde	pláss dě laa kō(ng)kord
Citroën	seetrō-énn (French) sitrō-ěn (English)
Pont de la Concorde	pō(ng) dě laa kō(ng)kord
Lapointe	laapwá(ng)t
Brandade de Morus	braa(ng)daád dě mőrüss (-ü as in Fr.'vu')
Truffles	As this is the English spelling we would suggest the English pronunciation 'trúffělz'
Torrance	tórraa(ng)ss
Comeliau (Maître)	méttr kómměl-yō
Quai Henri Quatre	kay aá(ng)ree káttr
Plat de Jour	plaá dě zhoór (-zh as 's' in 'measure')
Albert Rochain	albaír rōshá(ng)
Lucas	lükaá (-ü as in Fr.'vu')
Suze-Citron	süz-seetrō(ng) (-ü as in Fr.'vu')
Patron	pátrō(ng)
Vermouth Cassis	vairmoot kásseéss
Auteuil	ōtó-i (-ō as in Fr.'coeur')
Vincennes	va(ng)sénn
Brasserie	brass-reé
Rue St. Antoine	rü sa(ng)taa(ng)twaán (-ü as in Fr.'vu')
Quai de Bercy	káy dě bairsseé
Le Petit Albert	lě pětee talbaír
Theophile	tay-ōfeél
Clermont-Ferrand	klaírmŏ(ng) férraa(ng)
Calvados	kálvădoss
Simca	símkă
Fricandeau à l'Oseille	freékaa(ng)dō aa lōzáy
Muscadet	müskăday (-ü as in Fr.'vu')

Lille	leel
Nina Pejade of Toulouse	neenă pĕzhaád ŏv toŏloóz (-zh as 's' in 'measure')
Poste Restante	póst restáa(ng)t (-o as in 'lost')
Bastille	basteé
Rue de Rivoli	rú dĕ reévŏli (-ú as in Fr.'vu')
Jean Valner	zhaá(ng) valnaîr (-zh as 's' in 'measure')
Serge Madok	saírzh máddock (-zh as 's' in 'measure')
St. Antoine	să(ng) taa(ng)twaán
Peronne	pĕrónn
Montdidier	mŏ(ng)deéd-yay
Goderville	gŏdairveel
St. Denis	sa(ng) dĕneé
Francine Latour	fráa(ng)sseen latoór
Ferdinand Lemaire	faírdinaa(ng) lemaîr
Porte Maillot	pórt mī-yō (-I as in 'high')
Corbeil	kórbay
Raus!	rowss (-ow as in 'now')
Charenton	shárraa(ng)tō(ng)
Picardy	pínkărdi (This is the English spelling and pronunciation of the name)
Folies Bergère	fóllee bairzhaîr (-zh as 's' in 'measure')
Jeanine	zhánneen (-zh as 's' in 'measure')
Marchand	maárshaa(ng)
Jean Bronsky	zhaá(ng) brónski
Armagnac	áarmăn-yack
Hotel Beausejour	hōtéll bō sóazhoór
Dieppe	di-épp

1.6–1.7 (*opposite and above*). The pronunciation list for one episode, "The Winning Ticket" (BBC Written Archives Centre, T5/2, 185/1), © BBC, reproduced with kind permission.

1.8. Maigret in his office with the map of France over the fireplace and a framed portrait of Mme. Maigret on his desk ("Death in Mind").

Lady," tx. 28 November 1960), while remaining partly in shot. The set is dressed to be unremarkable: a little shabby with nothing to detract from the conversations and confrontations that take place therein. On occasion, adjacent spaces, such as the corridor outside the office, or the offices of superiors, are shown. The significance of this set is primarily generic. It provides a recognizable home for viewers' expectations about the type of fiction this is, the role of particular characters, and the likely narratives. Its novelty, for the non-French viewer, is its Parisianness, and it is the oscillation of the traditional pleasures of detection with the discovery of a new environment—which is itself, at the same time, familiar—that is the lure of the series. The commissaire investigates crime in his city—but in this process, he is also our guide in the display of the city and its inhabitants. As one of the reviewers commented, "It is always pleasant to look at Paris."[40]

If Maigret's office provides a generic home for the viewer, his apartment provides both reassurance and the fascination of difference. Always shown as an interior, the view from its window, shot in Boulevard Richard-Lenoir, shows similar apartments opposite.[41] The flat is comfortable and full of furnishings in a busy, continental style, and usually contains, not just furniture and ornaments, but also his wife. But it is

1.9. The Paris outside the window of Maigret's office ("Death in Mind").

most significantly a place in which Maigret both has meals prepared for him—by her—and eats, often with her. Food and drink are important signifiers of Maigret's nationality throughout the series. French habits of eating and drinking, and the importance of these pleasures within French culture, are notable indicators of setting, and take up much more screen time than is expected in equivalent British series, where a cup of tea or a pint of beer are the normal refreshments. Maigret is shown coming home for lunch—or occasionally, being unable to do this. He eats meals that include a dressed salad at lunchtime—very uncommon in British homes in this period. He has filtered coffee for breakfast and wine with his meals, often an apéritif, and the Maigrets sometimes have a tisane at bedtime. In this home, Maigret is shown to be a comfortably married man, well looked after, extended tolerance, and sometimes nagged a little. He is familiar as a husband—but he is also French, with French habits and expectations.

He also works in the French legal system, which requires some explication. "Sometimes I wish I was an English policeman," declares Maigret at the opening of "The Winning Ticket." "You would have to be nicer to your suspects," replies Lucas, his trusty subordinate with whom he is chatting in the office. Maigret agrees to this rather blatant flattery of a British audience, but then offers a careful account of the difference between British and French policing and the role of the magistrate within the French system, thus explaining the recent entrance of a magistrate into the office. As this magistrate had been speaking, it was clear from Maigret's expression that the character was unsympathetic; the magistrate's concern that a recent crime in the center of Paris might affect the tourist trade is treated with barely concealed contempt; the magistrate's performance is fussy and nitpicking. But as the production is organized for the non-French viewer, who will be unfamiliar with this role of the magistrate, Maigret must articulate his intermittent desire to be an English policeman in order to explain the powers of this unattractive character.

This explanatory sequence follows one in which Maigret addresses the question of his occupation in a different way. The scene has opened in the office with Maigret examining cuts and tears in two pieces of clothing. It is not clear what he is looking at or for, but that there is damage is evident. Maigret describes to Lucas what he has found: that the cuts in the two pieces of clothing are of different lengths. This is a moment in which Sherlock Holmes would be able to deduce a great deal from the damaged material. But Maigret is not that sort of detective, as is made clear in his answer to Lucas's question, "What does it mean?" "No idea," replies his boss.

"The Winning Ticket" thus considers the type of detective that Maigret is from two different angles. He is a detective who works under a system that he finds tiresome—here designated as a quality of its Frenchness, but actually an international generic condition of police officers in detective fiction—and he is not a Sherlock Holmes–type deductive investigator. But the magistrate explanation—a plot necessity—should not be taken to mean that the series assumes that the viewer needs everything French explained. On the contrary, the series assumes that its viewers can handle the foreignness of France with a little assistance now and then. So this episode moves straight into a discussion of a victim's stomach contents, which include the untranslated *brandade de morue* (a dish made with olive oil, potato, and dried salt cod).[42] "Brandade," says Maigret, "is a complicated dish," and therefore goes on to suggest that the victim will have eaten in a café.

Paris as the City of Sexual Attractions

The most pervasive of the images of Paris on which *Maigret* draws is that of the city of sexual attractions. The film critic Barry Norman characterizes this idea of Paris in his review, in 1969, of a one-off return of the Rupert Davies Maigret: "[*Maigret at Bay*] was a pleasant reminder of how very good the series used to be, particularly in the way it reflected Simenon's knack of conjuring up the exciting Paris—a place where something delicious and probably naughty is about to happen any minute. Actually, Paris isn't really like that at all. . . . Still, Simenon makes you feel that the mythical Paris does exist if only you knew where to look, and the *Maigret* series recreated that impression quite vividly."[43] As Norman points out, it is Georges Simenon's own interest in late-night Paris, and his repeated use of low-life milieus, that necessitates this engagement with a Paris of cabaret dancers and professional criminals. Jules Maigret is radically democratic in his concern with the humanity of all social classes affected by criminal acts, and the stories feature tramps and petty thieves, heroin addicts, countesses, and bar staff. But these settings of the Simenon stories coincide with the way in which "the Continent" has always meant sex and naughtiness to the British, so it is an indicatively British judgment that this is "exciting Paris" "where something delicious and probably naughty is about to happen." The question for the BBC was how to manage the presentation of the city through this most recognizable iconography, the *Moulin Rouge* version of Paris, which is both true to the source material and will serve, without ambiguity, to identify the setting of the television series. For this is the BBC, and this Parisian mise-en-scène is a matter of some delicacy for the producers, which, on occasion, is addressed through the invocation of high-art precedents for the representation of the Parisian demimonde (see fig. 1.12). Anxiety about this representation of Paris, particularly in relation to export markets, emerges just before transmission, when there was a long memo from the G.M.T.P. (General Manager, Television Promotions), Ronald Waldman, which refers to its "over-insistence and over-explicitness on sex," and also identifies a problem with "a lightness of

1.10–1.11. Two variants of naughty Paris, the first straightforward sexual display, the second, rather more highbrow, through the use of mirrors, framing, and the black velvet ribbon alluding to Edouard Manet's 1882 painting, *A Bar at the Folies-Bergère* ("Death in Mind").

voice in the young policeman which could lead to at least a suspicion of effeminacy."[44]

The choice to begin the British series with a nightclub-set story confronts these difficulties directly, while, as I discuss below, the follow-up second episode takes place in a far more bourgeois environment, which, nevertheless, represents French domestic life as rather more erotic than British. "Murder in Montmartre" ("Au Picratt's") has the double focus of a murdered nightclub dancer and the later murder of an old lady about which the dancer has warned the police. The internal BBC synopsis declares, "From out of the neon-lit jungle of Montmartre comes a frightened strip-tease dancer named Arlette," and the episode has an explicit thematic concern with the question of how seriously the testimony of such a young woman should be taken, and thus introduces the

1.12. Maigret with a Toulouse-Lautrec poster behind him in mise-en-scène that directly references the art historical representation of Paris as a city of sexual attractions ("Death in Mind").

inspector's attentiveness to characters often ignored by their social superiors.[45] As the first episode, "Murder in Montmartre" must establish the setting and tone of the series, and the location shooting is reserved for daylight exteriors of familiar, landmark sights within Montmartre. The instructions to the camera operators are precise—the shooting in Paris, "Corner of Sq. Montmartre. Show Sacre [sic] Coeur. M passes through shot," while the funicular must also be captured.[46] This location shooting serves to confirm the identity of setting that has already been established in the opening of the episode through "sexy Paris" footage. The stock nature of this imagery is confirmed by the careful detail in the archive demonstrating that all eight shots of the opening establishing sequence involved reused props. There was no need to waste expensive location shooting as the necessary material was already in stock from previous British Parises. Ealing Studios provided a flashing sign and photographs of nightclub artists while, thriftily, the production reused footage of street signs originally shot for the pilot episode (now lost), "Maigret and the Lost Life."[47]

The episode opens with a nighttime sequence of the neon-lit exterior of the Folies Pigalle, accordion music providing a soundtrack to an image dominated by the glistening rain on the pavements (shot in

1.13–1.16. Title sequence for "Maigret au Picratt's" in the Jean Richard *Maigret* showing the use of a Paris that preexists the narrative and includes other pedestrians such as a musician with a double bass (1.14). (The young policeman in 1.16 is not Jean Richard.)

Gough Square, Fleet Street), reflecting the neon promises of "Theatre Cabaret—Folies Pigalle—Naturistes—Nues—Striptease."[48] If this 1960 BBC version is compared to some of the other versions of this story, it becomes clear that the iconography of the nighttime economy of Pigalle (the neon, the club signs) is employed by each, but that this setting is mobilized differently. In the 1985 Jean Richard version, there are intermittent glimpses of the sign Le Picratt's poised above a street in which late-night citizens—including a musician, prostitutes, and

1.17–1.20. "Maigret et les plaisirs de la nuit." Bruno Cremer version of "Au Picratt's." In fig. **1.17**, the outline of Maigret's hat is just visible as he sits smoking his pipe in the title sequence. Figs. **1.18–1.20** show the nightclub, tightly framed, using neon and establishing milieu through casting.

policemen—go about their business (figs. 1.13–1.16).[49] A car of gendarmes draws up to exchange banter with a colleague on watch on the street, women stand in doorways, and passersby skirt puddles. Long shots show shop fronts, pavements, pedestrians, and cars. While the neon is present, it is located within a preexisting quartier in which life goes on. Unlike the BBC version, which must signal its setting with extreme economy, there is here a television rendition of Paris that, for nearly two minutes, exceeds the demands of the narrative, and preexists as a place. The 1991 Bruno Cremer version, "Maigret et les plaisirs de la nuit" (Maigret and the pleasures of the night), which was filmed by the distinguished cinematographer Raoul Coutard, again gives a brief shot of an illuminated sign, but uses stereotypical casting of "irregular" people—prostitutes, a doorman of restricted growth, an Afro-Caribbean man—to identify the demimonde, along with some tightly framed filming on a long curved flight of steps (figs. 1.17–1.20).

The Granada-Gambon version, "Maigret and the Nightclub Dancer," is selected to launch the second series, which again indicates a discernible judgment that the trope of sexy Paris functions as an establishing shot for the city, an economical way of summarizing what is on offer for the television tourist in the series to come.[50] However, here, as the series title sequence itself concentrates on the establishing of place and period through pans and zooms across sepia-toned photographs of Parisians at work and play (see figs. 1.28–1.30 later in this chapter), the Paris setting has already been established, and the episode opens with interior close-ups of the about-to-be-murdered striptease artiste (Minnie Driver) performing her routine in the shadowy, plush-red club. The combination of the initial title sequence and the strip club establish the Frenchness of the setting.

This first story, with its mise-en-scène of bars and clubs and workers who trade in late-night pleasures, identifies one of the recurrent milieus for the Simenon novels and thus the BBC series. However, with a junior policeman in love with a murdered striptease artiste, and Maigret's own pragmatic acceptance of this world, it also indicates how the series will deal with the demimonde. The neon outline of a sensual woman's body that lights up the club exterior conforms to the promise of Paris as the city of naughty attractions. But the particular manner in which Maigret interacts with the denizens of this world, the seriousness with which he takes them as people, inflects this location differently. He quietly corrects the assumptions of his colleague who observes, "Funny sort of girl to be house proud," when they are visiting the apartment of a murdered dancer by suggesting instead, "Funny sort of girl to be murdered." This alluring city is made recognizable by the use of familiar imagery, but within that recognition, the world is treated as mundane and unremarkable, inhabited by working people like any other. The relative discretion of the British version, which has much less nudity than either the Richard or the Cremer versions, and certainly no mention of whether the murdered woman shaved her pubis, is matched with a tolerance about the lifestyles of the demimonde that is less evident in both the Richard and Cremer versions. In the Richard world, Mme. Maigret is declaratively respectable, redeeming her husband from his excursions into the unrespectable, while in the Cremer episode, the casting of an unsavory character as a transvestite provokes considerable prejudice.

The British idea of the sensuality of French culture recurs in a rather different manner in the second episode of the BBC *Maigret* in relation to a pair of expensive, frilly silk knickers that exemplify the use of props, rather than location shooting, to signify place. These are purchased by Maigret's junior, La Pointe, as the cheapest item in an exclusive lingerie shop that he is investigating. The characters in this episode, "Unscheduled Departure" (tx. 7 November 1960) are much more petit bourgeois and respectable than those in the first episode, and the sequencing was clearly intended to indicate the social range of the series. However, as one of the characters manages the lingerie boutique ("We have nothing but silk"), and Le Pointe is embarrassed into making a purchase, there are two different moments in the program when these semitransparent, ruffled knickers are taken out of their little box and held up in the center of the image. In the second of these, in the police offices, the older men laugh—quite kindly—at La Pointe's embarrassment about his purchase. This is not a smutty moment as it would be in British comedy, but one in which La Pointe's reluctant expenditure of fifty francs on something for which he has no use provides diversion for all. Nevertheless, in effect, a striking pair of frilly knickers has been displayed twice in this otherwise impeccably bourgeois story—functioning to show that we are still in Paris, where even respectable women might wear sexy knickers like this. While the prop list for this episode is very careful to specify only that the garments should look expensive ("6 expensive looking negligees"), and the knickers were actually nylon ("1 dozen small-drum shaped boxes, one to contain pair nylon pants"[51]), the display of this luxury underwear mobilizes associations of the French capital with sensual pleasures, which both economically confirms the setting and invites the viewer into a more sophisticated world. These frilly knickers displayed in an expensive, prestigious drama series can be taken to symbolize the complex ambitions of the BBC's substantial investment in Maigret's Paris: on the one hand, the appeal to a more cosmopolitan viewer than might be watching its domestic rival's *Emergency Ward 10*; on the other, the consistent seediness of Simenon's Paris and the inextricable associations of the French capital with "something delicious and probably naughty."

Leaving Paris, Leaving Maigret

Long-running television series provide opportunities for characters to change and age alongside the audience. Rupert Davies was forty-four when he first started playing Maigret in 1960, and had almost reached the retirement age for French civil servants (fifty-five) on his final appearance as the commissaire in 1969. Nothing else in Davies's career touched his success as Maigret, and Georges Simenon remained as pleased as he had been with the original casting, although Davies was burdened by his success. The initial BBC agreements with the Simenons were for the rights to adapt twenty-six stories, with an option to extend for a further thirteen stories.[52] Many of the BBC production files refer to "the 39," which are the original contracted episodes broadcast in three thirteen-week series between 1960 and 1963. The popularity of the series led, after very protracted negotiations, to a fourth and final series that ran in the autumn of 1963, coming to a close on Christmas Eve. This final series is clearly structured to move to conclusion, and in the last episode, "Maigret's Little Joke," Lucas is promoted to inspector and the Maigrets set off on holiday: "his first for three years," observes Mme. Maigret. The lighter tone of this final episode, which included filming on the Côte d'Azur, after the dark penultimate one, "Peter the Lett" (tx. 17 December 1963), in which Maigret's lieutenant, Torrence, is murdered and Maigret himself injured, is nevertheless suffused with the melancholy of an ending. The invalided Jules Maigret is shown as displaced from his own story, reduced instead to watching and narrating from the side.

Instead of being the person the audience watches, Maigret joins the audience and watches the police. There is a formal self-consciousness through which Maigret himself becomes a marginal figure in the investigation so that the audience is readied for his departure. The character of Inspector Maigret assists in his own passing, which means that the episode is both poignant and terminal. The narrative structure and use of location function as a commentary on the preceding programs, and the Paris that has been created for the television audience is distilled into Maigret's home, his workplace, and a bar on the Left Bank.

When the episode opens, after an initial, location-shot scene that shows the inspector emerging from a subway to buy a newspaper on the banks of the Seine, Jules Maigret is shown at home, his arm in a sling, subject to the rule of his wife. Domestic power is symbolized through a little business with an old sweater that Mme. Maigret wants to throw out, but her husband wants to keep. The full extent of the apartment set is used—as Maigret rushes from bedroom to living room—to show the commissaire, investigator of many secrets, reduced to the domestic impotence of hiding an old garment from his wife by stuffing it in a drawer. This extravagant use of two adjacent domestic spaces, in a series that normally shows only the Maigrets' living room, indicates, in the opening scenes, the extent of the inspector's displacement from his normal routines.

The prominence of Maigret's domestic space is matched by the other most significant setting in the story, a bar notionally on the Quai Saint-Michel, from which the police headquarters, across the river, on the Quai des Orfèvres, is visible.[53] It is in this public, but homely, space that Maigret establishes an alternative office, observing the progress of the murder investigation, and intervening through the writing of enigmatic postcards to his subordinate, now in charge. This location is first established ten minutes into the episode, with a careful three-shot sequence, in which the relevant spatial relations are demonstrated between the opening boulevard location, the Quai des Orfèvres, and the bar, and it is shown that Maigret has a new daily routine in which he buys a paper on his way, not to work, but to the café. It is from here that Maigret, reading the newspapers, discussing with staff, and sometimes just sitting and thinking, is shown to deduce the progress of the case, which he narrates for the audience, while observing when the windows of his office are lit up and when they darken. Simultaneously, the audience is also privileged to witness how Lucas is handling being in charge, and the contrast with the methods and tone of "Le Patron" accentuate Maigret's skill—and his absence. Lucas is shown to be hasty, judgmental, and irascible, too often shouting at suspects in a manner destined to make them uncooperative. However, he has also learned well from his mentor, and the episode makes the character the gift of a trip to the South of France.[54] This sports car, yacht, and sunshine excursion thirty minutes into the plot offers a contrast between Maigret's limited mobility, going between home and the café, and the opportunities that greet Lucas on his promotion. It also inscribes "holiday" within a fiction that begins and ends with the Maigrets packing to go away, offering a pleasurable glimpse of a non-Parisian life of leisure— although the Maigrets are going to the less glamorous Concarneau.

It is the demotion of Maigret from his own professional life that is so skillful, though, producing a felt rendition of the difficult marginalities of retirement (although there is no mention of such). This is embodied through the clue cards that Maigret writes for his colleagues throughout, and through his gaze across the river at his former office. In the clue cards, Maigret offers suggestions to both his team and the viewer, literally writing out the progress of detection. In combination with his café commentary, Maigret's card writing turns him into something much more like the narrator than the protagonist of the fiction. In the gaze at the office window, the difference between inclusion—being part of the investigation—and exclusion is given the spatial form of a point-of-view shot. Because the police headquarters is a large, uniform building, with many identical windows, this desire is best figured in the evening, when the shining light of one illuminated window identifies the particular office. And herein lies the poignancy of the device, for the exclusion and loss that Maigret feels is shown to be both unique (the one window) and part of a much larger, impersonal, undifferentiated institution (all the other windows). It is a clever and aesthetically satisfying end to the four years of British Maigret to have the hero sitting in a Parisian bar commenting on how his junior is running an investigation. This television city has become familiar through the four series, and although it may still be foreign, it has become familiarly foreign through its weekly broadcast into the home. Paris has been confirmed as a city of landmarks and strip joints, bars and gendarmes; but also of ordinary streets, nondescript cafés, and proper meals at home. Just like the wives of British policemen, Mme. Maigret wishes her husband would work less hard and come home more often.

The Modernity of Maigret

Rupert Davies made one final appearance on the BBC as Maigret in a one-off 1969 production, *Maigret at Bay*, broadcast on a Sunday night in the Play of the Month slot, in which the themes of retirement are explicit. The play (it is billed in the *Radio Times* as a "television play" by Donald Bull[55]) was promoted as the key attraction of the week's viewing, scheduled at the prime time of 8:15 P.M., immediately following the BBC's big drama serial success of the period, *The Forsyte Saga*. The importance of the television event was signaled by the dedication of the front cover of the *Radio Times* to Rupert Davies, pipe in hand, posed in front of a Parisian *Colonne Morris* (advertising pillar), with the legend "Rupert Davies returns as Maigret."

At ninety minutes, this dramatization has more time for both character and spectacle than the usual fifty-minute episodes. Maigret's state of mind becomes more important than the robbery with which the drama commences, while Paris is displayed through locations from the Seine to Montmartre. The opening sequence, which begins with a low-angle shot of the glistening cobblestones of the Place de la Concorde to follow an audacious jewelry robbery, which is later referred to in a newspaper headline as "Rififi Place Vendôme," immediately invokes French cinema, rather than the British television play, as its peers.[56] The four-minute heist sequence filmed in a deserted early morning Paris introduces a story line that becomes much less significant than Maigret's own midlife melancholy, which is in turn augmented by false accusations of sexual assault made against him.

The flamboyant, generic use of location in the opening sequence is matched by a rather more subtle use of Maigret's routes in the city to express his state of mind. In particular, location shooting of the banks of the Seine, and the steep steps from the quays, are used expressively both to evoke his familiarity with the city as a workplace and to anticipate his retirement. Early in the episode, because of his insomnia, Maigret visits his doctor, who counsels him to recognize that his age means he faces "a spiritual climacteric." Aged fifty (with a state retirement age of fifty-five), Maigret reflects on his future. "Every time I see the anglers on the quay, I think that will be me in five years," he observes. In his final walk along the river, he is shown to have come to terms with the future as he talks to a young fisherman and attempts to cast a line.

This story is also dramatized in the later Granada Maigret, where it formed the third episode in the second series, "Maigret on the Defensive." Incorporated into this series as just another story, there is no particular melancholy in the Granada version. Instead, the story functions to demonstrate Maigret's success and reputation, his maverick position in relation to his superiors, and the loyalty of his subordinates. In contrast, the earlier version, as a Play of the Month return, reiterates the intimations of mortality present in the final episode of the fourth series and presents a hero who is both fallible and weary. The story line involves Maigret responding to a late-night telephone call for help from a young woman, and thus being set up for a disgraced resignation. While his behavior with her (all of which we are shown) does not involve the braggadocio she recounts in her case against him, it does entail vanity and the sense of being indispensable. Only this could take him from his wife's arms in the marital bed to a late-night bar and a beautiful, distressed young woman who insists that only he, of the great reputation, can help her. On the morning after the encounter, he is shown springing up the steps from the Seine, full of energy.

Alongside this melancholy, this double sense within the drama that not only Jules Maigret but also the audience must accept that it is time for him to attend to his wife and start thinking about a cottage in the country, there is a certain bravura display of the beauties of Paris. This is most notable in the opening sequence but is also demonstrated in the range of locations used, fifteen in all, which include the Place de la Concorde, the Place Vendôme, Rue Gabrielle, the banks of the Seine—and a garden in Caithness Road, Hammersmith ("this is assumed to be Paris").[57] What a reprimand about studio bookings refers to as "the heavy film content of the programme" distinguishes this Paris from the more studio-bound Paris of the earlier series, while at the same time reprising those earlier programs, making them seem as if they were more location shot than they actually were.[58] As the *Daily Telegraph*'s reviewer put it, in a comment that draws attention to the familiarity which I am arguing is a key aspect of the television city, "half the pleasure of the programme came from Maigret's familiar Paris, the anglers along the Seine, the cafés in Montmartre, his scruffy little office and Mme Maigret fussing solicitously as ever."[59] So Maigret returns, but in a form that is subtly different to the series, testifying to the different production circumstances of Plays of the Month within the BBC.[60] This difference is also discernible in the treatment of what turns out to be the motivating narrative drive within the drama, illegal abortion.

The Simenon story (*Maigret se défend*) identifies the murderer who seeks to discredit Maigret as a psychopathic dentist who "helps" young women, sometimes, unfortunately, murdering them during the abortion. The narrative involves a clever play on what can be seen from windows, and who stands at which windows, or in the street, to observe whom. The story dates from 1964, and abortion remained illegal in France until 1975. However, in Britain it had been legal since 1967, and there had been a significant public response to the 1965 Ken Loach–Tony Garnett Wednesday Play, *Up the Junction*, about the horrors of illegal abortion. In terms of institutional politics, returning to this topic four years later in the Play of the Month unavoidably recalls the earlier uproar and also demonstrates the way in which television fiction speaks to contemporary concerns, even as it dramatizes stories set in another time and place. Here, the combination of the liberalism of (parts of) the BBC in the 1960s is combined with Maigret's celebrated, nonjudgmental acceptance of human activity when his friend's daughter replies, with a shrug, to his enquiry as to whether she has ever had an abortion, "But of course."

I have argued that much of the pleasure of the BBC *Maigret* lies in the combination of the detective genre with what was for the British viewer a novel, if culturally recognizable, location. This is not to underestimate the importance of performance—particularly those of Rupert Davies and Ewen Solon—of script, and of Simenon's stories set in his own apprehension of Paris. But in this study of television cities, the 1960s BBC *Maigret* is interesting for the way in which it enables viewers to visit Simenon's Paris on a regular basis and become familiar with the types of people, the types of places, and the types of crime to be found there. If Simenon's Maigret novels are characterized by what Ginette Vincendeau has called a "social voyeurism" for a French audience, then this British version additionally provides a living-room tourism for a non-French one. This television city is foreign, but it is also deeply familiar. It has the topography of the police crime story. It is a city in which respectable women are usually, like Mme. Maigret, at home, or, if not, are (often avariciously) pursuing the interests of their menfolk, while out on the streets and in the clubs, the women who work the nighttime economy are bearing witness to Maigret—or being found dead. Pigalle, les Halles, Montmartre, 36 Quai d'Orfèvres: this is not Dock Green or Newtown, which would be the most familiar police territories for the British viewer at this time. "It is always pleasant to look at Paris," as the critic of the London *Times* observed, and this Paris involves looking at women as well as looking at the Seine.[61] There is an established identification between Europe and sex in the British cultural imaginary, and Simenon's Maigret stories provide many more plot devices and settings using bars, clubs, and ladies of the night than equivalent British crime drama.[62] But the law is still avuncular and paternalistic, just rather less judgmental than British policemen of the period, such as George Dixon.[63]

The location shooting is crucial to this familiar-unfamiliar tourist pleasure. As I have demonstrated, the location footage has a tendency toward the recognizable landmark—but there are also many sequences shot in a more banal and quotidian Paris, sometimes with the identifying flash of a passing Citroën DS (figs. 1.21–1.22).[64] These shots are often sandwiched between studio sequences that are dressed with unambiguous signifiers of Frenchness. But the quotidian location sequences themselves, although identified as Paris through this editing, retain their own mysterious thereness, prey to the contingency that partly defines the photographic arts. The vividly documented challenges of the production seem to have led to a predilection for Atget-style shots of empty streets. In the Location Breakdowns for episodes, which list location, shots, and artists for each location, most locations include a shot or two listed "Nil" or "Extras."[65] These were much easier to get in the can than shots that also included actors, and shooting instructions include notes such as "the odd cul-de-sac to get a good montage."[66] Additionally, in the episodes that I have viewed, there is a discernible inclination toward the long view—of a street, an alley, an apartment block, a busy junction, or a boulevard. It is almost as if the production circumstances—the busy three-to-five-day excursions to Paris—manifest themselves in a cinematographic desire to get as much of the city in a single shot as possible. Ginette Vincendeau has argued that the Jean Richard series, which also began production in Paris in the 1960s, bear witness to a way of life, focused on the community of the quartiers, that was already disappearing. The discussion of different versions of "Au Picratt's" above sketches how this might be done. The BBC *Maigret*s do also provide inadvertent testimony to 1960s Paris, but not in quite the same way. They do not have what Vincendeau characterizes as the almost ethnographic quality of the early Richard programs because they are not inward with the world they depict, a point noted by the representative of the French national broadcaster RTF in his comment, "Your Maigret series does not have the same atmosphere of authenticity to which we are accustomed in our programmes dealing with crime."[67] Nevertheless, in their combination of British ideas of Paris with scenes filmed in Paris, which both authenticate these ideas of Paris (through landmarks and stereotypes) and also offer material that is more recalcitrant (the one- or two-shot street scenes), they do provide an incidental photographic archive of early 1960s Paris. "The Trap," for example, has a montage sequence that includes, with "no artists in shot," Rue Pot de Fer, Passage Cottin, Rue Mouffetard, Passage des Postes, Passage de Patriarches, Rue Daubenton, the Montmartre Funicular, Place du Tertre, and Rue St. Rustique.[68]

What is at stake here can be considered in another way by returning briefly to the 1993 Granada version of "Maigret on the Defensive." These programs were filmed in Hungary, using Budapest for the 1950s-set Paris street scenes. The former Soviet colony offered unmodernized apartment buildings, empty streets, little traffic, and exceptionally good rates

1.21–1.25. Different types of location shooting in BBC *Maigret*, "Death in Mind." **1.21:** Street corner with Metro sign and Citroën DS in background. Location here is signified through these two general icons of Paris and France. **1.22:** Location footage of a 1960s underpass, part of the Périphérique, the nearest car a Citroën DS. **1.23** and **1.24:** Long view of unidentified street with French location identified through gendarmes after car breaks down.

for this expensive U.S.-U.K. coproduction.[69] The whole production took place in Hungary. There was no nipping over the Channel for the location shooting. But, interestingly, there is no sense of space in these programs, none of the thereness that permeates the BBC programs. Possibly because there was actually more location shooting, the shots themselves are much more constrained. They are tightly framed on the narratively significant—to exclude identifiably non-Parisian and

1.25. Use of landmark to signify location. The pursuit in "Death in Mind."

present-day elements—and edited together in a way that makes setting equivalent to costume or other elements of the mise-en-scène. The setting is inert. Location it may be, but it is location that can never be itself, and must instead always be framed and dressed as Paris of the 1950s. This later British *Maigret* was self-consciously retro, invoking a vanished Paris through location filming in unmodernized Hungary. But the nostalgia of this adaptation and the black-and-white images of the 1960s British series should not be muddled up.

Richard Cobb, in his wonderful short essay on Maigret's Paris, argues that the detective is "a historian of habit, of the déjà vu," and that this is why he was so reassuring to a certain generation.[70] This persistence in the attention to the déjà vu partly explains why Maigret is attractive for handsome retrospective coproductions, like the Cremer, Gambon, and lately, disastrously, the Rowan Atkinson versions.[71] However, these handsome productions, all carefully sourced retro-detail, precisely lack the perceptible contingency of the television cities of the Davies and Richard versions. As the credits of the 1993 Gambon version indicate, this Paris is already long gone.

In conclusion, I want to argue that the 1960s British *Maigret*, with its complicated mélange of methods to produce Paris, may have been judged inauthentic by the French—how could it not be?—but did signify modernity in the British context. This is a modernity that comes

1.26–1.27. Granada *Maigret*, 1993: The constraints of framing while location shooting in Budapest to avoid the intrusion of anachronistic or non-Parisian elements ("Maigret and the Nightclub Dancer").

precisely from the repetitions of the televisual city, the comfort and security of watching, from a British living room, a Paris in which ordinary people commit banal crimes and are investigated and understood by Inspector Maigret. Here, the modernity of the medium itself should not be forgotten. Only in 1957 did the proportion of homes in Britain with television come to exceed those without.[72] *Maigret* on British television in the early 1960s represented a new postwar world, a world in which many new experiences became possible for ordinary British citizens: watching television, going to Europe on foreign holidays, drinking wine, understanding a bit of French, considering the European Economic Community, watching European art cinema—and acknowledging the pleasures of sex.[73]

1.28–1.30. The title sequence for the 1993
Granada version of *Maigret*, which ties the series
to a fondly remembered Paris.

In histories of postwar Britain, the poet Philip Larkin's much-cited declaration that "sexual intercourse began in 1963 . . . between the end of the Chatterley ban and the Beatles' first LP" forms an emblematic inauguration of the "swinging sixties."[74] Recent historians of the period, such as Dominic Sandbrook, have argued that the swinging of the sixties has been much exaggerated, and, for most people, life continued with hardly a ripple of the concerns of the metropolitan elite.[75] However, perhaps the BBC *Maigret* was one such ripple, broadcast between 1960 and 1963, a precursor to the sexual intercourse that began in 1963, and the radical social liberalization of the 1964 and 1966 Labour governments—the French setting taken for granted, Paris watched in British living rooms by large audiences every week, and this British Paris exported worldwide. Maigret's attention to the pleasures of the table coincided with the slow introduction of more Mediterranean cuisine to Britain, particularly through the cookery books of Elizabeth David, and the attention to France, Italy, and Spain as desirable destinations with enviable lifestyles.[76] While the British upper classes have always enjoyed Paris and the Riviera, Ben Highmore has argued persuasively that a "new declension" of the modern is articulated in 1960s Britain through the import of everyday artifacts such as French earthenware dishes and Italian pasta jars, made available on the British high street by Terence Conran's Habitat shops.[77] While the artisan chic of the continental rustic kitchen might appeal mainly to the metropolitan new middle classes, setting detective genre fiction in France could be seen as an earlier, related move for the BBC, with a rather broader reach. It suggested a confidence in a popular engagement with the foreign. After a very long nineteenth century, Britain was beginning to get modern.

The awkwardness of the manner in which Rupert Davies inhabited Maigret's Frenchness can be seen to symbolize the awkwardness of these changes for Britain. Nevertheless, the composite French milieu of *Maigret* and Maigret's Paris meant modernity in this context, the beginning of the swinging sixties in London, and a period of extraordinary innovation in British television. And to support my point, let me draw attention to the end credits of the series. These elegant monochrome graphics are quite different to the opening titles, and draw on

1.31–1.33. Final titles to the BBC *Maigret* with 1960s graphic design.

the pop sensibility that also creates *The Avengers* and the art-school chic of British popular music. The screen is all white, with a band of gray stripped across the top of the bottom half.[78] Across this band of gray are laid the names of the credits, while isolated characters, one or two at a time, move and gesture in the abstraction of the white screen (figs. 1.31–1.33). The simplicity and cool of these 1960s credits demonstrates the modernity of television Paris and *Maigret* in midcentury Britain.

2 Living-Room London

A New Medium in an Old Country

Two images of London as a television city, one from approximately the beginning (1968) of the period discussed in this chapter and one from the end (2010), are emblematic of the transformations in both television and London during this time. The first, a logo for Thames Television (fig. 2.1), dates from the period of national broadcast television (the network era), normally watched in the living room, while the second comes from the title sequence of one of the BBC's most successful twenty-first-century programs, an updated Sherlock Holmes (fig. 2.2), which can be watched on a range of devices and sites. Each image mobilizes London landmark imagery, most notably the River Thames, to create a television London; however, they do this in different ways to serve slightly different purposes. I argue that there are some clear historical continuities for television Londons, which can usefully be traced through the interplay of three key factors: the heritage of British public service broadcasting, Britain's imperial history, and the hybridity of television as a medium. The chapter, which commences with a discussion of the peculiarities of the British broadcasting context, the cultural centrality of television, and the place of London within this, is then organized in three main parts that sandwich television's version of an everyday, multicultural London between the persistent apprehension of London as a dark, Victorian place. While there is a multitude of other Londons, the pattern I outline here is argued to be foundational for an understanding of this particular television city. The essence,

2.1. The Thames Television logo with its compression of London landmarks (Thames Television, 1968–91). **2.2.** The third shot of the *Sherlock* credits, a view west, inland, evading the new skyscrapers to the east (BBC, 2010).

the interest, and the complication of London as a television city lies in the juxtapositions of an old, imperial city and what was, in the mid-twentieth century, a new medium.

For the twenty-five years that Thames held the London weekday franchise, this logo and its theme were deeply familiar to British viewers, and this familiarity through repetition is among the most significant aspects of the televisual city. The Thames Television logo regularly popped up between programs and during continuity announcements to remind viewers of the identity of the television company broadcasting in their homes.[1] If the viewer was watching in London, the Thames logo announced both where programs came from and where they were being watched. However, as the logo is composed of a fantasy collage of famous London landmarks assembled on a bank of the River Thames, it also presents an image of that location, of London as a television city. This composite image, with the word THAMES in white capitals across it, brings together the London landmarks of Big Ben, the Post Office Tower, the Old Bailey, the Bank of England, St. Paul's, and Tower Bridge. All of these buildings are clustered impossibly together on what is presented as a landmark-rich riverbank, with the Thames in the foreground. Tower Bridge, on the extreme right, is open, so the right-hand side of the image seems open to the estuary and the sea beyond.

This image was seen far beyond the London region; it was familiar to viewers all over Britain from 1968 to 1993 as many Thames Television programs were broadcast nationally on the commercial ITV network, and they all began with the Thames TV London montage.[2] Many of these programs—huge hits such as *Minder* (1979–94) or innovative drama such as *The Naked Civil Servant* (1975)—were widely exported, and the eight notes of the Thames theme would have been known to viewers thousands of miles away. Box sets of DVDs have kept the image in circulation, as the Thames archive is marketed in a commodity form that always commences with the Thames logo, while digital and satellite television enable audiences all over the world to view and review this twentieth-century television.

The image from the title sequence of *Sherlock* seems, at first glance, with the prominent addition of London's Millennium Wheel on the left of the image, and the Big Ben clock tower nearer the center of the image, to be simply an updated image taken facing inland, rather than out to sea. This image is the third shot of the title sequence, which opens with two busy nighttime shots of Piccadilly Circus taken from above. These shots, in which the image is flooded with the contrasting, moving light from car headlights, street lamps, and Piccadilly Circus's enormous neon sign, function to signify an abstract, urban excitement and rush. This third shot, which maintains the buzz through the speeded-up traffic rushing across the bridges, anchors this abstract urbanness to somewhere clearly identifiable as London. Red London buses punctuate the foreground as they speed across Waterloo Bridge, and the Millennium Wheel frames part of the Victorian gothic of the Houses of Parliament, which take up half the midground of the image. The traffic, the wheel, and the plain concrete of Waterloo Bridge, which leads from the not-very-distinguishable concrete of the National Theatre and the South-bank Centre in the bottom left-hand corner of the image, are, though, the only hints of modernity in this twenty-first-century view. The wheel dresses the nineteenth-century riverside with a tourist icon, but as the view faces west, rather than east, the cluster of skyscrapers that signifies the new city of London in Docklands is completely avoided. This London remains dominated by the Victorian city. In contrast, the Thames logo consciously (if geographically impossibly) juxtaposes the Post Office Tower, which, with its revolving restaurant, was a key icon of the swinging London of the 1960s, with older, enduring symbols such as St. Paul's and the central criminal court, the Old Bailey. Significantly though, the Thames image eschews the Houses of Parliament, including only the clock tower, and thus separates the image of a modern, up-to-date 1960s metropolitan television station from the London of government, differentiating itself from the more official BBC. This slightly tricksy maneuver seeks to establish Thames—in contrast to the BBC, as we shall see—as the television station of a located capital city rather than an official, state broadcaster.

These are different types of image, called on to perform different tasks. The Thames logo combines several different views of London in one image and works to locate, not just individual programs, but the source or origin of television itself. Its use by a television station, rather than just an individual program, gives it a broader possessive and locative ambition (these are Thames programs, made here). The *Sherlock* shot is one from a title sequence that is used at the beginning of different seasons and episodes, and also appears as the home screen on series DVDs. Here, there is a branding of a franchise, a twenty-first-century Sherlock Holmes, rather than a television channel, and this franchise can be found on affiliated websites, publications, and merchandise. The Victorian gothic parliament buildings are essential to the pitch of the program; juxtaposed with the decorative modernity of the Millennium Wheel, and, within the sequence, the whizz of (speeded-up) traffic and editing, the image epitomizes its project. Set in an old place, this will be a speedy new experience. This is an image of adaptation that at the same time signifies the persistence of London as old city, and the marketable attractions of neo-Victorianism in the twenty-first century.

This mixture of old and new is characteristic of London as a television city, whether articulated as an aspirational project of modernity as in the Thames logo, or through the contrast of movement and building in the *Sherlock* image. In this chapter I explore some of the vectors that produce old and new television Londons as a widely exported television city. Developing some of the ideas about the recalcitrant British engagement with modernity raised at the end of chapter 1, my suggestion is that television London, in particular, is a privileged site on and through which Britain engages with the new realities of its changed place in the world. Television is one of the places where Britain works out what it might be to be modern, even as this new medium is often recruited to reimagine Britain's historical literary and dramatic culture. Capital cities represent nations; London additionally, for a complex set of historical reasons, is peculiarly resonant as a center and origin of British broadcasting, with both a national and an international reach, a claim that can be exemplified through the call sign of BBC Radio to occupied Europe during the Second World War: "This is London, this is London." This call sign had a global significance, and when British television restarted after the war, it too developed international ambitions, as the analysis of British *Maigret* in chapter 1 has demonstrated. The interplay of old and new Londons and old and new international audiences and markets is a complex one.[3] London, as a television city, tells some stories of much longer duration than the existence of the television medium, and it is with the BBC that the story must begin.

The Peculiarities of the British Broadcasting Context: This Is London

Britain is geographically small, not great, and the broadcasting industries are overwhelmingly concentrated in London.[4] So too are the Houses of Parliament, the press, and the monarchy. Most government departments and the Civil Service are based in London.[5] Government and state news is primarily both made and broadcast in London. News from London has its own ritualized "outside broadcasting (OB)" London topography, its customary locations, from which reporters speak. College Green, a tiny island of grass in the traffic outside the Houses of Parliament, is the traditional site for outside broadcast cameras to break parliamentary news. Ceremonial occasions involving the royal family are reported with camera teams in the Mall outside Buckingham Palace. Scotland Yard, the police headquarters with its revolving sign, provides a familiar backdrop for crime and police news, while the Old Bailey, the central criminal court, houses key trials. So on British television, and through the reporting of news from Britain worldwide, London is made and remade as center and origin. "This is London" indeed.

However, it is not just London as center and origin of the (still, just) United Kingdom that is made and remade in much British broadcasting. For most of the twentieth century, the BBC World Service (funded by the Foreign Office) broadcast worldwide from Bush House in the Strand.[6] Shaping the role and image of the BBC is the history of the British Empire, and London as an imperial capital. This matrix of relations can be exemplified through an instance from the early days of radio noted by John Reith, the first director general of the BBC. He noted that the BBC broadcast of the speech with which King George V opened the British Empire Exhibition in 1924 was the first time that the monarchy had been heard on radio, "making the nation as one man."[7] The elements of this first broadcast are significant: the BBC, the monarchy, and the enormously popular Empire Exhibition in the purpose-built Wembley Stadium on the outskirts of London.[8] It is not just one nation that is being made here, but a nation that is also an imperial center. Wembley

2.3. The placing of London in the world for BBC news broadcasts: 2016 news titles, BBC1.

Stadium may now be more familiar as the home of sporting fixtures, national and international rituals of another kind, but from its earliest days the BBC has been entwined with both state and empire, an entwining given broadcast form with the founding of the Empire Service in 1932.[9] The BBC's complex relation to the state, the historical funding of the World Service through the Foreign Office, the dominance of Reithian values—a whole set of historical structures, institutions, practices means that the London of the BBC is in some senses global. As one of the editors interviewed in a study of Bush House commented, "BBC Arabic is known across the Arab world as the London station. . . . It's a local way of referring to it. . . . Broadcasters started their bulletins with 'This is London' which is 'Hunah London.' I was just thinking about it because whenever I go to the Arab world, people refer to us as London."[10] While the Thames Television logo identifies London as the source of programming, the BBC logo has, characteristically, identified the BBC with London in the world. It is the globe, rather than the nation-state, that frames the BBC logos (see fig. 2.3), and, within this framing, the BBC and London are overlaid with each other, in both national broadcasts and international channels such as BBC News 24 and BBC World.

The Cultural Centrality of Television

The peculiarities of the British broadcasting context are not limited to the overdetermination, in a small country, of London as seat of national and formerly imperial government, center of the media industry, and home of the BBC, which means that unlike other international news providers such as CNN or Al Jazeera, the news broadcasts of the BBC are associated with a city.[11] There is also the long history of public service broadcasting and its significant institutional embodiment in the structure and practices of British broadcasting and the BBC in particular.[12] This is not a history that I recount here, but it is germane to the understanding of television London because of the place of television, and the BBC, within British culture. Only as the determining, but taken-for-granted structures of public service are being finally dismantled in the twenty-first century does the cultural centrality of twentieth-century British television, particularly from the 1960s through the 1980s, come more clearly into view.[13] For my purposes in this chapter, this claim for the cultural centrality of television, made most convincingly by John Caughie in 2000, means that it was on and through television that the meanings of twentieth-century postimperial modernity for this old country were articulated.[14] The very substantial resources devoted to television production outside a commercial remit (instead, "to inform, educate and entertain"), at a period when writers and program makers were excited by the possibilities of "the biggest theatre in the world," are germane here.[15] The cultural contexts of British television, which include a strong documentary–public service tradition, a significant literary-theatrical heritage, a vibrant working-class popular culture, deep ambivalence about U.S. cultural influence, and the transformations in educational opportunity and social mobility that followed the Second World War, are significant determinants in the making of British television culture, with its peculiar, rather uneven hybrid forms and tone. Television was certainly, for some, "a license to print money," but it was also an exciting new medium in which young, committed program makers wanted to work, inspired by the prospect of enormous audiences and the new democracies of culture.[16]

It is this mixed environment, partly patrician, partly innovatory, partly popular, partly profit driven, that produces some significant television Londons which can be found across a range of genres, including classic literary adaptation, contemporary drama, soap opera, and situation comedy. The new medium was called on both to create new forms, and also, very significantly, to transmit to wider national audiences versions and performances of already existing cultural forms, from literary and theatrical classics to music hall and orchestral symphonies. Television in Britain is a new medium in an old country, and one of its negotiations must be with the weight of this country's past. One aspect of this is a suggestive historical simultaneity between the early days of British television as a mass medium and the final days of the British Empire. Kobena Mercer describes it thus: "During the 1950s two events occurred which, between them, transformed everyday life and public culture in Britain. One was the mass migration and settlement of Caribbean, Asian and African citizens from the former colonies of an Empire who came to the metropolitan centre to start a new life and rebuild a war-torn economy; the other was the mass installation of television sets wired-up and tuned-in to receive broadcasts from the BBC and the newly formed ITV network."[17]

Mercer continues, "What has been the relationship between these two histories?," and I argue here that this question is particularly pertinent to an understanding of televisual London, and that a focus on London provides a privileged site through which the relationship between these histories can be explored. London's nineteenth-century preeminence proves a notable presence in British television programming, while the imperial history of the U.K. permeates its televisual output. In this chapter, my case studies are selected to investigate the ways in which different television Londons make and remake old Londons and old empires. The chapter moves through twentieth-century Victorian London in Dickens adaptations to the new neighbors of postimperial Britain in shows like *EastEnders*, *Desmond's*, and *Holding On*. In the final section, I look at the "new past" of the twenty-first century in some of the London-set dramas of the twenty-first century, where historic London is once again an important setting in series ranging from *Ripper Street* to *Call the Midwife*. This new old London speaks of and to a different televisual context and a very different city. The greatest city in the world in the Victorian period, old London has proved richly generative for the makers of television programs, and is paradoxically ubiquitous in the new twentieth-century medium, returning in digitally distributed versions in the twenty-first century, a constant, costumed counterpart to the twenty-four-hour news services of the news from London.

Old London: Charles Dickens and Victorian Television

Television as a medium has been much discussed in terms of its con-temporaneity and its ability to broadcast current events and affairs. It is frequently characterized as a banal, ephemeral medium through which everyday life flows—and is wasted. An important aspect of television in relation to London, though, has been its dramatization of London as an old city, particularly a nineteenth-century city, a place where the rich live in mansions and travel in carriages, while the poor haunt dark streets and grubby, crowded dwellings. If, as Iris Kleinecke-Bates has argued, the imaginative re-creation of the Victorian age is a domi-nant cultural preoccupation of late twentieth- and early twenty-first-century British culture, this finds one of its most privileged expressions in the television London of literary adaptation.[18] Fog swirls through the dark city of rookeries, opium dens, money lenders, lawyers, mer-chants, hansom cabs, barefoot children, wealthy nouveaux riches, and impoverished aristocrats. The most constant form for the appearance of this London on British television screens is through the adaptation of the novels of Charles Dickens, although the Sherlock Holmes sto-ries of Sir Arthur Conan Doyle, flamboyantly reworked in the recent period as *Sherlock*, are also a very significant source and are discussed in the final part of the chapter. In each of these cases, the oldness of the London shown in television adaptations can obscure the historical contemporaneity of the fictions. The very skill manifest in the aspira-tion to authenticity in the period mise-en-scène and costume in, for example, the 2005 BBC *Bleak House* or the 1984–94 Granada *Sherlock Holmes*, can make these fictional worlds seem as if they were always in the past. As Maxim Jakubowski observes of the Holmes stories, "Dur-ing the years Sherlock Holmes spent in London—from approximately 1878 to 1904—he lived through one of the greatest periods of change the city had ever known. . . . Many of the locations referred to in the Holmes stories are relatively new. . . . What we may now view through the golden fog of nostalgia as being quaint and historical was fresh and new to the young Holmes and Watson."[19] Similarly, Dickens's London was one in which the Georgian material structure of the city was being transformed by both the enormous growth in population and major works such as the main drainage sewage system, the embanking of the river, and the building of the railways and terminals.[20] Although we see these serials as set in the past, it was a past that was turbulent in its pace of change, rather than achieved in its pastness, and in my view the most interesting adaptations are those which render up some sense of the excitement and terror of modernity.

Dickens adaptations—although subject to the same ebbs and flows of fashion as the Victorian age more generally—have been a regular component of British broadcasting throughout its history, and in the form of television serials distinguished by high production values have been exported worldwide.[21] For the British viewer, the sight of well-known actors with flamboyant, muttonchop moustaches or elaborate, period coiffures, wearing authentically detailed costumes as they move through Victorian settings, is deeply familiar—even if a frequent response is to change channels.[22] This Dickensian world seems almost to live inside British televisions, just as its appearance in other contexts immediately signifies British television. If, as I propose in this book, the television city is characterized by repetition, domesticity, and familiarity, then the enormous number of Dickensian Londons that have been produced for television are one of the sites through which this may be explored, and here I concentrate on adaptations of the late novel *Our Mutual Friend*.[23] I consider some aspects of London as a Dickensian television city, before proceeding to analysis of the more hybrid Victorian Londons that currently contribute to the continuing staging of television London as an old city.

The adjective "Dickensian" has resonances, particularly in relation to ideas of the city, that extend far beyond specific references to the work of Charles Dickens or Britain. The circumstances of the urban poor, and particularly poor children, are most commonly evoked, and thus the term has a representational aspect. In this usage, "Dickensian" connotes living conditions that should arouse both horror and pity, and are in some sense premodern. Dickens, as an author both popular and highly regarded, is also often cited in a more formal sense, in relation to discussions of television as a medium, generally through a claim that Dickens would nowadays be writing for television.[24] In this move, the nineteenth-century novelist is invoked to win gravitas for the twentieth-century medium. Culturally legitimate literature is mobilized to establish the seriousness of the much more culturally troublesome medium of television.[25] Here, I want to undercut adjectival Dickensian television and analyze the television Londons of some actual television Dickens adaptations. My starting point is with the historian Raphael Samuel and his observations on the adaptation of Dickens, occasioned by the 1987 film of *Little Dorrit* (directed by Christine Edzard).[26] Samuel argues that particular Dickens adaptations must always be understood in relation to broader historical attitudes to the Victorian age, both contributing to and drawing on these images. He wants to demonstrate the dead hand of heritage on Edzard's film, while also recognizing the politics of an engagement with Victorian values in Mrs. Thatcher's Britain. The historical polemic of Samuel's interpretation demonstrates his point: there is not a single Dickensian London. Dickens, as many scholars have argued, is made and remade for different audiences and periods, sometimes a gothic figure, sometimes associated with Pickwickian Christmas cheer.[27] The history of Dickens on British television is thus a complex history, not just of which novels seem of the moment, but also of the way in which the history of the moment is presented through the novels. If, as Samuel argues, the 1940s David Lean Dickens films were significant, at the moment of the postwar settlement, in "fixing a notion of the Victorian as a time of oppression and fear," then the introduction of Dickens adaptations on Sunday afternoons by the BBC in the 1950s and 1960s further developed a distance between the period depicted and the modern, midcentury home in which they were viewed.[28] It might be modern to have television, but what was offered on television, particularly by the BBC, was often anything but, insisting instead on the repeated return to the period of Britain's industrial and imperial expansion. This dark Victorian age, transmitted on the most modern of domestic technologies, gave resonance to the contemporary rhetorics of progress and a new Elizabethan age. However, these Sunday Dickens serials should not be seen simply in relation to ideas of progress and the Victorian. They were also formative in the evolution of ideas about the role of television and what public service broadcasting offered the nation. This is extolled enthusiastically by Jeffrey Richards: "The BBC Sunday teatime serial . . . became the flagship of Dickens production in the 1950s and 1960s. Dickens as editor of *Household Words*, Dickens as family entertainer, perfectly fulfilled the Reithian image of television, of the family gathered round the wireless or television sharing the culture, a vision based on the premise not of freedom of choice but freedom of access to all that is great. The Sunday teatime serial was the epitome of television as an educational, uplifting, socially cohesive force."[29] Richards, whose chapter is titled "Dickens, Our Contemporary," wants—unexceptionally—to demonstrate that different Dickenses are invoked at different periods. Here, his point is the way in which the new medium can provide access to classic literature for all, and Richards celebrates these serials as embodying the public service ethos of the BBC in this period. Thus the mise-en-scène of Dickensian London, the costumes, the carriages, the fogs and gas lamps, not only becomes recognizable as a place (London in the past) but also signifies an attitude to both television and its audience. This often rather frightening fictional world is good for you.

The London of *Our Mutual Friend*

The BBC has undertaken three television versions of *Our Mutual Friend*. The first, in 1958, followed on very successful versions of *David Copperfield* (1956) and *Nicholas Nickleby* (1957).[30] While the programs no longer survive, BBC written archives preserve some details of the production, including audience reports about the twelve-part adaptation and records of the limited location filming. The novel is long and complicated, and has proved less attractive for adaptation than those Dickens books with single heroes, such as *Great Expectations* and *Oliver Twist*. The audience in 1958 evidently "found it much less easy to follow than the previous Dickens serials because of the profusion of subsidiary plots and characters."[31] It was not until 1976 that the novel was adapted again, this time in seven fifty-minute episodes that concentrate particularly on the double romances of Bella/Rokesmith and Lizzie Hexam and Eugene Wrayburn, as does the most recent, 1998 version, which was described, on first broadcast, as "two powerful love stories born of a society motivated by greed."[32] Here though, as each of only four episodes is feature-film length, the narrative pacing is rather different, and each episode is preceded by an increasingly lengthy résumé of previous events.

Our Mutual Friend is the last novel Dickens completed and offers a powerful image of late-Victorian London in its narrative of a vast fortune made through the rubbish of the dust heaps that the humble Mr. Boffin inherits.[33] But it is not so much for the dust heaps—which have perhaps become rather more vivid to readers in the twenty-first century than they were in the landfill glory days of the twentieth century—that *Our Mutual Friend* is most potent in the imaging of London, as in its treatment of the River Thames. For just as the dust heaps render up riches through the ceaseless activities of human scavengers, so too must the river be husbanded, its foreshores, waters, and sewer outlets monitored "with a most intent and searching gaze" for the flotsam and jetsam of the greatest city on earth.[34] The book opens with Gaffer Hexam and his daughter Lizzie out on the river in a small boat, "doing something that they often did" and "seeking what they often sought," and it is with this scene that the 1976 and the 1998 BBC adaptations start.[35] The inauguration of the narrative, as it has been with so many London tales, is the discovery of a body in the River Thames. This too was the hook at the end of the first episode of the 1958 version, with many audience members reported as displaying "considerable eagerness to find out which of the two men had managed to crawl out of the river."[36] The river's harvest, Gaffer Hexam's find, is the body of a young man wrongly identified as the intended heir to the dust heap fortunes.

The power of the Thames throughout the novel is recognized by both extant television versions, with the 1976 version using three shots of the dirty gray river for the credits. The opening back-in-time shot, an engraving of merchant sailing ships laid over moving water, is followed by a tight close-up of flowing tidal water and then a further close-up of the huge links of the ship chains, muddy and moving, but tethering an unseen ship to harbor (figs. 2.4–2.6). The 1998 version, which uses austere, white lettering on black for its titles, opens with Gaffer and Lizzie in their small boat on the river (figs. 2.7–2.9). In each, the production recognizes the significance of the River Thames to setting, plot, and mood, locating the action in a television London given coherence by the river. This watery setup then enables the contrast between the urban river and the rural canal lock, which appears later in the novel, to demonstrate the degradation of lives lived on the London river. In the 1976 produc-

2.4–2.6. The establishing of the River Thames setting in the opening titles for 1976 BBC adaptation of *Our Mutual Friend*.

2.7–2.9. The River Thames and Lizzie (Keeley Hawes) in the titles for 1998 BBC production of *Our Mutual Friend*.

tion, the significant, expressive use of the river setting, particularly in episode 4, contrasts strongly with the carefully framed, rather frontally styled rooms of many interior scenes, while the structure of the episodes gives both a watery opening and watery climaxes.[37] In the 1998 version, as I discuss below, the final scenes are set on the river, offering a contrast between the sunny pastoral of a riverside picnic at which all the sympathetic characters are gathered together, and a spectacular illuminated pleasure ship, a glittering hulk of excessive consumption where Society reflects on the story of a promising lawyer reputed to have married a penniless water woman.

If the river and the dust heaps are the persistent, generative setting for *Our Mutual Friend*, giving a visceral sense of late nineteenth-century London, some of its themes, particularly the proximity of poverty and great riches and the precariousness of social status, are common city stories, although given particular piquancy through the British class system. In each version, dramatic cuts are used early in the first episode to introduce the juxtaposition of the world of the river dwellers with London society. The muddy grays and browns of the river scenes contrast with the colorful silks and satins of the elite, the warm candlelight, and the spectacular displays of food, with the later version able to exploit a more mobile camera to produce a sense of being within, rather than looking at, the public rooms of an upper-class mansion. This theme of the contrast between the two worlds, introduced through editing, is then developed through the spatial movement of the underemployed upper-class lawyers, Mortimer Lightwood and his friend Eugene Wrayburn, who travel from the West to the East End of London by coach. In the 1976 version, this journey, which inaugurates Wrayburn's romantic class mobility, is achieved elegantly through the reflections of buildings that are shown on the coach windows. In the 1998 version, as they approach their destination, there is cutting between the destitute inhabitants of the streets and the ennui of the conversation in the coach, which is sharpened by Lightwood's recognition of how very far from the West End they have come: "We shall fall over the edge of the world if we don't stop soon." Wrayburn's journey downward, from the bright lights to the river shores, is matched, within the fiction, by the journeys of Mr. and Mrs. Boffin and Bella up into polite society, where they must wrestle with ambition, snobbery, and avarice (their own, and that of others) as they seek to understand their new status.

Docklands Dickens

The perennial questions about morality, money, and status with which both individual characters, and the novel as a whole, are concerned, are inflected rather differently in the 1976 and 1998 versions. In between these two productions comes the eighteen years of Conservative government, from 1979 to 1997, which were characterized by an assault on the postwar settlement and the values of public service and the welfare state. In this period occurred the deregulation of the financial markets (1986), the shift to financial as opposed to manufacturing capital, the sale of social housing, and the social validation of conspicuous consumption in figures such as the yuppie, or Harry Enfield's satirical character Loadsamoney. While property speculation has historically been a key motor for London's development and the fortunes made therein, the 1980s saw a spectacular transformation in property prices and the involvement of ordinary citizens in the boom and bust (1992) of speculative financial capital.[38] Huge fortunes were made and lost in this period, and the concern of *Our Mutual Friend* with the circulation of money and the winning and losing of riches spoke vividly to post-consensus, "no such thing as society" Britain.

In each production, the question of money is introduced in the opening river sequence as Gaffer, to his daughter Lizzie's distaste, retrieves coins from the pocket of the dead man they have harvested from the river. Gaffer's position is clear—a dead man has no call on money as the dead man is of the next world while money is of this world. This initial philosophizing about the worlds of money sets up the narrative concerns with inheritance and entitlement that structure much of the fiction, and, in the 1976 version, the love that Lizzie Hexam and Eugene Wrayburn have for each other is prohibited by their different social status, and the having and not having of money. However, the 1998 production introduces another aspect of money very early on, before Eugene first sets eyes on Lizzie, and thus matches Gaffer's philosophizing with upper-class financial morality and practices. This is done through the characters of the Lammles, a newly married couple whose wedding is the occasion for the initial luxurious banquet, where they are shown, behind the façade of wealth, demanding accusingly of each other, "Are you a man of fortune?" "Are you a woman of property?," only to discover the dreadful truth of their symmetrical mercenary miscalculations. In 1998, marrying for money, pretending to have money you do not possess, and being concerned avariciously with the display and consump-

2.10. The conspicuous consumption of the 1860s and the 1990s at the end of the final episode of *Our Mutual Friend*, 1998.

tion of wealth are foregrounded right at the beginning of the serial. It is not just Gaffer Hexam who is making calculations about the money of dead people. So if Raphael Samuel's reading of the 1987 version of *Little Dorrit* as "Docklands Dickens" is correct, then, ten years later, the 1998 *Our Mutual Friend* offers a Dickens for the post-Thatcher New Labour government of Tony Blair, a government which announced, memorably, that it was "intensely relaxed about people getting filthy rich."[39] The vulgarity and moral bankruptcy of the rich is returned to at the end of the 1998 version, when we see them feasting, drinking, and gossiping on an illuminated steamship (fig. 2.10), incredulous that anyone could hold values other than their own. This is a condemnatory rendition of the excesses, hypocrisies, and snobberies of both the 1860s and the 1980s–90s.

Writing in 2002, John Orr, who has argued that the 1990s saw a revival of London as a cinematic city, referred to a "neo-Dickensian art of the city . . . in film and in fiction," which he glossed thus:

London film has been in ferment—and fertile as an art form because of it—for the very good reason that the city has equally been in ferment over the last two decades. In film and in fiction, London has become the multi-ethnic capital of the world and one of the global financial centres for the electronic age. At the same time, it has reaped the harvest of the new looseness in social networks, the brittleness of identity and encounter which is both the curse and blessing of advanced modernity. More than ever before it has become a magnet for the homeless, the casual, the migrant, the criminal, the creative, the rich, the ambitious and the terrorist.[40]

Orr's interests lie in cinema and the novel, so it is not surprising that he omits television from his analysis. It is possible, though, that actual, rather than adjectival, Dickens on television was invisible to him simply because there has been so much of it, and the classic serial tradition is so taken for granted within British television culture. From the outside, with a cursory glance, it may not be easy to notice the differences in tone and attitude between different television productions—one set of costumed characters in a nineteenth-century setting may look much like another. However, if Orr's persuasive analysis of a new relevance for fictions founded in radical inequality—his neo-Dickensian London of the 1980s and 1990s—is expanded, then we might expect to find it on television too, not least in the tone and style of contemporary Dickens adaptations, most notably the acclaimed 2005 *Bleak House*, as well as the 1997 *Great Expectations* and the 1998 *Our Mutual Friend*. This harsh world of the Dickensian city, with its fleeting human connections, the inexorable machinery of capital and the law, and the random and not-so-random connections between characters, is also discernible, though, in a range of other contemporary television fiction, from Tony Marchant's ambitious, eight-part *Holding On* (BBC, 1997), discussed later in this chapter, to Channel 4's online-originated four-part drama, *Run* (2013). The Dickensian television city—hard times in the living room—speaks of more than nineteenth-century London, and to understand its persistence on British television it is necessary to explore another strand of British television and the creative reverberations of the public service mandate in the determination to use the new, and then ubiquitous, medium of television to tell stories of everyday life.

The Everyday City and the End of Empire

The Making of Multicultural London

The most obvious television London of last thirty years appears in the BBC television soap opera *EastEnders* (1985–). This is the first connection anyone has made when I have told them about this book, and the fictional East London borough of Walford provides a powerful and continuing version of London and Londoners. Taking place around Albert Square, originally organized through the stories of two families, the Beales and the Fowlers, *EastEnders* provides an exemplary instance of the television city: located, repetitious, full of incident but somehow always familiar. The generic demands of soap opera, which include much mulling over of incidents and relationships, means that women characters are more prominent than they are in many other city-set fictions, and also that this television city has as many interiors as streets. This is the television city as a place of well-lit homes and families, not lone flâneurs in shadowy streets. It is also, because of the inclusion of a map of London, which foregrounds the winding outline of the River Thames in its credits, one of the most recognizable contemporary ways—after the Tube map in which the geography of London is represented. The theme tune of *EastEnders*, nowadays calling viewers far outside the United Kingdom to a familiar corner of London, presents a current version of the old BBC call sign, "This is London."

EastEnders follows in a long and distinguished tradition in British television drama in which the medium is used to tell stories about everyday working-class life. It brings everyday serial drama to the capital city, to the south. Its most obvious precursor and model, popular television attracting huge audiences, is Granada television's Salford-set *Coronation Street*, which has dominated images of the north of England since 1960, and which was challenged, in 1982, by the new Channel 4's Liverpool-set, innovatory soap opera, *Brookside*. Partly because of the public service remit, British television drama has had a constant engagement with ordinary life, and *EastEnders* also draws on the pioneering television drama of the 1960s and 1970s with its commitment to "making it real" and using the new medium to represent its audience to itself. At the time of writing, *EastEnders* has been running

2.11. The shape of London and the River Thames in the *EastEnders* credits.

for thirty years, and in this period has passed through different phases and large numbers of cast, crew, and scriptwriters. Now, like *Coronation Street* in the 1980s, *EastEnders* too finds its own history constraining how it can handle and represent the extraordinarily rapid changes through which its ostensible setting is being transformed into part of a global city in which property is inconceivably expensive for ordinary Londoners. Paul Newland has drawn attention to the paradox of the program's project, beginning to broadcast a continuing drama of the traditional London East End while the redevelopment of the London Docks to become Docklands was already underway, so that these ideas of the East End are already under threat.[41]

When *EastEnders* started, in 1985, one of its direct challenges to both *Coronation Street* and *Brookside* was its determined ethnic diversity, with an initial cast including the African Caribbean Carpenter family, a Turkish café owner couple, and Asian corner-shop owners. These realist ambitions, to present both the traditional East End—there was also a Jewish doctor—and its changing composition, faltered quite quickly, for complex reasons, which Christine Geraghty summarizes as seeking to accommodate change but doing so "on the basis of suppressing difference rather than acknowledging and welcoming what it offers."[42] However, this original commitment to an ethnically diverse cast locates the vision of *EastEnders* to an identifiable multicultural moment in British television, one of the intermittent flickers in which Mercer's two histories, of the end of empire and the rise of television, seem directly in dialogue. The London historian Jerry White has proposed that the "entirely unanticipated" transformation of London's population in the second half of the twentieth century, so that "by the mid-1980s virtually any main street in the capital could cater for the needs and desires of every major culture round the globe," was the greatest change for London and Londoners in the twentieth century and identifies the end of empire as the motor of change: "The West Indian diaspora of the late 1940s and 1950s was the key event in the remaking of the Londoner. . . . The winds of change rattled windows in Notting Hill Gate and raised the dust on Brixton Hill. For the imperial citizens of Highgate and Middlesex (Jamaica), of Waterloo (Trinidad) and of Woodford (Grenada) were coming home to roost. And coming to colonize London."[43] And it is this journey, this return, this settlement, which both transforms and must be accommodated in the streets of London—and also on the television screens of the nation, and the initial casting of *EastEnders*. In comparison with dramatic newsworthy stories of arrival, preserved forever in the British imaginary by the newsreel film of the disembarkation of the *Empire Windrush* in 1948, or television images of the expelled Ugandan Asians on the Heathrow tarmac in 1972, settlement is a story of quotidian strangeness, hostility, difficulty, and accommodation. And television, the increasingly taken-for-granted medium through which something of these mundane encounters can be apprehended, is itself one of the sites in which the contradictory processes of decolonization, the coming to terms with the end of empire, is enacted.

New Neighbors

Following the pioneering research of scholars such as Jim Pines, Sarita Malik, Stephen Bourne, and June Givanni, there is now extensive documentation of the role of British television as both agent of, and site for, the negotiation of the understanding of postimperial Britishness and race and ethnicity in twentieth-century Britain.[44] The emerging institutional histories by scholars such as Darrell M. Newton and Gavin Schaffer also begin to track the significant preoccupation, particularly within the BBC, with policies for the address to, and representation of, "new citizens."[45] This hard labor of documentation makes it possible to move beyond counting the limitations of the representations of black and Asian citizens (and there are many), or of imposing a retrospective political correctness on the linguistic equivocations of television announcers in the use of terms such as "colored" and "Negro." Instead, it becomes possible to address British broadcasting as itself an environment formed within national and imperial assumptions that was, in the second half of the twentieth century, subject to its own transformations, while also resonating within the wider world. Here, the domesticity of the medium is critical. The inclusion of a regular topical calypso commentary by the Guyanese singer Cy Grant in the BBC's flagship early evening current affairs magazine program, *Tonight*, in the 1960s may have been conceptualized by *Tonight*'s producers mainly as a light entertainment punctuation in the fifty minutes of reporting, but it also introduced the rhythms of the Caribbean to many a British living room, rendering the exotic as ordinary.[46] The contours of the television world, in this argument, are responsive to, and formed by, the wider cultural context, in which, for example, immigration was conceptualized as a problem and race relations a focus of anxiety, but this increasingly popular medium also has its own institutional structures, conventions, and autonomy. For if, as Bill Schwarz has argued, it is in the encounter with the former colonial subjects of empire that the imperial heartland comes to see itself, the analytic question becomes, "Where, and in what terms, in British televisual output, does decolonization register?"[47]

Both the particularities of a nationally regulated, limited-channel public service system and the matter of television genre are significant, as are particular initiatives. As both Newton and Schaffer have demonstrated, key voices at the BBC (most notably the Director General, Hugh Carleton Greene in the 1960s) were committed to antiracism, although the resulting programming did not necessarily further those aims.[48] Similarly, the creation of Channel 4 in 1982, with a special remit to cater to those audiences not served by the existing three channels, led to the pioneering black and Asian current affairs programs of the early 1980s, of which Paul Gilroy queried, "Bridgehead or Bantustan?"[49] The British documentary tradition, which was protected by the public service project until the end of the century and flourished in programs such as *World in Action* (Granada, 1963–98), *Man Alive* (BBC, 1965–82), *This Week* (Associated Rediffusion/Thames, 1955–92), and *Panorama* (BBC, 1953–), as Sarita Malik has shown, returns repeatedly to questions of decolonization and empire (although not always conceived as such) and the "problems" of immigration and racial prejudice, while the news and current affairs programs report associated events in which London figures repeatedly, be it Rachmanism and riots in Notting Hill or dockers marching to support Enoch Powell.[50] Light entertainment provides a world in which blackness is imagined as an attribute of blackface white actors trailing memories of the American South, most notable in this context for the persistence of the extremely popular *Black and White Minstrel Show* until 1978. In terms of televisual London, however, it is situation comedy in which we can trace some significant negotiations, and what Stuart Hall has called "inevitably ambiguous achievements" by black media practitioners.[51]

The sitcom in British television has produced some memorable domestic situations in which the comedy is played out across social class, gender, ethnicity, and generation, with particular characters and catchphrases entering the wider popular culture and resonating far beyond the original audience. And it is the domesticity of the sitcom that is pertinent here, for the arguments about decolonization to which I allude briefly above are partly arguments about the way in which postcolonial immigration to the mother country brings the matter of empire into an often uncomfortable proximity. As Stuart Hall put it in 1978, "We are here because you were there."[52] Empire, and the end of empire, instead of being something taking place far away, overseas, and on the news, becomes instead something taking place in the street, next door, and, through television, in the living room. It is precisely not the world of the *Black and White Minstrel Show*—far away, and somehow timeless—but instead the complicated everyday interaction of expectation and reality that is accommodation with new neighbors. It is the intimacy of decolonization that was invoked by the infamous racist slogan in the 1964 Smethwick by-election, when the Conservative candidate, Peter Griffiths, campaigned successfully for election as an MP (in a former Labour seat) on the slogan, "If you want a nigger for your neighbour, vote Labour." As Malik has demonstrated, it is this invocation of new neighbors that is a significant formation in the British experience of the end of empire, and was addressed directly in programs such as *This Week*'s "The Negro Next Door" (Associated Rediffusion, 1965).[53] New neighbors too are a noticeable facet of twentieth-century British television sitcoms, from *Till Death Do Us Part* (BBC, 1965–68, 1972–75, which reappears in the United States as *All in the Family*), *Love Thy Neighbour* (ITV, 1972–76), and *The Fosters* (ITV, 1976–77) right through to the confident and successful *Goodness Gracious Me* (BBC, 1996–2001). The discourse of new neighbors has particular resonance in relation to the medium of television, for television, as it is in the home, gives new neighbors to everyone, as Rob Turnock has argued about the shock of the sudden intimate exposure to different class cultures with the commencement of ITV in the 1950s.[54] It is television that, as Stuart Hall put it in 1995, discussing the resistance to the changing realities of British culture, "is bringing this unwelcome message of cultural hybridisation into the domestic sanctuaries of British living rooms."[55]

What Schaffer calls the "racial sitcoms" of the 1970s are often as grim to watch now as they were then, and in the great flood of archive television that is now available in DVD form, it is noticeable that there is only a trickle of this programming. Schaffer, who argues that these programs provide a privileged access to "the racial values of the 1960s and 1970s," gives a contextualized examination of the extent to which this programming can be seen to construct race as the major problem of postwar Britain, as well as considering the extent to which it racialized difference.[56] Malik, who offers a history that is more televisually contextualized, concentrates on the ambivalence evoked by these programs and the varied reactions of audiences.[57] My interests are slightly different, in that I am concerned with the intimacy of the city in the living room, the new neighbors represented by performers such as Norman Beaton, Oscar James, Carmen Munroe, Thomas Baptiste, and Lenny Henry, who contributed to transforming ideas of the everyday. I will look in more detail at one of the few black-authored dramas on British television in the twentieth century, the Channel 4 sitcom *Desmond's*.

Desmond's, written by Trix Worrell, was broadcast on Channel 4 between 1989 and 1994, and was widely exported, both to the former British Empire and to the United States, where it was screened on Black Entertainment Television (BET).[58] The half-hour sitcom was set in a West Indian barbershop in Peckham, southeast London. In discussing the germination of the project, Worrell has recalled the barbershop that was round the corner from where he grew up, also in Peckham.[59] Peckham, with Rye Lane, its central shopping street, exemplifying many of the changes that Jerry White notes taking place in London, has a notable television presence in Britain through the enormously popular 1980s sitcom, *Only Fools and Horses*.[60] Written by John Sullivan, himself a working-class South Londoner, *Only Fools and Horses* introduced the nation to Del Trotter (David Jason) a London wide boy who makes a living for his family through the traditional city occupations of wheeling and dealing, ducking and diving.[61] Del deals in knockoff and dodgy goods as Trotters Independent Trading, a company epitomized in both ambition and actuality through its commercial vehicle, a little yellow three-wheeler Reliant Robin, which declares on its side that the company is based in "New York, Paris, Peckham," as I discuss in the introduction. *Only Fools and Horses*, which ran for ten years, with a very extended afterlife of Christmas specials and prequels, made Peckham a familiar location on British television screens, and Del Boy and his hapless brother Rodney immediately identifiable characters.[62] *Desmond's* Peckham, then, enriches and challenges an already generically familiar television London, sitcom Peckham, a place where a working-class population struggles to get by. The locations of *Only Fools and Horses* were the Trotters' living room in the resonantly named tower block Mandela House, their local pub, and, occasionally, the local streets and market shown in the title sequence.[63] To this, *Desmond's* adds its main studio location, the barbershop, and its other main set, the living room of the family's upstairs flat, as well as occasional excursions into nearby streets. *Desmond's* uses classic sitcom geography: a workplace and a living room set, with the workplace enabling narrative events through the visits of customers and friends while the domestic space caters particularly to dramas of generation and family.

These studio locations, the situation for the comedy, are very precisely located in Peckham through the filmed title sequence that opens each episode, and includes a shot of Peckham Rye railway station (figs. 2.12–2.19). This rapid montage sequence, which is cut to the rhythm of the soca-style theme tune, proposes the serious intent of the program through its documentation of a dynamic black London, presented with a commitment to a shared urban coexistence that is symbolized by the handshake at the end of the sequence, a close-up of two hands, one black, one white, grasping each other firmly. The use of a soca edit in sections of this sequence (with quick, rhythmic cuts that subordinate image to music), just like the calypso in *Tonight*, points to the enormous significance of black music traditions in the making of multicultural London: there is a soundtrack to these stories that surfaces only intermittently on television. Here though, the music transforms the image, while the *Tonight* calypso was a rather more mediated ventriloquism. In the final group of shots, Desmond (Norman Beaton) and Shirley (Carmen Munroe) seem to dance in the street in front of the barbershop.

This title sequence, which uses mainly images of young people, locates the program within a changing London, a city that is being given new energy by black music (the sequence opens with a shoulder-held boom box), youth culture (skateboarders), and young black professionals (a car-driving woman with the novel device of the period, a brick-size mobile phone), and a black woman barrister. But in the middle of the sequence, the images suddenly change from contemporary color film to black-and-white newsreel showing the iconic *Empire Windrush* arrival scenes.[64] As the words of the theme tune recall arrival, "We came from the sun to live in the cold," there are four images of the *Windrush* and its passengers, finishing with a medium close-up of a young boy, a child who will grow up in England and who, forty years later, could be hanging out at Desmond's. This *Windrush* sequence in the middle of the credits establishes that there is a history to the lives depicted in the sitcom, lives that are shown to be partly structured with questions of home and belonging (the place of origin, the West Indies, or that of arrival, the U.K.), recurring both in conversation and in aspects of the mise-en-scène, such as the photograph of a house in Guyana that Desmond

2.12–2.19. The title sequence of *Desmond's*, 1989, moving through contemporary Peckham (the boom box, the street, and the station) to archive images of the arrival of the *Empire Windrush*, back to a handshake on the present and the location for the sitcom with Desmond (Norman Beaton) and Shirley (Carmen Munroe).

keeps behind the mirror. The sense of an ever-present elsewhere that characterizes the sensibilities of, particularly, the old male characters such as Desmond and Porkpie, is embodied in a different way in the setting of the show in a barbershop.

West Indian barbershops, along with black churches, were significant public spaces for immigrants who found themselves unwelcome in existing institutions and have also been documented by other artists, including the notable series *Peter's* by the Birmingham-born painter, Hurvin Anderson.[65] Writing about Anderson's work, Eddie Chambers has suggested that these barbershops offered much more than a place to get one's hair cut: "Instead, it represented a space of comfort, of affirmation of self and a certain double consciousness. Within the Black barbershop, such things as current affairs, sport, and music in the UK could be passionately discussed and argued over at the same time that equally nuanced observations were being made on current affairs, sport and music in the Caribbean."[66]

The achievement of *Desmond's* lies in the manner in which it articulates this double consciousness across generations and nationalities with both humor and seriousness. The barbershop regulars include older immigrants, like Desmond himself, and Porkpie (Ram John Holder), who dream of return. Their backward glance is contrasted to that of Desmond and Shirley's British-born children, particularly assistant bank manager Michael (Geff Francis), keen to succeed in Mrs. Thatcher's Britain, and Matthew (Gyearbuor Asante), the perpetual-student African barbershop regular.

The inevitable ambiguousness of comedy—does the audience laugh with or at?—has been much discussed in relation to the politics of representation, and Trix Worrell, the writer of *Desmond's*, has described how many of his friends urged him not to "let the side down by going into sitcom territory."[67] The strains of Worrell's excursion are sometimes evident in the tone of *Desmond's*, which is not always confident, and some of the jokes don't work. But there are also moments of difficulty in which the experiences depicted almost rupture the conventions of the genre, in which what has been called the burden of representation proves too heavy for the sitcom. This is most obvious in episode 4 of the first series, when the program raises the question of cars, young black men, and the police, but can't quite handle the seriousness of the issues it has raised (figs. 2.20–2.24). The car theme emerges early in the episode when the sharply dressed Lee arrives at the barbershop, jangling his new car keys, and offers Desmond and Shirley's daughter Gloria a lift to school. There is a careful exposition of both the joke and the issue here, which is embedded within the fiction through Shirley's ignorance about the street slang in which the initials BMW have a double meaning. Lee has a new car, having sold his old BMW ("black man's wheels," as Lee and Gloria chorus to her mother) because the car was "too conspicuous, always being pulled over by the Old Bill." This setup is then intercut with another story about the incompetence of men undertaking domestic labor when Desmond and Porkpie, sent out by Shirley to do some shopping as the barbershop is quiet, prove themselves unable to operate a shopping trolley. This scene is played for laughs beneath a sign advertising "BURRELL English and Empire Fruiterer," but the tone then changes as a cut reveals Lee and Gloria in a white Golf GTI turning a corner and being stopped by the police. Desmond's concern, "What do the police want with my Gloria?," suddenly dramatizes the coming together of the everyday life of young black men ("always being pulled over by the Old Bill") with the less conspicuous lives of their parents' generation. Desmond rushes over to the car and the police, distressed, agitated—evidently not going to make things better, and possibly likely himself to get arrested. And suddenly the scene cuts and we're back to the barbershop, where the incident is not referred to again (fig. 2.25). So the constant harassment of young black men, particularly those in expensive cars, which has been so well documented in the British context, is purposefully illustrated within the episode in a manner that demonstrates the older, immigrant generation's ignorance of street life for the young. Desmond is shown to be both shocked and naive about what life is like for younger people, and the cut, from an external scene to the familiar barbershop set, epitomizes the producers' problem. In this cut, the show holds back from the alarming generic consequences of an arrest for its lead character. Not so funny.

This narrative paralysis provides a clear example of the imbrication of questions of genre, access, and the burden of representation. The show displays clear evidence of a desire to present everyday black British life

2.20–2.25. Desmond (Norman Beaton) and Porkpie (Ram John Holder) become involved in the police stopping Lee, and the sudden cut back to the barbershop (*Desmond's*, episode 1.4).

as normal, as not a problem. It recognizes a responsibility to the community in which it is set, hence both the loving attention to everyday generational conflicts and the introduction of more serious plots alluding to a broader racism. However, the condition of access to the airwaves is the generic form: comedy. And comedy has to stay funny to get broadcast.

Desmond's is important for several reasons. Institutionally, its commissioning marks a conscious effort within British broadcasting to diversify its creative personnel, and it was the first multiprogram black-authored drama since Michael Abbensetts's pioneering Birmingham-set *Empire Road* (BBC, 1978, 1979).[68] Commissioned in the mid-1980s, *Desmond's* is one of a tranche of programs and initiatives informed by aspirations toward multiculturalism on (some parts of) British television.[69] Other London-set dramas from this phase, such as *King of the Ghetto* (1986), *EastEnders* (1985), and *South of the Border* (1988–90), also contribute to a changing presentation of the city, and the involvement of new creative personnel, enabled by policies from which there has been, as Lenny Henry has argued forcibly, a subsequent retreat.[70] For my argument, though, *Desmond's* is important for its combination of its location and its everydayness. Because the drama is so evidently situated in a recognizable contemporary London and its humor is the humor of a family and friends within this context enacted through confident performances, the program has an ease with itself that marks it out as an instance of a banal postimperial neighborliness.

Hard Times in the Living Room: *Holding On* in the Neo-Dickensian City

Ten years later, the writer Tony Marchant explores fin-de-siècle urban culture in *Holding On* (1997), an eight-part drama that slices through late-1990s London, exploring the intersections of the post-Thatcherite city. I started this central section of the chapter with *EastEnders*, pointing to its formation within a public service project at a multicultural moment, and conclude with *Holding On*, which, while having recognizable origins within this formation, embodied most obviously in public sector workers Shaun (David Morrissey) and his wife, and the tower block/pirate radio story strand, marks an anticipation of the new, global city. *Holding On* embodies both the end of a certain type of

London, an ordinary city housed, schooled, and employed in ways that persist from the postwar settlement, and a certain type of television.[71] This is discernibly a London in which postimperial public service is a residual formation, embodied in the contrasted story arcs of the two characters who work for Her Majesty's Revenue and Customs, central character Shaun, a tax inspector, and his colleague, Zahid (Ahsen Bhatti), losing ground to the new brutalism of the global city of gated communities, service economies, and personal tax deals. Both individual characters, and certain ideas of citizenship and neighborliness, are shown to be barely holding on.

Explicitly modeled by Marchant on multithread city narratives such as *Our Mutual Friend* and Robert Altman's Los Angeles city film *Short Cuts* (which is shown playing at a cinema at the end of the first episode), *Holding On* seeks to anatomize London in the mid- to late 1990s when power shifted from eighteen years of Conservative government to Tony Blair's New Labour, elected in 1997.[72] This is recognizably the same city as the Dickensian London of the 1998 *Our Mutual Friend* discussed earlier, but staged within the tradition of British television contemporary drama. *Holding On*'s vision of the city, which is determinedly cross-class and multiethnic, draws on the work of pioneers such as Trix Worrell (*Desmond's*), but its generic inheritance is far from sitcom. Its characters, which include a tax inspector, a bulimic restaurant critic, a pirate radio operator, a nurse, a public relations consultant—who has an affair with her security guard—and a taxi driver, provide a range of stories that intersect, just miss, and turn out to be more deeply connected with each other. The eight-episode work has clear themes that ebb and flow across its hour-long weekly installments. Some, such as the catastrophic effect of Care in Community (the changed policy for mental health patients), the erosion of public morality in combination with the excesses of conspicuous consumption, or the employment prospects for young black men, are historically specific. Others, such as the unpredictable path crossings of city life and the radical contrasts of poverty and luxury, are more generic city stories, but always, here, given specific inflections through, for example, the use of location filming on the London Underground (repeatedly), or in palaces of self-display such as the fashionable Soho restaurant Quaglino's.

The title of the series gives a sense of the precariousness of the London lives it depicts. With two murders early on, and a suicide in the final episode, it is evident that not everyone successfully "makes their own luck" (episode 8).[73] The scale of the production, the number of story lines, and the space of the eight hours enables the creation of London as an incessant city, one that plausibly preexists and persists outside the drama. The variation in tone and the cutting between story lines are key strategies in this production of a television city where there are innumerable stories in process. Thus in the penultimate episode, in which several central characters are shown to reach an accommodation with their situations, a little group of three scenes midway through the episode exemplifies the aesthetic ambition and method of the drama, as it brings together a two-and-a-half-minute somber radio interview with Florrie (Ellen Thomas), the mother of the murdered pirate radio entrepreneur Chris; a nasty end to an evening for Brenda's flatmate (five minutes, ten seconds); and the hasty, sweaty sex of Chris's sister and friend (one minute). The variation of tone and scene length here, between the seriousness of the interview, the fury and distress at Brenda's flat, and the erotic pleasure of the sex, accentuates the parallel different individual lives in the city, while the sequence also shows, more literally—by cutting from the awake to the asleep—different activities taking place at the same time. As a televisual city, *Holding On*'s London is relatively unusual in that it does not much depend on the repetition of shots and locations that I have argued is so characteristic of the twentieth-century television city. It is the simultaneity of the cross-cut stories that makes the city. London the city is changing, and so is the manner of television storytelling. Instead of repetitions, its many stories are held together by the story of Shaun, the tax inspector, who roams—increasingly desperately—over a city that is shown to be ceaseless and various. Scenes are set in football grounds and on the roof of tower blocks, in London clubs and London cabs, in cemeteries and travel agencies.

The series uses a noticeable combination of different scene lengths and pace, confident in combining exposition and atmosphere, and always attracted to filling the screen space, often in unexpected ways, so that the viewer too is subject to that slightly panicky claustrophobia manifested by so many characters. The journalist Gary Rickey (Phil

Daniels) is often filmed in extreme, distorting close-up while he confides to the camera, most notably in a Tube carriage filled with Chelsea supporters in episode 7. This is an urban aesthetic of the image: too close, too tight, too many bodies—too much like any rush hour, an experience that every city dweller blocks out of consciousness in order to carry on traveling (fig. 2.26). But it is the experience of the middle-aged Annie (Sandra Voe), mother of a schizophrenic son, that most clearly depends on this willingness to fill the image up. She is shown taunted by local youths shouting "nutter's mother" outside her home, and when she takes refuge inside, they climb on the windowsill, blocking out the light—and filling the screen—to continue their abuse. They both menace Annie inside her home and block out light for the viewer, closing down our window on the world, threatening both Annie and us; the city in the living room (fig. 2.27). This willingness to crowd the image, to make it uncomfortable to watch, which is juxtaposed with other, longer and wider shots, is an important strategy in conveying the relentlessness of London life. Pace and composition create a London which never stops, which is always liable to get too close, in which it is difficult to hold on.

Holding On, as its title suggests, is a transitional text, a text of a city and a television system in transition—crisis, even. Retrospectively, it can perhaps now also be seen as a drama that engages with London, and its demands on its inhabitants, at a moment in which the city was becoming more separate from the rest of the country. "Making your own luck" is the appropriate description of opportunities in a city where the increasing hegemony of financial service industries means that gambling with other people's money on the stock market is one of the most highly rewarded professions, and the new superrich require concierged daily life. In terms of television series, *Holding On* is broadcast eighteen months before the first season of HBO's *The Sopranos* in 1999, a more widely recognized moment of transition in the production of television drama. Since its 1997 depiction of London, the city has grown significantly and now has a population estimated at about 8,500,000. British television has continued to set television series in London, but, as I explore in the next section, it has all too rarely followed *Holding On*'s impulse to dramatize the contemporary. Stepping back from the global

2.26–2.27. *Holding On*. **2.26:** Gary (Phil Daniels) acknowledges the viewer from a crowded underground train (*Holding On*, episode 7, BBC, 1997). **2.27:** Annie (Sandra Voe), "nutter's mother," being harassed in her home, the light blocked out for both character and viewer in a composition that crowds the frame.

city, British television has turned again and again to old, familiar—and globally exportable—Londons.

Returning to the Past in Twenty-First-Century London

Twenty-first-century television has moved a long way from the BBC's Sunday teatime serials, although the much-heralded death of television has yet to take place. The twenty-first-century living room is a multi-screen environment in which some viewers may be negotiating several screens, tweeting and messaging while monitoring the larger screen, while much television drama is watched by viewers alone and on the move. Aspirations to digital commissioning are apparent in the range of website modalities across which contemporary programs exist, and one of the BBC's most notable successes has been the updated *Sherlock* (2010–), which is indicative of the BBC's global ambitions in the twenty-first century.[74] My interest in this third and final section of the chapter lies in the apparently strengthening lure of the past for British program makers and the rather different, and sometimes contradictory, attitude to old Londons manifest.[75] The point about *Sherlock*, of course, is that it is updated to the present, but it is a curious present in which the audience has the privilege of something like hindsight, just as it does more explicitly in *Ripper Street* (2013–16).[76] The aggressive techno-textuality of *Sherlock*, with its mobile phone detection and its helicopter shots, is not the only type of new old London being made in the twenty-first century, though, and one of the other BBC successes of the period has been the East End drama set in the 1950s *Call the Midwife* (2012–), which combines nostalgia for working-class community with celebration of the welfare state. *Call the Midwife* joins a long line of comforting Sunday night television drama in Britain but is notable in this context for the warmth of its evocation of female agency, which challenges the televisually dominant characterization of the East End of London as a killing ground, as seen in the contemporary *Ripper Street* and *Whitechapel* (2009–13).

The BBC's *Sherlock* has been successful worldwide, and has been hailed as a stylish updating of a venerable and much-adapted source, Sir Arthur Conan Doyle's Sherlock Holmes stories. Before Holmes was adapted by the team associated with the revival of another classic property, the BBC's *Doctor Who*, the definitive television version was the one made by Granada Television in the 1980s, starring Jeremy Brett as Holmes.[77] These programs displayed the meticulous attention to period detail characteristic of British television heritage drama (it was Granada who made *Brideshead Revisited*) and used mainly studio work with excursion location filming for particular episodes. The large Baker Street set, which took five months to build and included at least ten shops and an asphalt street surface—and was, wonderfully, located next to the venerable *Coronation Street* set outside Manchester—was a key element of the production, as the producer, Michael Cox, recalled: "We also decided to spend the larger part of our budget on what we call street level detail. . . . We wanted the front doors and the shop windows and what was in them to stand up to the closest scrutiny."[78] This attention to "the closest scrutiny" resonated well with Holmes's forensic method in the stories, while, as Kim Newman points out, Brett provided a "modernist . . . psychologically intense performance."[79]

In contrast, *Sherlock* seems to move flamboyantly out of the studio, favoring aerial shots of landmark London, location shooting in distinctive buildings, and, through the dramatic use of movement, the sense of a city that never sleeps. Its panache is evident within the first ten minutes of the first episode. This moves from simulated war footage of the Afghan war (all bright, overexposed images, indecipherable fighting, and a just-audible reference to "Watson") to the classic landmark London title sequence (Piccadilly Circus, Big Ben, the Wheel), which follows the revelation that Dr. John Watson is being encouraged by his therapist to write a blog after being invalided out of the army. The pace of the pretitle opener anticipates the pace of the whole ninety minutes, but it is the first manifestation of the appearance of Sherlock Holmes that indicates how this Steven Moffat–Mark Gatiss version of Sherlock Holmes positions itself confidently within a multiscreen world. At a press conference in which Inspector Lestrade (Rupert Graves) is announcing the latest developments in a series of apparent suicides to a hungry crowd of journalists, simulated texting—from, we deduce, Holmes—appears across the screen: "Wrong!" This device, in one move, updates Holmes to the twenty-first century while also including its audience in this modernity. What is particularly well judged is pace. Given that the Holmes-Watson pairing has a substantial extratextual life, that the show is called *Sherlock*, and that we have been introduced to a Watson who is writing a blog, the audience needs no help with identifying the source of the text messages and can do this much faster than anyone within the fictional press conference. When, after the second "Wrong!," Lestrade receives a message signed "SH"—"You know where to find me"—many in the audience will already know that the answer is 221B Baker Street. So these may be stories about a very clever man, but at the series' inception the audience's position too is flattered: a very clever man, maybe, but also a pleasingly clever audience.

My interest in the possibility for a certain self-satisfaction on the part of the audience for *Sherlock* is the first thread in the arguments with which I wish to conclude this chapter and is pursued in more detail in relation to the roughly contemporary *Ripper Street*. At its baldest, I argue that twenty-first-century television London is notably and repeatedly set in the past. While this has always been a strong strand of television Londons—and I have already discussed the television adaptation of nineteenth-century literature—more recently, other factors drive the repeated production of a London that is both detailed in its pastness, in terms of mise-en-scène, and also, paradoxically, often emptier or more vacant in relation to contemporary concerns. "This is London" seems now more commonly exported as "This was London." Changes to the television industries worldwide are well documented, and the increased pressure to produce exportable content that will generate multiplatform revenues cannot here be my detailed concern, although it is partly in relation to these changes that I have selected *Ripper Street* for discussion. This Tiger Aspect production was initially commissioned by, and shown on, the BBC, but was canceled after two series. It was then taken up by Amazon Prime, one of the newer entries to content provision, and in the summer of 2015 appeared back on the BBC.[80] *Ripper Street*, like its contemporary, *Whitechapel*, is set in one of the most familiar London topoi, the East End. This is a London that is by now a curious composite of sources that include television's own *EastEnders*, myths of the London Blitz, and the continuing fascination with the murders committed by Jack the Ripper, often with a bit of Kray twins mythology thrown in for good measure. I have argued elsewhere that this mélange produces the London East End as a privileged site in which certain narrative events are predictable.[81] That is, as soon as you see a certain kind of foggy, often cobbled street and a Victorian street lamp, you know that female characters are likely to end up dead. This is London as the site of perverse sexual murder. This London, too, has a global reach and is widely recognized—and, more importantly for the television production companies, is a very attractive export. On first broadcast, *Ripper Street* was marketed to British and U.S. audiences with particular attention to setting. The British version of the BBC website tracked the labor of production with slide shows comparing set sketches and pictures of completed sets.[82] The website for BBC America, in contrast, promoted the connection between the series and the real Whitechapel, offering both a virtual tour of the sites of the Ripper murders ("Jack the Ripper: The Virtual Tour") with twenty-first-century photographs and a collection of nineteenth-century images and Ripper-related ephemera titled "The Real Whitechapel."[83]

This type of extratextual material seeks to anchor the location of the fiction through the authenticity of the sets and historical reference, but much of the sense of place actually comes from people. *Sherlock*'s London is produced, not unlike Maigret's Paris, partly through the resonant associations of the detective with the city. Audiovisual locations are made through the filming of city streets, exteriors, and studio sets, but these locations are often identified and made coherent through character and performance. *Sherlock*'s London is mainly filmed in Cardiff, partly in the previously decaying area of Bute Town, with its couple of streets of untouched early nineteenth-century houses. The space becomes London because Sherlock Holmes and Dr. Watson are detecting there. The East End–set *Ripper Street*, which had funding from the Irish Film Board, uses an absent persona, that of Jack the Ripper, to secure its location as London, while filming in the disused Clancy Barracks in Dublin.[84] Character, performance, and the resonance of previously told tales are as important in creating the London of these programs as any location filming.

The project of *Ripper Street* is most clearly discernible from its female characters. While the casting of the male roles—Matthew Macfadyen, an actor with a wide range of leading television roles from Mr. Darcy to *Spooks*, as Inspector Reid, Jerome Flynn providing working-class authenticity as his sergeant, and Adam Rothenburg as an American surgeon making a shameless appeal to a U.S. market—reveals a transparent attempt to provide three different types of men in the core triangle of the main action, it is in the female roles, rather than their casting, that both the ambition and the difficulties of this Victorian-set drama are revealed. The two central continuing female roles in the first series are each associated with one of the male principals and embody dominant ideas of Victorian womanhood. Reid's wife is respectable, pious, charitable, and in mourning for their lost daughter for the duration of the first series. She is played, by Amanda Hale, with nervous intensity and controlled, modest physical movement, shot often with downcast eyes, her empty hands at her side or clasped. She is contrasted with Long Susan (MyAnna Buring), the associate of the American, who runs a "cathouse," shown as flamboyant in both her dress and her undress. Susan, a character who actively contributes to this reimagining of the East End of London as part Wild West, embodies the enduring fantasy of the woman who works as a prostitute but still enjoys flamboyant sex with her man, and functions within the fiction to accentuate the sexlessness of Reid's relations with his wife.

Within the study of adaptation, it has been frequently observed that it is the female characters who are most subject to updating. The ambition and sensibility of Jane Austen's heroines is rendered modern to a later audience through aspects of performance and casting, while the problem of Dickens's propensity for child-women makes his works more difficult for the contemporary adapator.[85] *Ripper Street*, though no adaptation, is formed within this same dynamic as it seeks to appeal to a female audience who may well remember Macfadyen as Mr. Darcy in *Pride and Prejudice*; it endeavors to render its female characters both recognizable in a Victorian world and sympathetic to a postfeminist era. For its fin-de-siècle London to become a popular television destination ("We wanted to create a TV series that might run and run, a gritty, period version of *Hill Street Blues* or *NYPD Blue*," as its writer remembered[86]), something had to be done about the women, so that female characters do more than walk the streets and then be disemboweled. While it is undoubtedly a show focused on relations between the three central men, there are female characters in *Ripper Street* who seek fulfillment in their work and personal lives and intermittently use a vocabulary of needs and self-esteem that would not be out of place in twenty-first-century Manhattan. This concern with female agency, which is manifest in the regular appearance of female entrepreneurs of various kinds (directors of orphanages, refuges, and brothels; engineers and owners of mills), counterpoints the visceral and narrative emphasis of the series on blood, bodies, and bodily fluids, and particularly the invasive damaging of women's bodies through domestic violence, snuff movies, and Ripper look-alike killings. The heart of the series and much of its visual energy is with the splatter of blood, "shitting yourself to death," and the removal of body parts, but it self-consciously stages this material within a broader view of the nineteenth century, the Victorian age, as being a problem for women.[87] A cynical reading would suggest that the repeated, explicit verbal and narrative recognition of the plight of Victorian women legitimates the reveling in the image's violence against them. This television London is one that provides the gore and visual shocks associated with cinematic horror, while also addressing another audience through its cast of Victorian women struggling with their subordination.

The self-conscious framing of the series' gory and repeated violence against women, which attracted some protest on broadcast, is just one aspect of the way of its knowingness.[88] This is a program that knows it is rehashing some very familiar stories and both winks at and flatters the audience in the display of this knowledge. This is immediately apparent in its opening, which is structured as an East End slum tour for well-dressed Victorian ladies and gentlemen. Their—and the audience's—host is a corpulent, cheery fellow much like Mr. Pickwick, with his muttonchop moustaches and the bonhomie of a showman. He gestures theatrically in the confined spaces of slum alleys and courts, inviting in both his tour and the viewer. The program thus announces that it too is a species of this type of entertainment for the comfortably off, and, with the discovery of the body of a murdered woman, tourist, audience, and generic expectations are satisfied, and we set off into the drama of what one commentator has called "CSI: Whitechapel."[89]

The cleverness of the conceit of *Ripper Street* is to set the drama in the streets of Whitechapel immediately after the Ripper murders. The writer of the show describes arriving at this conceit as the key moment in the creation of the series: "Constructing our stories to run alongside the Ripper investigation was a terrible constriction, so we dug him up, threw him out, and decided to start our stories once he'd gone. Pretty much everything flowed out of that moment."[90] What flows is an example of twenty-first-century generic hybridity on television—and, as it is television of the digital age, on many other screens too. The series produces a version of London that is one of the dominant modes in which it is broadcast and exported in the twenty-first century, the dark Victorian city, and one of the determining features of this London is the partnership of its producers. The Irish funding, in particular, can be seen onscreen with the use of eighteenth- and nineteenth-century Dublin exteriors. This means that the buildings in some of the street scenes have a solidity sometimes absent in period cities, while there are also some unexpected—and beautiful—locations, such as the decadent mansion used to stage the invention of snuff movies in the first episode. But it is the generic inheritance that I want to address, because I want to argue that this is a program which makes its viewers feel complacently modern.

Ripper Street is a precinct crime drama in costume. It combines the traditions of British heritage television, manifest in details from the women's underclothing to the lighting and plumbing of the autopsy room, with the locus and iconography of Jack the Ripper's East End, and the continuing, week-by-week policing of the station-based cop show. Inspector Fred Abberline, the inspector in the Ripper case, is here present as a hangover from that other story, a former policeman scarred by his obsession, unable to relinquish his unsuccessful pursuit and always vulnerable to misinterpreting evidence to see the Ripper's work again. Perhaps most significant though is the familiarity with forensic procedures of the post-*CSI* audience. It is tropes associated with investigation and traces of crime that are most flattering to the audience. Post-*CSI*—

and a good twenty years of autopsy crime drama—the crime drama audience is expert in the preservation of evidence, the reading of crime scenes, and the mute testimony of the corpse. We know how important it is to look under the fingernails of victims; we understand about the revelations of blood splatter and not moving the body. So when Inspector Reid (Macfadyen) insists on the importance of these procedures, we know both that he is right and that he is an enlightened, modern, Victorian man. However, we also know about many other things that the Victorians either didn't know, or discovered, or found too avant-garde to be credible. The series is positioned within a miasma of half-known and remembered aspects of Victorian history: some of these are directly related to questions of science and the body, and include the identification of water as the source of cholera outbreaks; surgical experiments on hysterical women; attitudes to human deformity; and questions of inheritance. This audience hindsight weights the dice in relation to the fictional world. Extratextual historical knowledge repeatedly informs the audience about which characters are sympathetic (those with twenty-first-century attitudes), while providing a kind of detached pleasure in watching these nineteenth-century mortals struggling with ignorance and prejudice. And here, in this repeated construction of the superior position of the audience, which is much amplified by the plots' brisk march through key historical events in Victorian London such as the building of the Underground and the strike for the Dockers' Tanner, *Ripper Street* produces the East End of London as a piquant tourist site, a history that has been transcended and can now thrill and fascinate. As does *Sherlock*'s London, the London of *Ripper Street* flatters the viewer. However little history of Victorian London one knows, it is surely more than the poor souls living the fiction.

Call the Midwife and Nostalgia for the Future

While the most obvious companion to *Ripper Street* is the contemporary *Whitechapel*, with its "toff and pleb" pairing of Rupert Penry-Jones and Phil Davis as detectives in a twenty-first-century East London afflicted by a variety of grotesque and bloody murders, the contrast of tone and genre with *Call the Midwife* will prove more instructive in relation to twenty-first-century television Londons.[91] *Call the Midwife*, which, with its creator and main writer Heidi Thomas, working from the memoirs of Jennifer Worth, had significant female input to the production, was set in Poplar, east London.[92] The stories are based in the community of, and around, the convent of Nonnatus House in the 1950s and 1960s, the early decades of the National Health Service. From this large, dark house, all polished wood, devotional spaces, and precise period detail in costume and furnishings, the young midwives go forth to attend to the births of the working classes that surround them. As the title indicates, this is a show that includes at least one birth or labor scene every episode, and perhaps it was the assumption that childbirth was a minority interest that explains the BBC's evident surprise at the enormous returning audiences the show attracted.[93]

The London of *Call the Midwife* has three main elements: street shots and exterior scenes, Nonnatus House interiors (where the midwives lodge with the nuns), and working-class home interiors. Its world is initially located through the title sequence, which uses black-and-white photographs of working-class street life interspersed with overlapping handwritten manuscript pages. The outdoors of the East End is created through what are usually long and medium-long shots using high brick warehouse walls, cobbled ground, and numbers of extras performing either dock-related tasks (carrying sacks and loads) or demonstrating street life (children playing, women gossiping, laundry drying). Through these cobbled streets cycle the midwives, bringing succor, medical knowledge, shock, compassion, revulsion, and, through the device of a narrated voiceover (read by Vanessa Redgrave), an explicit commentary on middle-class responses to the working-class lives they encounter in all their intimacies. While there is occasional location work outside Chatham Docks (which now host *Call the Midwife* tours), where most of the filming for the first three series was done, the external spaces of the show are extremely constricted.[94] While this can be interpreted expressively (constrained lives, limited horizons), it is more useful to see these limitations as indicative of the priorities of the production. Although *Call the Midwife* is set in the East End of London, this setting is only important insofar as it provides a historically resonant and quite unmistakable location for working-class characters to live. The priority of the show is the drama of the interaction between the fully

2.28. The midwives bicycling through the East London streets (*Call the Midwife*, episode 1.2, BBC, 2012).

realized and differentiated middle-class characters and the figures in a landscape, their patients. Estella Tincknell makes a robust case for the program's political defense of the benefits of nationalized health care at a time (of broadcast) when this is under threat.[95] She also draws attention to the influence and significance of older female characters within the fiction, and this is certainly unusual, even more so for East End–set drama, where not being murdered is the major challenge for female characters. However, in terms of television Londons, what is most striking is that *Call the Midwife* too uses the familiar trope of the middle-class explorer-missionary making reports from darkest East London. While some episodes, such as 1.2, explicitly use darkest London/prostitution images, so that the uniformed midwife is like a latter-day Salvation Army visitor, more commonly, the narration recounts the shocked response of Jenny (Jessica Raine) to the living conditions and material deprivations of the poor.

Like *Sherlock*, *Call the Midwife* has been an extremely successful export for the BBC.[96] Its post–Second World War old London, with its mid-twentieth-century vision of a benign state that would care for its citizens from cradle to grave, has proved enormously attractive worldwide. It turns out that childbirth and newly socialized health care was not such a minority interest, and, as Tincknell argues, the series presents an impassioned defense of the welfare state that is all too resonant as twenty-first-century austerity seeks to further reduce the remaining pitiful provision. However, while I don't disagree with Tincknell's identification of *Call the Midwife*'s polemic, its appeal might lie elsewhere. Here, Svetlana Boym's analysis of the complexity of nostalgia proves useful.[97] In her notion of "reflexive nostalgia," she insists on the possibility for the coexistence of longing and critical thinking. For the world of *Call the Midwife*, paradoxically both paternalistic and women centered, is, above all, a structured world in which hope may flourish. While the conditions and behavior of the working classes within the fiction are depicted as both shocking and unruly, help, usually in the form of a nice young woman on a bicycle, is at hand. Improvement is promised and administered. Women may not have to just keep on having babies, year in, year out, with dirt, disease, and domestic violence inevitable. An ordered—and better—future beckons. Things will get better. And this sense of a future, in a curious way, *Call the Midwife* shares with *Ripper Street*. The unmistakable decency (in the early series) of Inspector Reid, as played by Matthew Macfadyen, with his big, watery eyes and his acne-scarred skin, as he seeks to bring a progressive vision of the role of the state to the lawless streets of East London, also embodies a dream of order and a benign state, even though his endeavors are repeatedly drowned in bloody debauchery. In extremely contradictory ways, both series display a longing, not so much for the past, but for a time when there was, as part of the texture of everyday life, a better future imaginable, and when the state and its agencies would contribute to this. If this is nostalgia, it is nostalgia for the future imagined in the twentieth century.

But this benign state and promising future are nowhere to be found in contemporary-set twenty-first-century London drama, nor indeed is there that much of a London-dwelling working class. Instead, the ordinary Londons of shows like *EastEnders*, *The Bill*, *Luther*, and *Casualty* show a city in which services are stretched to breaking point, and citizens are anxious, overworked, desperate, and often unsupported and alone. *Holding On*, in 1997, created a London with a visceral and precipitous sense of the imminent danger of not doing so. Since then, dramas such as *Top Boy* (2011) and *Run* (2013), with their location in the various illegal economies of the global city, re-create London as Dickensian city for the twenty-first century.[98] Instead of nice girls on bicycles, there are diminutive drug runners speeding on cycles out of anomic council estates and illegal immigrants bonded into endless labor for their traffickers. Most significantly, though, there is no sense of a future with hope.[99]

This Was London

Television is now an old medium. Twenty-first-century television drama often seeks to quarantine itself from the associations of the twentieth-century medium. If television, as I have argued, is one of the sites through which an old country makes sense of what it might be to be modern in the twentieth century, then the rapid changes of the post-broadcast/postnetwork era are also emblematic of profound changes in that society. In the British context, the most significant challenges posed by the transition to digital delivery concern the effect of these changes on the legitimacy—and funding—of the public service broadcasting project. This can be exemplified through the lost art of the television schedule, with its commitment to a nationally provided mixed diet of programming.[100] Whatever the shortcomings of this model, the ideological commitment to a varied provision, accessible to all, is important, and of a piece with the raft of post-1945 legislation affecting health, housing, and education that constitutes the welfare state. As I have suggested, one element within this provision was the representation of the historical literary and dramatic canon, while another was a commitment to the representation of ordinary lives in contemporary drama. Across these two strands—as well as through a range of other programming—some memorable television Londons have been produced. However, the new pressures on television producers produce a much more fragmented television landscape, in which extremely expensive international coproductions (often, as Helen Wheatley has argued, "spectacular television") jostle with much cheaper reality-based formats.[101] The wider issues here far exceed the concerns of this short book, but, in relation to television London, it is possible to proceed a little further.

For, at the same time as these momentous changes to television production—content provision—are taking place, the particular history of London too has definitely entered a new stage. At its simplest, this entails the disproportionate shift toward the use of residential property for investment purposes. As is evident from the discussion of the Dickens adaptations earlier in the chapter, property speculation has long been a motor of London life. However, the last few years have seen a governmentally supported inflation of the London property market (through tax relief on buy-to-let mortgages and nondomiciled property ownership), in tandem with the reduction of social housing provision. In a context of comparatively weakened sterling (as a global currency, which makes cheaper international investment in what is regarded as the safe market of London property) and increased immigration, both legal and illegal, the city becomes home to only the very rich and the very poor, with a diminishing residential residue of those who had London homes when the city was simply a national capital, rather than a global city. It is not just, as the popular press puts it, that London property prices have gone mad, or that young people are condemned to be part of "generation rent" for all their lives. As commentators as different as the geographer Danny Dorling and the novelist John Lanchester have observed, property prices in London are maintained, and continue to rise, through the use of London housing stock as high-yielding capital investment opportunities within a global market.[102] How this will develop as the U.K. negotiates its departure from the EU is unclear. However, this use of London property, as Chris Hamnett describes it, for "global asset diversification," in combination with the consequences of government policies such as the sale of social housing, help to buy, and caps on rental support, is leading inexorably to a social cleansing, particularly of central and inner London.[103] The transformation, in particular, of the south bank of the River Thames, long the working-class side of the river, is breathtaking.[104] The established working-class communities that feature in shows like *Desmond's*, or Euston Films' South London epic *Fox* (1980, Thames), are becoming increasingly residual. Prestige developments with designer architects abound, nowadays often incorporating a "poor door" for the inhabitants of the statutorily required affordable housing.[105]

It is possible to see an analogy between what is happening to television and what is happening to London. Bling apartment blocks and enormously expensive coproductions aimed at an international market may have something in common if they represent a wider abandonment of universal provision, leaving the rest of us to use the poor door. The recognized icons of domestic modernity in the twentieth century are the refrigerator, the television, and the car. But in Britain, perhaps it was also the dream of a planned and fair future as embodied in the welfare state and the public service television schedule. These dreams were simultaneous with twentieth-century television as a national broadcast system, and London as a postimperial rather than a global city. In the twenty-first century, while still (forever) postimperial, London is now more of a global city, although one uncertain about its own future and that of the financial services that have nestled in an English-speaking access to the European Union. No wonder that television producers in search of new program ideas that will run and run, as well as travel, find themselves looking backward. Vintage costume in a vintage city: so much easier to handle.

3 Portable Cities

BALTIMORE

The final television city of this book is Baltimore, seen worldwide on news media because of days of protest, civic unrest, and rioting in April 2015 after the death of Freddie Gray following his arrest and hospitalization. Gray's death is another tombstone in the long, unresolved story of racialized citizenship—and its exclusions—in the United States, a story that has already moved on and, despite the protest movement Black Lives Matter, has proved inexorable in its accretion of further deaths.[1] The Baltimore in these news broadcasts both is and isn't particular, because it draws on established conventions in news reporting. The television city of riot is not nationally specific, and can be found, as a generic type of television city (comparable to, for example, the ceremonial television city, or the television city of victorious sporting homecoming), across a range of national broadcasting systems.[2] The account of these generic television cities has yet to be written; my concern here is with the fictional Baltimore constructed at the turn of the century, and that would, I speculate, provide a framework of understanding, an assumed familiarity with "Baltimore," for those audiences who then heard news about Freddie Gray's death and subsequent events.[3]

The disproportion of the move from Paris and London to Baltimore requires some commentary to demonstrate that it is less perverse—and parochial—than it might at first appear. In the United States, New York, Los Angeles, and Chicago offer themselves much more obviously as television cities, while some of the most interesting scholarship on U.S. television cities has concerned New Orleans.[4] Baltimore, though, has established itself as the television city of the early twenty-first century, as it was the setting for an extended long-form drama, *The Wire* (HBO, 2002–8). This show has attracted extensive, enthusiastic critical commentary on topics ranging from the suitability of television serial drama to "demonstrate the interconnectedness of systemic urban inequality," to its "new and complex portraits of many aspects of black urban life," to its exemplification of complex narrative form, and its elaborations of both realist and melodramatic modes.[5] Baltimore is the final television city of this book because the visibility of *The Wire*'s Baltimore has rendered comprehensible some part of this book's project. As *The Wire* is in some senses about Baltimore, and because its narrative structure is cumulative and analytic, it demonstrates the power and resonance of television serial storytelling in the narration of cities. This formal consonance has already been explored in chapter 2 in relation to dramas such as *Holding On* and *EastEnders*, as well as the Dickens adaptations so important to British television. I have also argued that the repetitions of less serialized forms, such as the sitcom, produce their own sense of particular places becoming familiar and known. But it is the heralding of *The Wire* as exceptional in its production of knowledge about lives in a television city, in combination with the disavowal of its televisionness, that partly provokes the investigation of television cities which preceded the show.

There is thus a methodological, rather than referential, piquancy to the choice of Baltimore as the final television city of this book. Baltimore is not a capital city, nor does it have the extensive television history of Los Angeles or New York, which would require, as did London, a complex combination of periodization with institutional, generic, formal, and thematic analysis, in addition to particular case studies. Baltimore provides an exceptionally discrete case study as its television identity is principally bound up with two shows, *Homicide* and *The Wire*. Each of these shows has attracted considerable critical discussion, while the extensive commentaries provided by those involved in their production makes the type of production archaeology of my first chapter, on the BBC's Paris, unnecessary. Instead, as these two shows straddle the transformation from twentieth- to twenty-first-century television, and their critical reception exemplifies some of the changing attitudes to the medium, it is possible here both to track the increasingly visibility of Baltimore as a television city and to explore the construction of *The Wire* as an object of cultural distinction. It is Baltimore, not New York, not Los Angeles, not Chicago, that provides the most appropriate case study with which to close, a city relatively new to international television, produced over a period in which both television and ideas about television are in transition.

At Fell's Point

At Fell's Point in Baltimore, right on the edge of the quay, there was, until 2015, a cavernous empty building with a memorial plaque reading: "In this building from 1992–1999, a group of talented people created a television legend *Homicide: Life on the Street*." The building, the former city Recreation Pier, clearly identifiable as the main station set for *Homicide*, faces into the now-gentrified Fell's Point (with its streets of small, terraced former dockworkers' houses), but has the water of the Inner Harbor behind it. In the redeveloping of the port city of Baltimore, a television series is memorialized as a tourist attraction just opposite the Fell's Point Visitor Center, where the city's long maritime history, along with the clippers and cargo ships essential to Baltimore's past, is celebrated. Traces of the television production persisted on the pier building until its redevelopment began in 2015. The plaque was on the right-hand side of the huge central archway that leads to the empty lot used for car parking in the show, while on the left, above a monumental door framed by nineteenth-century classical pillars, were the words "Baltimore City Police."

It is not *Homicide* that is now the best-known television series set in Baltimore, though. It is *The Wire*, sixty hours of programming that has attracted critical and scholarly attention to the extent that the program's name functions as shorthand for a new type of U.S. television. There is no memorial to this series discernible in Baltimore—for understandable reasons, as it depicts the city as subject to corruption at all levels, its governance and redevelopment subtended by the drug trade, which determines the life patterns of its poor, particularly African American, inhabitants, while also perverting all the city's major institutions. *The Wire's* Baltimore explicitly renders another side to the much-touted success of the redevelopment of Baltimore's Inner Harbor as a tourist attraction and is—necessarily—ignored by the institutions and publications associated with marketing Charm City. The large visitor center on the Inner Harbor quayside, with its displays of Baltimore's history and heritage, makes no reference to television. The stories told to attract tourists and inform them of the making of the city emphasize a quite different history, one in which Baltimore is central to the Underground Railroad used by escaped slaves from Maryland and further south. There are maps of routes, highlighting shelters and crossings, and a foregrounding of key figures such as Harriet Tubman and Frederick Douglass.[6] While Baltimore itself has a long and contested history in relation to racial zoning, which has meant that the spatial development of the drug trade has a clear racial profile, the official version of the city instead presents Maryland as traversed by the routes to liberty, while the freely available tourist maps actually erase the Federal Street–Milton Avenue area of East Baltimore through a design that places the large-scale insert map of the redeveloped Inner Harbor over this now drug-ravaged area.[7]

If the City of Baltimore chooses to occlude the spaces and histories presented in *The Wire*, this has not been true of the academy, and the series has been extensively discussed in journals and conferences and incorporated into a wide range of courses.[8] There is also an extensive engagement by fans outside the academy, much of which is clever, witty, and well informed, demonstrating creative and intellectual responses to the programs, which are quite often more interesting than the academic literature. One of the outstanding artifacts of this huge penumbra of *Wire*-related material is *The Wire* Monopoly game, in which the (trademarked) Monopoly franchise, which is itself marketed in many different versions, is resituated in Baltimore, with the Monopoly board redesigned to feature places and narrative possibilities from the show.[9] This reimagining of the diegetic world of *The Wire*, with its stoops and corners, is particularly apposite because of the way in which it embodies the series' own concern with the spatiality of the city, the interlocking of legal and illegal trades, the role of chance, and the propinquity of urban devastation and redevelopment. This is an example of a television city that is sufficiently engaging, and seems so real, that viewers want to keep on returning to it and to imagine themselves as players of the game.

I watched *The Wire* on DVD, and in this I was surely not alone—but, in a way, I was. Steve Busfield, one of the editors of *The Wire Re-up*, a collection of blogs and posts about the show from the *Guardian* newspaper, describes what he calls "a common problem" when he started watching the show: "No one else I knew was watching the show at the same time as I was. When encountering another *Wire*-ite, the first question was always: 'Where are you up to.' Fear of spoilers was a conversation killer."[10] Busfield's common problem is the discrepancy between the memory of television as a national broadcast medium (the network era), when the previous night's television really could dominate conversation the following day, and television fiction in the age of download and DVD, which is watched at times of choice, separately from the national public. Busfield's conversation killer is the literal silence of the loss of a certain type of shared temporal experience, discussed within the academy through investigations of the end of television, or "mourning television."[11] As the passionate engagement with a television program evidenced in *The Wire Re-up*, or the Monopoly *Wire* suggests, television hasn't ended, but it has changed, and the television city of *The Wire* is different to the earlier television cities discussed in this book—but not perhaps quite as different as *Wire*-ites would like to claim—and the modality of this difference is one of the topics of this chapter, which considers Baltimore as the preeminent television city of the early twenty-first century, analyzing what is at stake in *The Wire*'s critical celebrity and the rise of postbroadcast television. While much of the existing scholarship on *The Wire* can be characterized as concerned primarily with either its innovation in television form or the world it presents, I wish to hold these two together, while also paying attention to some other contexts for this television city.

It is significant that the show has been widely watched, particularly internationally, on DVD, but not simply because that has made conversations about it more cautious. I do not argue that this is the greatest TV show ever made, or that it provides unparalleled insights into the twenty-first-century postindustrial U.S. city, but I am concerned with the grounds on which these claims are made and what they reveal about attitudes to television as well as to urban crisis. It is this television city, the Baltimore of *The Wire*, that has made feasible the idea of taking television cities seriously and, in a way, has prepared the conditions in which this book can be undertaken. Because *The Wire* itself has been taken so very seriously by many who don't generally engage with television, and because it has been seen to generate knowledge about Baltimore, and problems endemic to certain kinds of cities, the very idea of the television city has become comprehensible. But what of Baltimore before *The Wire*? What of the city as presented in earlier, formally distinct, Baltimore-set television, the seven-season, network *Homicide* (NBC, 1993–99) and the six-part HBO miniseries *The Corner* (2000), each of which can be seen to begin to establish Baltimore as a television city, contributing to an audiovisual imaginary that already includes the films of John Waters and Barry Levinson?

These three programs between them bridge a period of convulsive change in television, from the end of network dominance to the rise of cable and DVD box sets, themselves replaced by streaming and downloads. Across these changes, different rhythms and narrative pacing and structure become possible, and this affects the making of television cities, as I will explore. First, though, I want to map some of the changing metaphors of viewing that have accompanied these changes in program making, delivery, and viewing, as these produce the contextual climate into which each of these programs is received.

From Addiction to Bingeing: Changing Metaphors of Viewing

In the United States, *The Wire* was first available in 2002 through its cable channel producer, HBO. In Britain, it was only available as a DVD and downloads before it was broadcast late at night on BBC2 in 2009. "We literally know of no one, and we both know many people who have seen the show in its entirety, who watched it on television when broadcast," declare two scholars from Britain.[12] Despite the overconfident sense of the cultural centrality of their own social circle, these two writers are correct about how most of the audience of the program viewed—and how this audience increased. It is by now a truism to observe that the critical reputation of *The Wire* has developed in an inverse relation to its original television viewing statistics. Equally significant, though, is these scholars' tone. I think one could say that they are proud not to have watched *The Wire* on television, and, in this, they are perhaps even more representative. Where *The Sopranos* led the way, *The Wire* has followed, as the television that people who don't watch television— sometimes, proudly, don't even own television sets—are delighted to discuss.[13]

If the DVD, as Derek Kompare has argued, "finally enabled television to achieve what film had by the mid-1980s, namely, a viable direct-to-consumer market for its programming," it has also enabled these consumers to separate their purchase from its institutional origin, tele-vision.[14] *The Wire* may turn out to be one of the great achievements of what Clive James has called "the box-set years," a format already past its peak in the second decade of the twenty-first century, overtaken by postobject viewing access through streaming and download cultures.[15] As hindsight becomes possible, the DVD box set begins to appear as a transitional object in the migration of television from single-function domestic furniture to multipurpose screen and streaming. For, much more successfully than video, DVD box sets enabled the commodifica-tion of back catalogs as well as the release of new programming produced with this platform in mind. And these back catalogs of past favorites, box sets of a nation's audiovisual memories, both assuage and create amne-sia. For while it became possible to view again characters and contexts that had persisted only in memory, their new formats obliterate both their original broadcast context and, often, their broadcast temporal structure.[16] In a telling phrase, Kompare suggested that DVD box sets "provide the content of television without the 'noise' and limitations of the institution of television."[17] This noise is not just the temporal structure and immediate peripheral surroundings of a program, the advertising, the continuity announcements, and the channel identifi-cations, so particularly prominent in the U.S. commercial networks in comparison with the European public service broadcasting systems. It is also the cultural connotations of television and the noise of the nation-states (for example, the weather forecast or news headlines) that were the primary structural organization within which television was produced and regulated. And this in turn means that this noise was crucial in the twentieth-century interpretation of television in primarily national terms, or as a cultural forum, as speaking to and of the nation-state and its citizens. Television has been studied as a national medium, for what it might reveal about particular national cultures, and television scholarship has been dominated by national assumptions.[18] In the twenty-first century, as Graeme Turner has pointed out, even if one does not want to go all the way with the "end of broadcast television" narrative, television studies is now confronted with what he characterizes as "the increasingly contingent relationship between television, broadcasting and the nation-state."[19] The DVD box set, the portable commodity form, emblematizes this new contingency that renders unstable the developed scholarly methods of interpretation, and this noiseless television is a sweet irony for *The Wire*, which does, in such detail, seek to tell a specific and national story.

The impressive speed with which the DVD has penetrated the home has been accompanied by the adoption of new metaphors to describe home television viewing. Most notable has been the emergence of the somatic metaphor of bingeing to describe the domestic viewing of multiple episodes sequentially.[20] This popular usage offers a rather more complex apprehension of what has happened to television than may first appear, especially if considered in relation to the previously widespread characterization of regular viewing as addiction. Addiction, a metaphor prominent in the twentieth century in relation to soap -opera viewers, and particularly housewives, condenses judgments about television fiction and its viewers. It proposes an involuntary, noncerebral relation to the medium, an out-of-control habit. The contempt of this metaphor for television and its viewers was often shared by cinema scholars, who have, however, in the twenty-first century, noticeably turned to the medium to explore U.S. quality television in forms such as *The Sopranos* and *Mad Men*. Here we could note the inclusion of an epigraph from Chris Marker at the beginning of Linda Williams's monograph on *The Wire* in this book series. The plangent loss of cinema in the opening line, "But to tell the truth, I no longer watch many films," inscribes a reluctant yearning into the project of attending to television. There is in this new scholarship on prestige television often a stress on the way in which television has become more cinematic or, at least, less televisual, as well as an erasure of the history of television and television scholarship.[21] This new, good television, in contrast to old, bad, addictive television, is not broadcast network television, but television that one either pays to see or watches from box sets. Instead of being associated with housebound women, this new television is young, smart, and on the move, downloaded or purchased to watch at will. Arguably, this is men's television, a television emancipated from domesticity and the feminine.[22]

Difficult Men is the title of Brett Martin's 2013 book about recent U.S. television, which has an image of Tony Soprano (James Gandolfini) on the cover and proclaims it will go "Behind the scenes of a creative revolution: From *The Sopranos* and *The Wire* to *Mad Men* and *Breaking Bad*." The difficult men, we learn, are the showrunners such as David Chase, Steven Bochco, David Milch, and David Simon, as well as their creations. *Violence Is Power* is the title of Jason P. Vest's 2011 study of *The Wire, Deadwood, Homicide*, and *NYPD Blue* and the two Davids, Milch and Simon. These are definitely boys' books about boys. Martin's title is clever, as in addition to signaling something of the particular resilience necessary to succeed in the television industry (as well as being a mafia boss, a principled policeman, or a drug baron), it has the air of being familiar with feminist complaint. Men are so often difficult, it seems to recognize, before proceeding with its paean of (often critically very astute) praise for these particular difficult men and the third golden age of U.S. television.

It is in these discursive contexts, in which certain kinds of nonbroadcast television viewing are signs of distinction, that we find the metaphor of bingeing on serial drama. The move from addiction to bingeing offers a very economical, popular description of what in the academy are called changing modes of delivery and the shift away from the unquestioned dominance of broadcast television.[23] The metaphors demonstrate the shift from something that is rationed temporally (broadcast television), and which you must therefore get a fix from regularly, to something more like a box of chocolates that you purchase and consume in your own time.[24] But there is also a recalibration of agency and the location of badness. For bingeing describes bad television watching as opposed to the watching of bad television and has been imported into descriptions of television viewing from the now-extensive vocabulary of bad eating and bad drinking. So it is both a moral and a somatic metaphor, and perhaps it is not too far fetched to say that it has contemporary neoliberal connotations in its implied good opposite: self-disciplined non- or limited TV watching. To binge on television drama is to abandon aspiration, to be stuck on the sofa in the living room. These meanings were vividly enacted in the summer of 2014, when the *Wall Street Journal*, covering the acquisition of the LA Clippers by the former CEO of Microsoft, Steve Ballmer, reported that Ballmer had spent the two weeks after he first left Microsoft binge viewing *The Good Wife*.[25] This story was picked up in other media that demonstrated no doubt about the type of viewing Ballmer had undertaken. For example, in Britain, a relevant article was titled "Steve Ballmer Recovers from Losing Microsoft Job by Binge-Watching 100 Episodes of The Good Wife," reporting that Ballmer found himself in an "atypical glum mood" when he resorted to binge viewing.[26]

This anecdote points to a paradox at the heart of the new, valorized not-television box-set television, which has attracted scholarship within critical paradigms of exceptional authorship rather than national broadcast economies, while at the same time further devaluing ordinary television. For, despite this valorization within traditional aesthetic discourse, there is, in this metaphor of bingeing, the trace of a persistent cultural shame at absorption in an audiovisual, fictional world. Steve Ballmer absorbed himself in the fictional world of *The Good Wife* because there was a postemployment emptiness to his actual world. He temporarily left his life before reemerging to take on new challenges, and it is clear that it is better to be back there in the real. In this context, in which there is manifest cultural anxiety about watching too much television, realist fiction with an explicitly didactic aim—such as *The Wire*, rather than *The Good Wife*—may be particularly well placed to redeem the bingeing. Self-improvement has taken place. Learning while absenting yourself from your life may be culturally more acceptable than just taking time out. Sue Turnbull has demonstrated the historical consistency with which realist crime drama has been more critically esteemed, and *The Wire*, in this long history, is the perfect televisual object. Bingeing on Baltimore may be more culturally prestigious than bingeing on *The Good Wife*, even though *The Good Wife* is at least concerned with realpolitik.[27] Or to put it another way, one of the reasons that *The Wire* has been so extravagantly applauded—and don't get me wrong, I think it's a great show—is that its downbeat analysis, its plain style, its focus on labor, its unremitting revelation of cycles—makes it really seem unlike the television that housewives were addicted to. And that is why there is something about Linda Williams's brilliant, forensic demonstration that the show is not tragedy but melodrama which slightly misses the point. I completely agree that it is melodrama, not tragedy. But I think that only people who want it not to be television want it to be tragedy to begin with.

Homicide *and "Very Real Baltimore"*

Until the success of *The Wire*, the Baltimore-shot *Homicide: Life on the Street* was generally seen as an innovative 1990s development of the U.S. television police crime genre, following pioneers such as the Los Angeles–set *Dragnet* (1951–59), New York–set *Naked City*, *Miami Vice* (1984–89), and *Hill Street Blues* (1981–87). Of these precursors, it is *Hill Street Blues* that is most often cited for its transformation of genre, shifting the balance between crime fighting and the personal lives of the cops, while also exploiting the serial possibilities of network television with unresolved and multiple story lines. That is, *Homicide* was seen as part of a history of a television genre, albeit an innovative member of this genre and one, in the production involvement of Barry Levinson, Paul Attanasio, and Tom Fontana, with some identifiable name creative contributions. However, in the twenty-first century, *Homicide*'s critical genealogy has perceptibly shifted, and it now appears, in accounts such as those by Martin and Vest, within paradigms of authorship, as the first act in the television career of David Simon.[28] Once Simon's 1991 account of his year following the detectives in Baltimore's homicide squad is optioned by Levinson, and then Simon begins to contribute to writing the show, his transition from journalist to TV writer and producer commences.[29] This version is most interestingly explored by

Linda Williams, who argues that Simon's year-long journalistic observations of the police and street drug trade provide an ethnographic
bedrock to the fictional world enabled by the long-form drama of *The
Wire*, while Simon as a writer, through its precursors, *Homicide* and
The Corner, learns to preach less and dramatize more.[30] This shift of
critical emphasis, in which a genealogy of authorship succeeds one
of genre, condenses succinctly changes in the television industry, in
the marketing of television, and in television criticism.[31] The story I
wish to trace, however, is one in which Baltimore comes to visibility,
internationally, as a television city, and the importance to this of claims
about realism. In this, I will be exploring the ways in which different
television forms, such as the miniseries and the episodic multiseason
drama, affect the presentation of the television city.

Raymond Williams argues that realist texts can be characterized as
concerned with the contemporary, the secular (it is a godless world),
and the socially extensive, by which he means that the makers of realist
texts are often concerned to bring to attention aspects of contemporary
social life that are unknown or neglected.[32] Williams is very careful to
describe the historical, national, and medium-specific complexity of realism, and uses the notion of "many different variations in method" to
explain how texts that look so different can all be characterized as realist through sharing that impulse to present the real to contemporary
viewers. Baltimore, as a television city, has been brought to the screen
through three different television series that look different from each
other, but which each aspire toward realism. Taken together, they exemplify Williams's "different variations in method" of realism, while also
demonstrating the contextual character of what is understood to be a
realist textual strategy at a particular historical moment. *Homicide*,
for reasons discussed below, was widely perceived as realist within the
tradition of the police genre of the 1990s; *The Corner* solicits belief in
its veracity through both its framing devices and its use of naturalist
strategies. *The Wire* is different again and has been hailed as innovatory television while also being, in the astute judgment of Erlend Lavik,
stylistically "uncompromisingly old-fashioned."[33]

In the second half of the twentieth century, Baltimore existed as a
cinematic city known in the work of the directors Barry Levinson and

John Waters, both of whom display repeated attention to their hometown and, in their very different ways, a commitment to documenting something of its resilience in films such as *Tin Men* (1987) and *Hairspray* (1988). While the tone of the work of these two directors is quite different, between them, using varied degrees of location shooting in Baltimore-set dramas, they work and rework the post–Second World War history of Baltimore, most notably, the class and ethnic mix of the city, the population growth of Baltimore County, and the impact of desegregation. The cinematic city of John Waters, in all its excess and energy, credits Vincent Peranio as art director from the beginning.[34] Peranio appears in this capacity also in Levinson's later work, most notably *Liberty Heights* and *Homicide*. Peranio too is a Baltimore native and, "since [he] was kind of the only production designer in town," is best considered "gatekeeper" to audiovisual Baltimore.[35] His significance becomes apparent when we note that in addition to working with Waters and Levinson on films and *Homicide*, he is also the production designer for *The Corner* and *The Wire*. So while the *Wire*-led new emphases in television criticism privilege David Simon in creating television Baltimore, attention to the collaborative effort that is necessary in all film and television production reveals Peranio working across nearly all significant Baltimore-set film and television—as does the casting director Pat Moran.

Before *Homicide*, Baltimore was, as a televisual city, a local place. In the U.S. context, this means that local television stations, mainly wholly owned by the big commercial networks and PBS, showed nationally broadcast network fare with local weather and news segments. Local PBS programming, some of which is very local indeed and funded by local citizens and viewers, is rarely exported or even seen outside its local area. Baltimore existed televisually within Maryland, and within the context of certain kinds of national news (such as sports and election coverage), but, nationally and internationally, as a setting for television fiction, it was absent. It is in this context that *Homicide*'s first claim to generic innovation lies. Baltimore provided a fresh setting for a familiar and popular television genre that had historically been set mainly in either New York or Los Angeles.[36] Just like Miami in the 1980s, Baltimore provides new representational possibilities, while the very different color palettes of the two shows—*Miami Vice*'s ice-cream colors in contrast to the muted, bleached tones of *Homicide*—hints at the different aesthetic approaches.

So *Homicide*, before script, camera work, and narrative structure are even considered, in bringing a less well-known, more local city to the networked television screen, makes a realist claim—"you've never seen this before"; its freshness and novelty exist partly in relation to what has become conventional. It is to this which Jonathan Nichols-Pethick is responding when he writes of *Homicide* "being set in the very real location of Baltimore, Maryland."[37] Evidently, Baltimore is no more real than New York or Chicago—but on its appearance as a television city in the 1990s there is something about it as a television city that makes Nichols-Pethick want to claim it as "very real," and this, putatively, is its televisual novelty, its repeated use of a number of black actors, as well as its use of location. Here, the role of Peranio is crucial—as he observes, "I enjoy showing Baltimore to people, even if they are murder sites."[38] Because he is so deeply embedded in the city ("We have a location manager who I go with. . . . But in many cases, because I'm so familiar, I know I'll want to go Calvert and 33rd Street or this delicatessen in this neighborhood"), and such an enthusiast for it, he is able to make location choices that keep the city imagery fresh.[39] *Homicide* clearly provided an opportunity he relished: "In *Homicide* especially, since it was all about murder, you could have murder anywhere in the city. We went everywhere. We went to the B&O train museum, we had murders in Ruxton, we also went to the drug dealer neighborhoods. I probably went to 20,000 locations for that show alone. Of course that was seven years worth of scouting."[40] As Peranio has worked on most significant Baltimore productions, he knows which locations have been used for what; he knows what can be used as Paris, what as old New York, but also, in addition to his work for the three key figures of his career—Waters, Levinson, and Simon—he can point out-of-town directors "to other places that haven't been filmed so much."[41] It is in this sense that Peranio is the gatekeeper of location Baltimore, and his work, in combination with that of other Baltimore natives such as producer Barry Levinson, who insisted that writers on *Homicide* work in Baltimore, gives a particularity to this television city.[42]

There are other particularities to this city which are significant. In comparison to New York or Los Angeles, so familiar and at the same time so exceptional, Baltimore can represent more than itself because it is smaller and more ordinary.[43] This is perhaps the point about Hannibal Lecter living there: the grotesqueness of the crimes of this serial killer rather overshadows his place of residence. In the Lecter oeuvre, Baltimore is an ordinary setting for exceptional crime.[44] In *Homicide* and *The Wire*, it is an ordinary setting for ordinary murder, with a constant undertow of concern that one category of murder, in which the dead are young black men, has become too ordinary to be noticed. Baltimore has its own particularities, but it also has many features that enable it to function metonymically to represent other towns, both in the United States and further afield, which struggle with their future in a twenty-first-century globalized world.

An East Coast harbor city, with a history as a key distribution node for the East Coast and further afield, the city had a range of associated industries, from the docks themselves through to (food) canning and railways. The late twentieth century sees Baltimore hit by the same global transitions as the rest of the West, particularly after the oil crisis of 1973. The massive decline in U.S. manufacturing, the rise in imported goods, the consequent loss in well-paid blue-collar jobs—so far, so rust belt. For this port city though, the containerization of the global shipping trade, which is especially significant for sheltered natural harbors like the Chesapeake Bay (as it has been for the port of London), delivers a particular blow. The huge ships required by containerization just can't enter the smaller harbors and docks that have served for centuries, and, when they do, the scale of the workforce required is enormously reduced. This has happened to port cities all over the world, particularly those with what have historically been well-protected natural harbors. So Baltimore is in some ways typical of both the late twentieth-century U.S. former manufacturing city, and of international port cities.

However, Baltimore is also what Sherry Olson has described as "a strategic place" in the civil rights movement, "a great frontier city, an outpost of the North in the South," as well as "a beachhead against the de facto segregation typical of metropoles of the North."[45] This complex history, in which the city has been the site for a series of key contestations about segregation in employment, schooling, and housing, is largely obscured by the spatialization of ethnic privilege (white flight), itself enabled by discriminatory mortgage and housing policies, which in turn racializes poverty. In the latter part of the twentieth-century, residential patterns, which include massive federal funding for suburban highways and freeways into the city, become consolidated as an African American majority city/inner city and a majority white county. This county-city contrast recurs in Baltimore-set fiction, from the work of Waters and Levinson (who has his own concerns with Jewish Baltimore) to *Homicide*.[46] In the fictional world, this is what underlies the audacity of Thomas Carcetti's bid to stand for mayor in the third season of *The Wire*. As all involved recognize, often to the point of ridiculing his ambitions, he is "white in a brown town," and this population profile determines the kind of taxes that can be raised and the type of investment possible. It is onto this divided city-county that the regeneration schemes associated with redevelopment of Camden Yards and the harbor have been grafted, providing a tourist attraction at the heart of the city and subsequent, controversial, residential redevelopment of former industrial sites. What amounts to the racial zoning of Baltimore has been brought about through complex histories, initiatives, and, as George Lipsitz puts it, inheritance of white spatial privilege.[47] Its relevance for the setting of a television police series in Baltimore is that large parts of the city administration and many city employees are African American, and that therefore any type of realist impulse requires a differentiation between African American characters, rather than the more common casting strategy that provides one or two representatives of diversity. As Bambi Haggins notes, "The characters reflect the police force one might expect to find in a city with a majority black population."[48] Theoretically, it is possible to be different kinds of black in Baltimore-set drama.[49] Perhaps Baltimore—neither in the South nor one of the great destinations for the migration North like Chicago—has the potential to be a privileged site within U.S. cultural geography for a relatively rare type of U.S. story, one that takes for granted ethnically divided cultures, banal racisms, and a certain pragmatic coexistence.[50] A television city with and of difference.

A concern with the banality of racist assumptions about ethnicity and power is signaled immediately in the opening episode of *Homicide*, when the white college-educated new arrival to the homicide squad, Bayliss (Kyle Secor), misidentifies his superior officer as he searches for Lieutenant Giardello (Yaphet Kotto). Bayliss, with eye-line matches which demonstrate that he is addressing the seated white man rather than his standing African American colleague (Giardello), is shown to assume that it is the white man, rather than the African American, who is the lieutenant. This incident serves as a clear warning to any audience member who might make a similar mistake. Similarly, the detail and specificity of ethnicized public space forms a recurrent theme in *Homicide*. This too can be addressed in a very straightforward way, such as the first episode of season 2, "Bop Gun," which opens with parallel cutting between a family of visiting white tourists and three young African American men, with a third thread of match cuts between the "ghetto boys" and the police in which each throw missiles (to a basketball hoop and a wastepaper bin) and are shown picking up a gun. As the family, guidebook in hand, wander round the outskirts of the newly built Orioles stadium in Camden Yards, the young men from West Baltimore spot them, wandering unseeingly through contested territory, and the orange-red ball is abandoned in the alley as the tallest of them puts on his shades, the last shot before the cold open cuts to the titles. In a match that is characteristic of the series, the ball with which the young men are playing is matched with the police description of this type of case, a "Red Ball"; this term identifies the case, the murder of the mother, as special, as opposed to ordinary, homicide, and its specialness lies in both the ethnic and the economic identity of the white tourist victims.

Spaces of power are addressed in a different way in the three-part story with which the sixth season opened, "Blood Ties" (October 1997). Here, James Earl Jones guest stars as a wealthy and respected Baltimore resident, Felix Wilson, who has made his fortune from cookies and contributed significantly to the city as a benefactor. The investigation of a murder associated with his household proves difficult for the homicide squad because different team members have different notions of the respect with which his family should be treated, and these differences are articulated across ethnicity, so that Giardello and Detective Pembleton (Andre Braugher) are accused of going soft on the suspect. Race, affiliation, loyalty, respect: all of these are shown to structure the everyday lives and investigations of the detectives, just as wealth and influence determine the outcome of the case. And the arguments within the unit, and the discomfort the case occasions, are another example of the way in which the series uses a realist register. For these matters are, at the very least, uncomfortable, and the show chooses to address rather than evade them.

The end credits of *Homicide* give special thanks to the City of Baltimore and the Fell's Point Community. The production was based in the city Recreation Pier with which this chapter opened, with production offices on the first floor of the pier, while the whole of the *Homicide* set was built on the second floor and staff parked underneath.[51] Over its seven seasons (1993–99), the program ranged over the city, with scenes in both banal and landmark venues. Characters perform Baltimore landmark activities—mainly eating crab with gusto, which is first introduced in the second episode—in a range of settings from restaurants to benches, and crime scenes explore the leafy suburbs and the county as well as the hotels, the bars, the sidewalks, the alleys, and the row houses of the city itself. This variety of murder scenes is counterpointed by the repeated return to the workplace, the offices, corridors, restrooms, roof, and parking lot of the police station. And the rhythm of this return—the one thing, along with the constant conversation between colleagues, which can be depended on narratively—produces what is *heimlich*, or homely, in *Homicide*. Every episode takes the viewer back, repeatedly, to this place from which investigations of the city originate.

The police station interiors are rendered with considerable attention to what it might feel like to work there every day. Temperatures fluctuate; arguments are observed if not fully audible; desks are squabbled over and maintained differently; interrogation rooms seem almost to smell. In the ninth episode of the first season, "Night of the Dead

3.1. Mapping the city inside the office (*Homicide*, episode 1.9, "Night of the Dead Living").

Living," there is a bravura recognition of the centrality of the squad office to the series, with the whole episode filmed inside until the end, when the detectives are hosed down on the roof of the building (figs. 3.1–3.3). The failure of the air conditioning on a hot September night is both metaphoric and actual: we see the detectives sweat their frustration, one spending his time working on a diagram of some row houses and a yard to deduce how a body was moved. Homicidal Baltimore is outside, but in this hot, sweaty, airless set of offices, it is the constant subject of concern. The rooftop scene at the end, with the cast in underpants against a backdrop of the harbor, renders surprised relief to the detectives from the heat while also giving that same relief to the viewers through the escape from the offices and the sudden opening up of the horizon.

Helen Piper, in an interesting analysis of British television police series, has argued that police drama is about paid work as much as it is about crime, and this is useful in relation to *Homicide*.[52] It is certainly the working relationships, the hierarchies, the catastrophic personal lives, the ambition, and the frustration that provide the continuities across the seasons. But the characters involved in these interactions are partly created through their individual responses to the crime, which is their labor. The crime is significant because it provides a narrative stimulus to which

3.2–3.3. Police on the roof: relief after the hot night with the harbor in the background (*Homicide*, episode 1.9, "Night of the Dead Living").

individual characters can be shown to have different moral and practical responses. And viewers, in the best tradition of television soap opera, must negotiate their own judgments, partly based on what they know about these characters. The punchy editing, both between scenes and within, when the camera seems to focus in staccato bursts over a shot, repeating it from slightly different angles (but keeping the soundtrack continuous), accentuates these demands on the viewer, producing a visual equivalent to the contextual demands on the police officers. Tom Fontana describes the look of the show as follows: "[Barry Levinson] wanted it done in a documentary style, using editing techniques like jump cutting or repeating the same shot three times, to give the audience the same sense of stimulation as gun battles and car chases, but more in line with the kind of stories we were trying to tell."[53] Camera work and editing within the building are often flamboyant, presenting the familiar generic sets with unexpectedly long swift pans and sudden cuts, or violent close-ups. The squad offices may be familiar, but the style of the show anticipates and expresses the unpredictability and volatility of the homicide office environment so that the comfortable generic familiarity is made a little edgy. Nichols-Pethick characterizes the style of *Homicide* as seemingly "springing forth from the unlikely union of Frederick Wiseman and MTV," capturing both the uncompromising, steady determination of aspects of the style and its investment in the potential of the music track.[54]

Because of the location shooting, though, this place is more than simply generic—it is particular. As the pier, the principal set, is built out into the harbor, the building has water on three sides, and can thus be used for a range of punctuations and backdrops, as well as, always, to anchor the show in the reality of Baltimore, as we have seen with "Night of the Dead Living." There are certain standard views of the pier building and the water, first introduced in the second episode, which recur throughout the series, although often with slight variation in angle or position. However, my interest lies particularly in the way in which glimpses of this water, or the breathtaking view out to sea, is used as a regular background to the one-to-one colleague conversations that form such a significant part of the drama. For example, toward the end of "Saigon Rose" (U.S. episode 6.6), there is a lengthy and difficult conversation between two colleagues that is framed with the harbor in the background (figs. 3.4–3.5). There is no narrative need for the exterior view, but it transforms the dialogue scene. The sunlight glancing off the water, constantly and irregularly, distracts the eye, repeatedly placing the conversation in a particular location at a particular time of day, and also giving a little more room for what is being discussed to be considered by the viewer. In the later episode, "All Is Bright," this view is reprised in the "previously" opening, where it is juxtaposed with another use of the water (fig. 3.6). Here, geography is used differently. This shot is taken from the other side of the bay, looking out from near Federal Hill. The female character who dominates the image is associated with drug trade profit, and the fact that the tall building, the Grainery,

3.4–3.6. The use of the harbor in *Homicide* to give
a sense of a real geography (U.S. episode 6.6,
"Saigon Rose"; U.S. episode 6.8, "All Is Bright").

that dominates the space is a controversial condominium development arguably associates her with bad development. The fact that the same building appears in all the images also points to the accumulative geographical placing of the action of *Homicide*, the repeated use of the real Baltimore to guarantee the located authenticity of the fiction.

Nichols-Pethick argues that "no real formula ever emerged over the course of the series," and this unpredictability, in which the series retained a willingness to structure story lines differently over both individual and groups of episodes throughout its run, is a factor in what was perceived as the show's innovation and engagement with the real.[55] However, the series' television city, the fundamental rhythm of the alternation between the home of the squad office and the attractions of the different murder scenes, persists in a way which is very similar to that of Maigret's Paris for the BBC. It is also striking, as with *Maigret*, how various the locations used can be when the pretext is murder. Characters can be murdered anywhere, as Peranio notes, and *Homicide* ranges much more widely over Baltimore city and county than does *The Wire*. Here, *Homicide*'s contextual circumstances are significant. For *Maigret*, there was no possibility for viewers to access its Paris other than through sitting down at the scheduled time each week. The viewer could be modern and continental on a regular weekly basis, watching police officers who had aperitifs in bars instead of half-pints in pubs. *Homicide*, commissioned by NBC, the weakest of the three television networks in the early 1990s as the full significance of cable was beginning to become apparent, was given some latitude to enable competition with cable. Stylistic innovation (particularly camera style, editing, and the use of popular music), in combination with some experimentation in narrative structure and seriality, produces a less predictable squad and murder/investigation scene alternation, but this core rhythm is still there to match something of the rhythms of reception. Baltimore, in *Homicide*, is produced through this rhythm of repetitions, and it is my argument that this would become a little bit too much if you binge watched—now possible—too many. Too much repetition, not enough progression. This is a television city that is still structured through something like a weekly rhythm of reception, although much less so than *Maigret*. One tunes in, and it is there again, fairly reliably recognizable, even though—Frederick Wiseman crossed with MTV—its stylistic distinctiveness makes the television set jump a little.

The Corner

Homicide's Baltimore is produced—innovatively—within the recognizable rhythm of the alternation between the home of the squad office and the attractions of the murder scenes. The next significant television Baltimore, *The Corner*, is much more spatially coherent. This six-part series, as its title suggests, is set in and around one of the corners of West Baltimore drug culture. The series focuses on the McCullough family, parents Gary (T. K. Carter) and Fran (Khandi Alexander), and their teenage son, DeAndre (Sean Nelson), who, within the year of the drama, himself becomes a father. Each of the first three hour-long episodes takes one central protagonist ("Gary's Blues," "DeAndre's Blues"), while the second three, when the family characters have become more familiar, interweave their stories within the broader milieu characterized as "Dope Fiend Blues," "Corner Boy Blues," and "Everyman's Blues." The series is partly location shot with a verité style, preceding this documentary look with a title reading "True Stories" and a concluding title that once again testifies to the truth of the stories, and dedicates the programs to those who "lived and struggled on West Fayette Street in 1993." Sound is naturalistic, and the editing between sequences is often unexpected and abrupt, giving an impression that the footage shown is just part of much more recorded material, edited together for the purposes of exposition.

Generically, *The Corner* is set up against the formula of *Homicide*. Instead of a multitude of stories set all over Baltimore, it deals in the detail of one family's stories in one place. My interest lies both in *The Corner*'s Baltimore and in the way in which this miniseries throws into relief some of the strategies used in the longer, more explicitly fictional work, *The Wire*. The difference between the two, at its simplest, could be characterized as a move from the naturalist observation of *The Corner* to the ambitious, multi-institutional realist analysis of *The Wire*. The titles of the series, one a situated particular place, the other a technology through which connections can be traced, embody this distinction. However, it is a distinction that runs some danger of underemphasizing the careful shaping, structure, and performances of *The Corner*. The slice of life that is each episode is pointedly framed by interviews or straight-to-camera pieces in which the director, Charles S. Dutton, himself mainly off-screen, talks to different characters in turn, asking them questions and sometimes making judgments. This produces a series of reflections about both the life portrayed and the means of representation, as the actor responds directly to questions in character, sometimes looking straight to camera, sometimes to the questioner. These episode frames, which include interviews with the committed local police officer, Bob Brown, and with Gary McCullough's father, who talks about moving in as one of the first black families to Vine Street in the 1950s, are in turn framed by the series' introduction and conclusion. This is modeled as the journey from filmmaker to audience. At the beginning of the first episode, before the titles, Dutton, filmed standing against a wall on a Baltimore street, with the long prospect of the road behind him, introduces himself, claiming insider knowledge by outlining his own familiarity with the environment: "I grew up and hung out on a corner just like this one, not too far from here, on a corner like thousands of others across the country." He then proposes the hypothesis of the series: "On the one hand, the corner pulses with life, the energy of people trying to make it to the next stage, but also it is the place of death, be it the slow death of addiction, or the suddenness of gunshots."

The corner on which Dutton grew up thirty years earlier, and the one on which he has been filming, are proposed as typical of the open-air drug markets that can be found all over America, markets that have flourished despite the enormous increase in penitential institutions in that period, and so the project becomes to tell the "too rarely heard" stories of "the men, women and children living in the midst of the drug trade." This is an explicitly and conventionally realist project, to reveal stories "too rarely heard," and there is a clear ameliorist intention, in that the dominant contemporary government policy of simply incarcerating people associated with the drug trade (by building more and more prisons) is identified as a failure. The emphasis on the contradiction that characterizes the corner—both life and death—indicates that the approach of the filmmakers does not just involve pitying the downtrodden drug addicts but also recognizing the courage and struggle of many of those in the locality. So the series will pose for the viewer the question of what is to be done, of how the lives they watch, in their comfortable HBO-cabled homes, or through their DVD player or computer, can be made better, and who can do this making better.

In relation to this question, the little interview sequences at the end of each episode are significant, as they canvas the opinions of persons differently placed in the life of the corner, while some characters, particularly Mrs. Taylor (Jacqui Allen), who runs the Rec (the Martin Luther King Recreation Center) and who explicitly argues that she feels a responsibility to stay in the area, can be seen as working on the ground to provide some support for the children. Similarly, the various sequences of Narcotics Anonymous meetings provide a familiarity with the rituals of coming clean, as does the shortage of rehab beds, while even the dealer Curt (Clarke Peters), in the final episode, encourages his potential customer Fran to eschew his product and get back to the straight life she has maintained for some months. At the end of the final episode, "Everyman's Blues," the director moves back into the frame and introduces the viewer to some of the real people—Fran, Blue, Tyreeka, and DeAndre—who have been played by actors in the drama. They are addressed as a first, privileged audience for "the movie" and are asked to give their views on what they have seen. Each of the first three identifies the importance of the film as being to encourage both themselves and others to stay off drugs. DeAndre is more ambivalent, and the series has shown the concentrated pressure on young African American men to work the corners, and so his ambivalence can be apprehended more sympathetically. It is the absence of the real Gary (now dead) that speaks to the alternative strategy.

As a television city, the Baltimore of *The Corner* is constructed as profoundly local. Nearly all of the action is set in the Franklin Square area, around Monroe and Fayette, and most of the action consists of the trading, the consuming, and the relinquishing of drugs, with extended sequences devoted to the various kinds of associated theft and deception. The parameters of this local world are set by the exceptional excursions elsewhere: Fran goes to visit her ten-years-clean brother who lives in a more suburban street; DeAndre penetrates a couple of restaurants when looking for a job; and, most notably, in episode 4, Gary goes downtown to the Inner Harbor. This trip, in which Gary wanders along the new quayside, past restaurants and the water taxi, entering a couple of shops and mingling with other citizens and tourists, gives him a moment of flâneur-like mobility in the city. The range of visual stimuli in this sequence serves to accentuate the closed-in quality of the open-air drug market, its monotony and claustrophobia, while also demonstrating the manner in which that space is constructed partly through the contrast with other spaces. Gary's visit to the Baltimore of the Inner Harbor redevelopment, the widely advertised public face of Baltimore's regeneration, reverses the tourist literature. For the very exceptional quality of Gary's outing renders tourist, landmark Baltimore strange—a whole world of apparently trouble-free consumption, so near and yet so far from the corner.

Redeveloped Baltimore is more alien to the denizens of *The Corner* than the more vivid other space of the program, which is the space of the past. This space, a richly colored space of memory, erupts suddenly, without warning, into the grayish brownish tones of the present, particularly in the first three episodes. This remembered space, which includes a clean neighborly street, a garden with a swing, college, and parties, is a complex space as it condenses both individual memories and the invocation of an American dream. It serves, within the fiction, to explain that Gary and Fran were not always like this, that West Baltimore wasn't always like this, but also works rather like a fantasy, as the color and graining are quite different to the present.

Space in *The Corner* is not just local, it is territorial and contested. And in this contestation—which includes several different, similar corners and nearby streets and back alleys, and is played out between different parties—something of the particular capacities of audiovisual media in the presentation of space become visible. For the moving image can show both the physical space and the stories that partly determine what it is and how it is lived in. Film can reveal the way in which space can simultaneously be several different places, while narrative structure and generic echoes shape the persistence of certain kinds of probability. The most obvious example of this is the regular, violent eruption of the squad cars of the Baltimore Police Department into the area. Shot from the street spaces into which the police will arrive (rather than from the police cars, a more familiar generic space that will reappear in *The Wire*), the arrival of the cars initiates a routine which runs from the warning shouts through the discarding of drugs to the aggressive searching of residents, made to stand either hands up against the wall or lying on the pavement. This routine disrupts the pattern and pace of corner interaction, displaying its spaces as subject to, if not control, at least harassment and regulation from elsewhere. However, as the raids start on the corner among characters with whom the viewer is familiar, the spatial invasion is more palpable and the deliberate humiliation of the coercive display of bodies-for-searching more visceral. The police invasion sequences invert the characteristic dominance of the police genre in making the meaning of this type of space.

But there are more subtle interrogations of the social relations that structure the significance of place, of which I will discuss two. The first is an analysis of the space of the corner provided by the fifteen-year-old DeAndre, at this stage in the narrative poised on the edge of postadolescent involvement in the drug trade, and reflecting on corner strategies with his friends. Halfway through "DeAndre's Blues," standing in an upstairs room, looking out onto the corner, he gives a perceptive analysis of the personnel deployment across the trading space, observing, "This ain't brain surgery—you just gotta think about it a bit," proceeding to demonstrate his grasp of the separation of functions across different agents—"those two are muscle," all of whom just look as if they're standing about doing nothing. DeAndre concludes his analysis with a comment that could be taken as an epigraph for the project of the series as a whole: "Lot of people don't see there's much thought, but that's because they don't think." The space of the corner is produced through social relationships—it is not a place where bad things just happen. The poignancy of the ability to think which DeAndre has just demonstrated is that it is already evident to the viewer that this will make him more, rather than less, likely to become involved in running a corner.

The second demonstration of the socially constructed nature of the space of the corner comes in "Fran's Blues," when Mrs. Taylor is shown organizing "a moment" in the trade of the corner, so that she can bring a class of little children across the road. This scene commences with the children told to wait against a wall while in a series of close-up and medium-shot shot-reverse-shots between Mrs. Taylor and the corner habitués she explains that she is going to be crossing with "the little ones" every Thursday. Familiar corner characters, both addicts and traders, are shown to recognize the justice of her firmly made request and bring each other into order, at which point there is a cut to a much longer shot, opening out the space, revealing the spatial relations between different characters and showing the long prospect of the street, which is then crossed by a line of small children holding on to each other's hands. The social contract which Mrs. Taylor has invoked, the assumption that the corner people will recognize the innocence of the children, has transformed the space itself, with the longer, wider shot letting in light and positioning individuals in a broader social context than their own drug needs.

This lighter, more spacious image, so unusual for *The Corner* as whole, can also be read as a comment on the project of the series itself: to reveal and contextualize lives usually ignored.

The Corner provides, within the tradition of nineteenth-century naturalism, with its emphasis on the environmental and contextual determination of human agency, first sketches of characters, narrative trajectories, and struggles that reappear recognizably in *The Wire* (for example, Cutty's return from prison in the first episode of season 3 and Gary's living space; the young man who in *The Corner* is DeAndre and is variously embodied in *The Wire* as D'Angelo and Namond). The traditional critique of naturalism is that it shows only the detail of the appearances of things and does not provide the structural analysis of how these things come to be as they are. Thus, in this argument, the depressing impossibility of overcoming difficult circumstance is enacted in the very form in which it is presented, for the reader or viewer is

3.7–3.8. Mrs. Taylor (Jacqui Allen) makes space through negotiation and framing (*The Corner*, episode 3, "Fran's Blues").

not provided with the intellectual resources with which to understand causality and must therefore bow to what is environmentally inevitable. Revelatory the detail of this previously unfamiliar everyday life might be, but the reader or viewer, like the characters depicted, will remain trapped in it, able only to shed tears, or feel pity, or despair. In these terms, *The Corner* is recognizably a naturalist work, although the self-reflexive framing of individual episodes in the DVD presentation provides a more analytic context. Despite this framing, it remains a depressing watch, and I have lost count of the number of *Wire* fans who have revealed to me that they did purchase *The Corner* in the desolation of having finally finished the sixty-hour viewing commitment that is the later series, only to find themselves unable to watch the earlier six hours through to the end. One of the reasons for this may be the different kinds of spaces offered in the two shows. The very situatedness of *The Corner*, its localness, its sense of characters caught up in repetitions, the impossibility of escape, the apparent inevitability of certain destinies makes a viewing experience that is also constrained. Mrs. Taylor's sequence discussed above, Gary's excursion to the harbor, and the memory montages are among the only moments in which protagonists and viewers see a wider sky. In contrast, the much more explicitly generic premise of *The Wire* permits a much greater variety of responses, while its investigative structure (and length) grants an alibi to the realist project, so that its viewers are caught up in an investigation, rather than simply subject to an exposition.

The Wire *and Baltimore*

There are jokes about viewers of *The Wire* who think they would know how to sell drugs in West Baltimore. These jokes juxtapose the white privilege of some of the program's audience with the brutality and extremity of the world of the street corners dramatized in the show. They entail acute observations about the white fascination with African American culture that defines the genealogies of cool and can also be found documented in the evolving lists of websites such as *Stuff White People Like*.[56] While being confident about drug-merchandising skills learned from watching television fiction is evidently a category mistake of some gravity, there is something in this mistake that is an appropriate response to the style and concerns of *The Wire*. For *The Wire* is a realist text. It may not be only this, and much of the extensive criticism of the show is concerned with how to characterize its genre and mode, but its primary self-presentation is as a complex, wide-ranging narrative which reveals to its viewers something of a social reality that exists outside the text. This core revelatory-pedagogic project is shared by all realist texts, but the way in which it is realized varies, both historically and across different texts in the same period.

The Wire, particularly in the first season, does seek to show the minutiae of everyday drug dealing, the hierarchies of the street, the separation of the elements (stash and cash), the supply chains, the territorial defenses, the recruitment and dispatch of soldiers. It is quite straightforwardly didactic, and one of the reasons that it has attracted such passionate critical advocacy is because it is successfully so: it is apparent from both fan and scholarly writing that viewers not only feel thrilled and moved but that they have learned something. Perhaps it is ingenuous to describe *The Wire* as straightforwardly didactic. Perhaps that is the luxury of hindsight, of repeated viewing, of having learned about its world through the complex, often difficult investigation and narrative unfolding of the series, in which viewers and investigating team are aligned together so skillfully—listening, watching, checking, recording, remembering, connecting, looking again. For the realist textual strategies of *The Wire* are deployed within a generic context. As Sue Turnbull insists, *The Wire* is, at one level, simply the latest in a long line of crime shows that make significant claims for their own realism.[57] And each of these shows, such as *Naked City* (ABC, 1958–63) or, in the U.K., *Law and Order* (BBC, 1978), used audiovisual techniques that were seen as pioneering at the time in the way they brought the reality depicted into the living room of the television viewer. The impulse of the successful realist text, in its historical moment, is always to direct attention away from the textuality of the text and toward the reality that is represented. That is why people think they know how to deal drugs after watching *The Wire*.

In comparison with the stylistic self-consciousness of *Homicide*, *The Wire* uses rather different textual strategies. If *Homicide* is all "Fred Wiseman meets MTV," *The Wire*'s use of camera and editing is much more like Roland Barthes's notion of "writing degree zero." The image, instead of being buzzy and busy, is often carefully and elegantly framed within the already old-fashioned 4:3 ratio, so that the eye seems naturally to fall on what is significant or to understand the relative power of protagonists within the image, without a sense of mediation or direction. This is writing degree zero, a filmic style that seems to efface itself, although evidently the use of 4:3 indicates a very clear compositional choice.[58] Erlend Lavik's discussion and video essay exposition of *The Wire*'s plainness is pertinent here, and enables us to see why it might be particularly appropriate to consider the referential worlds of

Baltimore of *The Wire* as the primary topic for analysis, as the style of the show directs our attention to what is being shown.[59] Lavik demonstrates that there is little expressive fanciness to shot composition and editing, little formal self-identification of clever or well-framed shots, although there are certainly many of those. One of the most common shot sequences, from a close-up to a wider view, serves an analytic, contextualizing purpose. Narrative time is rarely complex: events move forward; there are no flashbacks; and although different narrative threads are edited together with considerable expressive adroitness, these individual stories too take place in unified and coherent space and time. The challenge, and the promise, that the show makes is that it is worth concentrating to see how all the different bits fit together. This is a demand for close attention on the part of the viewer that is made at a formal level, but which is not directed toward form. As Lavik argues, "*The Wire* does not so much invite us to become amateur narratologists as amateur sociologists."[60]

The program uses, and abuses, generic convention to make a realist point. The police investigate; the drug economy is anatomized; and the viewer learns. The generically conventional alignment of the viewer with the law becomes increasingly nuanced as the sophistication of the Barksdale operation is revealed and the parallels between institutions of crime and policing unfold. The didactic realist point of the first season is something like, "any particular drug-related killing in West Baltimore is only the tip of an iceberg of complex social and financial relations, and agents on both sides of the law are constrained by institutional structures and contexts." This develops, as the show proceeds, through both its own ambitious logic and utopian stagings such as the free drug market of "Hamsterdam" in the third season, to a more developed critique of the feasibility of the war on drugs.[61] Just as the police learn, so does the viewer—as also do individual characters, such as Bodie (J. D. Williams) and Pryzbylewski (Jim True-Frost). But the viewer does not just learn: although instruction takes place, the formal qualities of the text are not instructional. It is through emotional engagement with the characters, the lure of chasing the money for natural police, and the skillfully deployed serial pleasures of suspense that the learning takes place.[62]

The Wire is not just a realist text, but both its utopian and its melo-dramatic elements appear within a vocabulary and look of realism.[63] My concern is with the way in which its television city is produced in a particular medium that has particular histories and conventions. It is also—always—a television program, a long-form television drama with its roots, and first season, firmly with the police genre. It is a multipart, five-season television program, made for and broadcast on a particular cable channel early in the twenty-first century, and subsequently viewed on both DVD and online. What is most notable for my purposes—and the complexity of *The Wire* has permitted those with many different purposes to claim it in other ways—is that all five seasons of this show are set in one city, Baltimore, and that its narrative structure is cumu-lative. The television city that is the Baltimore of *The Wire* is produced through accretion, through a thickening of connections and textures. This Baltimore is still made through repetition—it is still a police detail, housed in a range of temporary offices trying to trace Baltimore graft—but part of this repetition is analytic as the scope of the inquiry broadens: the proposition that in any institutional setting (legal or illegal), individ-uals are enmeshed within determining social relations and structures. Publicity associated with *The Wire* has tended to eschew its television heritage, instead vociferously claiming the nineteenth-century novel, rather than TV, as an antecedent, and one of the consequences of this strategy is that it emphasizes narrative progression and develop-ment, rather than repetition. While it is true that the Baltimore of *The Wire* is not like the Oxford of *Inspector Morse*, for which each visit is somehow to the same place where it will all begin again with another murder to be solved within two hours, there are precedents within televisual storytelling that this genealogy ignores. Serial narrative in television since the 1980s has extended over the long form through a range of significant dramas such as *Heimat, Holding On, Our Friends in the North*, and *The Sopranos*, which have demonstrated the poten-tial for the medium to stage national bildungsromans of considerable analytic and affective complexity.[64] This makes the references to Vic-torian novels more significant as claims to the cultural high ground than as an accurate genealogy. Discussion of the genealogy of the pro-gram is one of the sites on which arguments about the most appropriate critical approach to *The Wire*—as well as its cultural status—is conducted, as is debate about mode and genre.[65]

Put baldly, the extensive critical discussion of *The Wire* can generally be organized across a spectrum, of which one end is the real and the other is television serials.[66] Precisely what is taken to be the real varies. It can be the drug trade, the inner city or ghetto, the decline of the docks, the corruptions of public office, the organization of the police service, the school system, the prison system, the justice system, the newspaper industry, or, more broadly, neoliberalism and postindustrial Baltimore within a global system.[67] The real of *The Wire* is defined differently by different scholars but is significantly informed by the stories and settings established in the first season and what, in the context of U.S. television, is the shock of the extended and often sympathetic narrative depiction of differentiated, but mainly drug-involved, African American (mainly male) lives. It is testimony to the achieved complexity of the drama that it can be invoked to serve a range of arguments and contexts. For example, the work of Anmol Chaddha and William Julius Wilson identifies the program's importance as its description and analysis of lives lived in the inner city in neoliberal times and draws on social science literature to both amplify and corroborate the analysis presented in *The Wire*.[68] The crux of their engagement with the drama, though, is their argument that the fiction can provide a more holistic, connected analysis than this social science scholarship. In this context, when *The Wire* is being discussed in terms of the knowledge of the real that it produces, a more common reference is to the work of the cultural geographer David Harvey, who is often called on by literary and cultural scholars to provide facts to back up their exposition of what is depicted in the show.[69]

Although British born, Harvey is a long-term Baltimore resident ("I have lived in Baltimore City for most of my adult life"[70]), and Baltimore haunts his published works, concerned, as much of it is, with the analysis of the residential housing market, patterns of urbanization, deindustrialization, and redevelopment. Whether his topic is nineteenth-century Paris or the American urban experience, Harvey's work always displays a self-conscious concern with method, for it seeks to produce analyses of the spatially transformative power of capital that can be debated and tested for their explanatory power. Baltimore appears often as an example. Sometimes, this is in the most general sense through the invocation of Baltimore to exemplify particular, generalizable trends with the phrase "a city like Baltimore," or "a place like Baltimore."[71] At others, it is more specific, as in a grouping with Liverpool and Lille as cities that did not possess necessary attributes in the brutal transformations from postwar Keynesian economic strategy, or its Inner Harbor can figure with London Docklands to exemplify new consumer playgrounds within strategies of competitive urbanism.[72] Although Harvey himself displays little interest in television, his work is referenced by *Wire* scholars with interests in the series' depiction of Baltimore and is cited, for example, by Peter Clandfield in his suggestive discussion of the resonance of the empty row houses ("Poe houses") which emerge to their full narrative potential in season 4, as concealed burial chambers, or by Sherryl Vint in her careful analysis of the contradictory pressure of journalistic and dramatic conventions on the work.[73]

While my interest is indeed in the Baltimore represented in *The Wire*, I am reluctant to invoke Harvey's Baltimore as a truth that the series represents, which can, in turn, in a circular move, be invoked to validate the representation of the city shown in the series. This seems a move that repays Harvey's own methodological scruple with a certain reductiveness. For what I know about Baltimore I have learned mainly from Harvey, and *The Wire*, and other historians such as Sherry Olson and Patricia Fields, and my own visits.[74] Instead, I prefer to work with the idea of juxtaposing different Baltimores, so that Harvey's Baltimore takes its place alongside the versions of the city we find in *The Wire*— and *Homicide*—and, theoretically at least, although I won't deal with them here, the novels of Anne Tyler. Each of these texts narrates the city, and something of the experience of living there, and I concentrate here on how *The Wire*'s sense of place is achieved, rather than comparing its account of the city with that of Harvey, or Anmal and Wilson—or Tyler.

The Wire is explicitly concerned with place, with the investigation and narration of a particular city through television. It is a show that is militantly set in a particular place, Baltimore, and much concerned with local horizons, expectations, and ambitions. Much of the plot is

driven by macho jostling for local power, be it as commissioner of police, mayor, or the bearer of, in Marlo's words, "the crown" of the drug
connect. And what is contested is often territory, be it drug corners, estates, or voter wards, just as real estate is the legitimate prize. The use,
for example, of the opening of the luxury condo development of the
Grainery in the closing montage of season 2 is a specific reference to a
particular redevelopment of part of the port. The detail of the drama's
local referential world, though, does not confine its story to the local.[75]
Instead, it provides, in Clifford Geertz's phrase, a "thick description"
of the particular that enables the viewer to provide a wider contextu-
alization, just like the characteristic shot movement from close-up to
a wider view.

Place is a significant element in the much-discussed opening of the
show, when Detective Jimmy McNulty (Dominic West) asks a teenage witness what happened to cause a murder and elicits the story of
"Snot" Boogie, the young man lying in a pool of blood in front of them
in the street. In this scene, the generic heritage of the show is established through the use of blue flashing light illuminating the conversation and reflected in the blood on the road, and it has its only spoken
identification of place as its frequently cited closing line: "This is America." The claim is immediately to the epic and the metonymic. However,
the identification, in the fifth shot, through a passing close-up of the
Baltimore city shield on the badge of an attending officer, also specifies
a place that is both particular and generic. It may be America, but it is
also Baltimore and a police drama. McNulty's curiosity about why the
murder occurred cues the viewer to understand the type of place this
is. It is a narrative place in which events of this type occur, and generic
expectation would lead one to expect that more will be done to investigate this murder. However, the facts of the situation have been laid
out very plainly without obfuscation, and so, in a sense, that murder
is already solved. The murder, it turns out, is merely symptomatic. It
is not the fact of the murder that will be the topic, but its representa-
tiveness, which recasts the epic claim about America, articulated by
a young African American man engaged in the drug trade who will
be lucky to live till he is thirty. "This is America" is taken both ironically, to anticipate how the series will demonstrate the very inequality

of opportunity in the land of the free, and to suggest that what will be shown in this particular diegetic world may be true of America more widely. So *The Wire* is set in a particular place, Baltimore (the badge), a national and mythic place (America), but also a generic place (the blue light, the dead body, the police). It is the interplay of these places that merits further attention.

The credits of each episode of *The Wire* finish with a declaration about the provenance of the fiction: "Filmed on location in Baltimore, Maryland." The production was based in Baltimore; cast and crew lived in the city; and many of those involved in making the program were Baltimore residents. The location shooting is evident throughout, from the concentration on West Baltimore in the first season to the judicious use of downtown, the Inner Harbor, views across the water and the port.[76] There are many shots of both typical (back alleys, row houses) and identifiable Baltimore locations (the Museum of Industry, the City Hall), and the show deals in many stories that are Baltimore specific (the redevelopment of the Inner Harbor, the gentrification of Federal Hill). The intricate local knowledge of the art director Vincent Peranio gives detail and variation to locations such as back alleys and drug corners, which makes the settings themselves expressive. Peranio himself observed of his work, "TV is really about close-ups and the actors, and so much of what I do ends up being fuzzy background."[77] In the way in which *The Wire* is shot, though, what might start as background often moves into focus toward the end of the shot, and the detail of the location work creates this contextualizing option. This Baltimore shooting, which gives the whole production a grounded and located feel, obscures the fact that a great many of the sets for *The Wire* are generic staples: police squad rooms, holding cells, interview rooms, cars, courts, prisons, clubs, bars, strip joints. As the generic mix expands, so that committee rooms, government offices, classrooms, and newspaper offices are added, the genres shift and mutate, and cumulatively become more intertwined.

What makes the generic sets seem more than this, what makes people want to go on *Wire* tours, is that they are made narratively significant and, through the judicious use of Vincent Peranio's local knowledge, knitted into a sense of a specific place, which is in turn made meaningful, as what is happening there turns out to be the topic of investigation.[78] The sense of the city that emerges comes from narrative and analysis, rather than simply the use of a Baltimore setting (although, as I have suggested, the use of the Baltimore setting only looks simple because of the skill of its achievement). The openings of the fourth and fifth seasons provide different examples of this in practice. In the fourth, most of the cold open to the season takes place inside a hardware store, opening with a close-up on the face of Snoop (Felicia Pearson) as she examines nail guns. In the setting of the location-shot store, which is never allowed to obtrude, never made the explicit subject of the camera's attention, single close-ups and two shots are used to show a quite technical conversation between a young African American woman (Snoop) and a middle-aged white man (the shop worker) about the relative merits of different models. Each is shown to have the technical knowledge to make the conversation worthwhile, and it is only when Snoop moves to payment—on the spot, in hundred-dollar bills—that the encounter is signaled as exceptional for the store. Snoop rejoins her companion, Chris, waiting outside in an SUV, pleased with her purchase and her discriminating exercise of consumer choice. It is for the viewer to work out what the nail gun will be used for. There is a single shot of the vehicle stationary outside the store, locating the shopping scene in a particular, but quite unremarkable, location, with a parking lot where Chris waits patiently for his colleague who has been buying a nail gun to more securely conceal bodies in empty houses. Although Snoop is not a customer who pays at a cash register, banal parking regulations might as well be observed, and the SUV is surrounded by other cars and customers.

In contrast to this unemphasized use of a particular location, the open to season 5 is all set within the police headquarters, and involves several familiar police officers duping a young man into confessing to a murder. The emphasis in this scene is on repetitions. The setting is generically familiar; the configuration of characters is familiar; and the police involved joke with each other about the twenty years or so that they have been using this particular fake lie detector test, as they explain to a new team member how it works. The familiarity of the whole setup, including the unethical but effective treatment of a suspect, is the point. The viewer is back in the same place, and the same old things are going on, with the same old roles being filled by new recruits. The narrative project of the previous four seasons is to enable the viewer to understand this scene as symptomatic.

Baltimore here is a city of people, transactions, and relationships. This may seem an obvious point, but much discussion of the cinematic city addresses the topic as if it is solely a matter of shots of the streets and buildings. Consequently, the television city, which has, historically, had less location work, particularly outside program titles, is seen as somehow less real, and less meriting of discussion. *The Wire*'s Baltimore certainly does use shots of streets, buildings, and Baltimore landmarks, and the contrast between the different spaces to which different characters have access is one of its most significant strategies in the production of the city. As important though in its incremental portrait of the city are the networks of trade and affiliation, which the viewer, like the police, must decipher. As both Williams and Bramall and Pitcher argue, although from rather different positions, it is the promise of intelligibility that lures the viewer on.[79] One form of assistance that is provided here is the use of the cold open as character study. This is particularly prominent in the first season, when a very large range of characters is being introduced, and is striking in the sixth episode of season 1, which, although it opens with an exterior shot looking down on a mutilated body spread-eagled on a car, is mainly spent in the interior of the row house where viewer sympathy is actively solicited for one of the young corner boys, Wallace (Michael B. Jordan). In a depiction that any viewer familiar with melodramatic codes will understand as potentially fatal, we are shown that Wallace in fact looks after a troupe of younger children, waking them for school, giving each a bag of chips and a carton of juice, his nurturing behavior symbolized by both the provisions and his insistence on toothbrushing. The row houses may be derelict, but they are also shown to be homes.

This was preceded in season 1, episode 4 by a portrait of "Herc" (Dominick Lombardozzi, playing Thomas Hauk, one of the police detail), who is shown trying his hardest to move a desk that has got wedged into the office door. This scene is a literal drama of place, when the dimensions of the office space are dramatized in a way that reveals character. Herc's muscularity, his sweaty efforts with this large piece of furniture, to which he recruits other team members as they arrive at work, is juxtaposed with Lester Freamon's (Clarke Peters) silent composure as he sits at his desk, delicately painting a very small piece of dollhouse furniture and observing the commotion and effort. Only at the end of the scene does it become clear that the desk is impossible to move because half the people are trying to move it in, while the others are trying to move it out. This scene is both metaphor for the team that is not yet one and a shrewd character study of Herc, who is too unimaginative to realize that others may not know what is to him obvious, and Lester, who may, and may not, have understood what is happening all along but chooses to say nothing.

The intellectual and representational project of *The Wire* could be seen as the analysis of the back story to a crime series set in Baltimore. Its achievement, as Lavik argues, is the organization of this analysis so that it is produced through the generic skills of the viewer as "amateur sociologist."[80] The pleasures of the text are mobilized to produce a feeling of something understood, and the feeling, as Linda Williams has demonstrated, is crucial. The terms of this analysis, what causes what, how what Bramall and Pitcher call the show's "fantasy of intelligibility" is realized, have attracted two significant critiques—both of which recognize the show's accomplishments—which engage with the spatiality of the represented world.[81] George Lipsitz has argued that the analysis is flawed because it does not address the structuring role of white spatial privilege.[82] His point is that the ghetto has been produced by systematic discriminatory housing policy and associated, seemingly unrelated initiatives such as the building of freeways, so to focus only on relationships within that context produced by what he calls "the white spatial imaginary" is, in fact, to make an analysis from within the restrictions of that imaginary. Brutal masculinities are demonstrated to be very understandable responses to brutal and unforgiving circumstances, but this sympathetic depiction concentrates only on appearances and symptoms, not their long-term causes. What is persuasive about Lipsitz's analysis is the way in which it attends to the overweening masculinity of the series' concerns and identifies its potential for sentimentality. What is trickier is the question of the dramatic form that would satisfy his analysis. If the relationship between *The Corner* and *The Wire* is one in which *The Wire* is a realist extrapolation from the raw material that finds its first form in the naturalism of *The Corner*, Lipsitz's argument can be characterized as one which sees *The Wire* too as limited by its naturalist failure to grasp the spatial modalities of inherited ethnic privilege. Paradoxically, it is the much more explicitly generic *Homicide*, with its expansive geographical reach into country clubs and suburbs for murder settings, which gives a more extensive sense of the terrain on which ethnicized spatial privilege is played out, although the final sequences of *The Wire*'s fourth season, showing the "rescued" (fostered) Namond (Julito McCullum) on the porch of ex–police chief Bunny Colvin's (Robert Wisdom) more suburban house, gives some intimation of a wider Baltimore, just as, ironically, do Jimmy McNulty's final words in the show as a whole, "Let's go home."[83]

The second critique concerns the depiction of African American motherhood on the show, and Elizabeth Ault notes, while setting up the terms of its analysis, "The world of *The Wire*, focused as it is on the public sphere of street economies and urban police forces, is notably, if not unrealistically, devoid of women."[84] Ault's argument is that the individuated pathos of the stories of the four boys who form the focus of the fourth season, and the slow tracing of the inevitability of the repetitions in their destinies, is achieved partly at the cost of their mothers. She connects the characterization of the neglectful, addicted, and status-conscious mothers of *The Wire* to a continuum in the representation of black women that ranges across popular and official sites (such as the 1965 Moynihan Report and the 1990s ghetto movies). Thus while the authenticity of the show in other spheres is produced through countering the "racial hegemony of television," in relation to mothers, this long-established image of emasculating black women / welfare queens is confirmed.[85] Ault is fully sensitive to the constraints of both genre and television institutions: she understands that generic conventions produce what are seen as plausible realities: "It's understandable that a show focused on male dominated spheres like street crime and city politics would focus primarily on telling the stories of men," but she still teases out a complicity between *The Wire*'s treatment of African American mothers and some of the ideologies it in other spheres opposes.[86] This analysis points to one of the abiding problems of telling a different city story, particularly in a genre, like the *policier* (police fiction), which is built on the encounters between men in the city's mean streets. Would a season devoted to the family or the home, alongside those on the drug trade, the docks, the city council, schooling, and the press, have been able to maintain generic plausibility? Would more time at characters' homes still count as a series about Baltimore? If the central protagonists within the drug world had been women, not men, would there ever have been any doubt about whether the show was melodrama, not tragedy? These questions, which are mine, not Ault's, although asked in relation to a particular, highly regarded and aesthetically successful series, return us to some of the questions underlying the project of this book about the relationship between the inside and outside of the television city, and about the intertwining of generic convention and spatial representation in the constraining of character mobility and the making of aesthetic judgments.

Endings

The end of each season of *The Wire* is a moment when the demands of the medium, and the conventions of seasonality, come back into prominence. The extended, multithread complex narrative of the preceding ten to thirteen episodes needs some sort of resolution, and this is mainly done through an accelerated montage, in three cases cut to single songs, which summarize past and in some cases future developments. These synoptic montage sequences perform several functions in relation to the television city.

First, there is the matter of generic space. This is dealt with most simply at the end of the first season when the generic complexity of the whole enterprise has not yet been revealed. Freamon and Pryzbylewski are shown, in the basement-set office (with its allusions to the outside city through the high windows), dismantling the hard-assembled investigative wall of photographs, names, connecting arrows, and question marks. Without much speech, the two men take down photographs, sometimes pausing on a particular face, and allowing the viewer to review the role of the individual. The generic space of investigation is being closed down, and the sober tone of the scene echoes the disappointing final settlements. This procedural trope recurs in other season conclusions, but in a much more abbreviated form. In season 2, it is simply the turning out of the light in the squad room. In season 3, the dismantling of another investigative wall, the light again turned out, and in season 4, a new wall is being set up. This dismantling/light trope condenses referential meaning (the investigation being closed down) and self-reflexive commentary on the end of the season.

The balance between this generic space and the space of the city shifts as the series develops, with more and more of the final montages devoted to views of characters and cityscapes. The police investigation produces the real—makes individual characters and places meaningful—and then the real can stand alone as significant for the viewer who can revise the past episodes. Two of these final montages are given subjective framings: in the second season, Nicky Sobotka (Pablo Schreiber) gazes out to the harbor, peering through a chain-link fence, and, in the final season, Jimmy McNulty exits his car on a freeway and looks at the city. In Nicky's sequence, while it initially seems as if the cut from Nicky's face is to the remembered past shown in the preceding episodes, the images, which include the port in much greater disrepair and unionized dockworkers now drinking on the streets, soon shift to an anticipated future. The cut back to Nicky's face at the end of the sequence moves back to the present, and Nicky walks down an empty road by the waterside fence, away from the camera into the middle distance.[87] This future montage, an exceptional departure from the series' habitual present-tense narration, is vulnerable to Lipsitz's charge of sentimentality, as is the treatment of the newspaper industry in the final season. Nicky, who has proved himself a rather weaker, more volatile, and potentially more selfishly venal trade unionist than his now-murdered uncle, is privileged with a view into the future of the devastation of the further decline of the docks to which his own actions have contributed. While this is a grim future, granting it to Nicky, a character whose actions throughout have been characterized by a lack of foresight, tips the text into sentimentality because the emotion evoked is implausible for the character to whom it is attributed. In contrast, McNulty's final view of Baltimore, which follows an extended fake Irish wake for this "natural police" at the end of the last episode of the last season, opens up questions of what has been learned in the long sixty-hour watch that can legitimately be associated with the character.[88] As McNulty gazes out at the city, and then a montage of characters and events commences, the generic city of the investigation and the location-shot city are shown to have become one. The viewer can use the montage like one of the investigation walls: she is offered a chance to recall particular faces and plot points and to demonstrate an understanding of how these fit together. The arrows and the question marks of the investigation have been transformed into an analytic understanding. Here, the future tense of some scenes (more girls being unloaded from containers; younger children being arrested) is justified by the key argument of the piece as a whole about the inevitability of repetition and escalation with current policies in place. The move at the end of the sequence, away from the narrative constituents and back to views of Baltimore, leaves space for the audience to reflect on what they have learned about the city, but also takes this reflection to the third term of the place of this television city: America.

Finally, I return to where I started, with the disused Recreation Pier at Fell's Point, on which there is a plaque commemorating *Homicide*. As I have been writing this book, the Recreation Pier has been transformed into expensive waterside apartments. One of my justifications for choosing Baltimore as the third television city of this book was that the critical success of *The Wire*, a show which stages a portrait of Baltimore, had made feasible the idea of taking television cities seriously. The significant and growing scholarship on the cinematic city had seemed repeatedly to ignore the television city in a genealogy that jumped from the great 1920s city symphonies to the digital city. Television, as so often, I argued, was, for reasons of relative cultural prestige, forgotten.[89] However, Michael Curtin challenged my ideas about the neglect of the television city by arguing that the early twenty-first century was proving a time of quite extraordinarily interesting U.S. television cities, and this made me think about the difference, and the similarities, between contemporary television cities and their history.[90] When I, like many other teachers, brought the Baltimore of *The Wire* into the seminar room, I was struck by how immediately students were attracted to exploring the real Baltimore, trying to anchor their dramatic experience of the fiction into the city's mapped geography.[91] As one part of my *Wire* classes, students worked together to explore *Wire*-related Internet sites (in the classroom, using different computers linked to large screens). The first time I did this, there was a moment when all the large screens, independently under the control of different groups of students, were showing Google street view maps of Baltimore. Given the freedom to explore the paratexts of *The Wire*, the students searched, in the first instance, not for discussion threads or Monopoly games, but for real locations. It was this teaching experience that led me to privilege realism as the key term in my analysis of *The Wire*—the form of the fiction clearly convinced its viewers that they were learning something about the real Baltimore. Researching Baltimore as an audiovisual city led me to the art director and production designer Vincent Peranio and his exceptional history as a gatekeeper for the audiovisual city across film and television. In his words: "I've always felt that the different films I've done here were, in a way, chronicling Baltimore. It was my own little thing, that I was showing Baltimore to as many people as possible. And showing them as real a version as possible, even though one might be more colorful or more nostalgic or more realistic. It was still the city." Peranio's work in Baltimore has extended from the 1960s to the present day. He has designed films and television programs set in the city throughout the period of deindustrialization. He has designed films set in the past, taking advantage of the mixture of period building that still survives in this comparatively poor city, and he has designed films in which Baltimore stands in for other Eastern Seaboard cities, particularly New York. But most notably, as he puts it himself, he has "in a way, chronicl[ed] Baltimore." If *The Wire* seeks to present a thick, horizontal analysis of the city and the drug trade, Peranio's work provides a long, vertical chronology that in some ways enacts what it records, from when he first worked with John Waters in the late 1960s.[92]

Peranio was already living in Fell's Point, which he describes as like a ghost town at the time, when he met Waters (and Pat Moran, who works as casting director on so much Baltimore audiovisual work). Speaking of those early years of filming with John Waters (when he was still thinking of himself as a painter), he draws attention to Baltimore's cinematic virginity, observing, "It was a great time. It was a great freedom because there was no filming done in Baltimore. They didn't have any permit system or anything like that." The area round the docks and harbor was being transformed externally by the beginning of containerization and internally by the city's decision to expand the road network. Peranio, part of a group of young artists, was one of those first waves of incomers so well documented in the story of gentrification in other cities.[93] He has described the city as they found it then:

> This was right when the city was moving everybody out because of the road, buying people out, buying houses out, boarding them up. So it was like we had the whole place to ourselves. It was almost a little ghost town of just *On the Waterfront* kind of look, very industrial, which is what we liked very much. . . . There wasn't a tree in Fells Point. It was very bleak . . . and I just fell in love with it. I loved the trains coming down the streets, you know, stopping in the middle of the streets. It had a great look to it.[94]

Homicide breaks Baltimore as a location for filming; however, it also marks a more institutionalized relationship between film location, production company, and real place. Waters's films were low-budget affairs, funded on a one-off basis and often involving a continuing core grouping of cast and crew, many of them Baltimore based. Television drama production is rather different. Even a long shoot on a feature film is nothing like the months and years of a continuing drama. *Homicide* was filmed in Fell's Point (and other parts of Baltimore), but it was also produced and run from there. The long business of television production, the many people involved—all this took place in Fell's Point and contributed to the changes in the area. The bars, the restaurants, the rents, the parking: all were affected. There has been some interesting scholarship about the post-Katrina city of New Orleans and the industry associated with the production of *Treme*, which both is set there and endeavored to use local labor.[95] The question becomes how to conceptualize the relationship between a site-specific show and a particular location when the very making of the program is transforming the location. As the Fell's Point memorial plaque states, the city Recreation Pier hosted this newer type of industry for seven years, and when *Homicide* finished, Baltimore was no longer a city in which "they didn't have a permit system or anything like that." *The Wire* is made in a much less innocent Baltimore, a Baltimore with a film commission, with permits, with designated officials to promote and manage filming within the city. As the acknowledgment at the end of *The Wire* states, "The producers wish to thank the Baltimore Film Commission, the Maryland Film Office and the Maryland Historical Society." Television has changed Baltimore. But has Baltimore changed television? Yes and no. It has changed certain perceptions of what can be done in the medium and attracted the attention of viewers who have not previously discussed or analyzed their viewing. *The Wire* will have an unchallenged place as an exceptional realization of the storytelling possibilities of the medium, although not necessarily a model that can be successfully emulated. But one of the side effects of its success has been, in many accounts, to obscure the previous history of the medium, and this book has sought to demonstrate that there have been television cities before the Baltimore of *The Wire*, and there will be afterward.

Television, with its history of the use of the formal qualities of both repetition and seriality across genres and modes, has made many more television cities than I have been able to discuss in this short book. The sitcom city and the soap opera city are different types of city, with different spatialities and different types of plausibility, as shown in chapter 2, than the city of the investigator from which most of my case studies are drawn. However, the specificity of the television city, across genres, is that of a city to which one returns. The modality and possibilities of this return are both generic and subject to the transformations in the medium's modes of delivery. The television city can be both domestic and intimate in exactly the moment that it is also scary. From the temporally constrained television city of the twentieth century, when you had to be there, in front of the screen in your living room, to

explore the mean streets, to the portable TV cities of the urban com-
muter, downloading another place to absent yourself from the one you
are in, the television city is rendered familiar in its repetitions. This city
of repetitions is one that should be attended to in any understanding
of cities both audiovisual and architectural, and I hope this book will
stimulate further scholarship on many other television cities.

Notes

Introduction

1. Written by John Sullivan for the BBC, *Only Fools and Horses* was broadcast for seven series and also appeared on British screens in the form of Christmas specials, sketches, and a prequel. Full details are available in Sullivan, *"Only Fools and Horses"*; and Clark, *"Only Fools and Horses."* U.S. usage divides a television series into seasons, whereas British usage, at least until the twenty-first century, is "series" throughout. For most twentieth-century British television, the original usage "series" is retained throughout this book.

2. *Only Fools and Horses*, exported, like much British television, to its former empire, has also established significant audiences in former Eastern Bloc territories such as Yugoslavia. The Netherlands, in addition to broadcasting the British series, made its own version, *Wat schulft 't* (What's it worth?). Attempts in the 1990s to produce a U.S. version with NBC were less successful. Graham McCann, *"Only Fools and Horses,"* 261.

3. *Sex and the City* was notable for its use of Manhattan locations (40 percent location filming is the figure given by Sohn, *"Sex and the City,"* 14), and also for its departure from the multicamera setup typical of television production, instead using film and a single camera (Simon, *"Sex and the City,"* 194).

4. This book is not principally concerned with the question of what television now is. Graeme Turner has made—with others—a convincing series of arguments against the "end of television/convergence hypothesis." See Turner and Tay, *Television Studies after TV*; Pertierra and Turner, *Locating Television*.

5. As Yoshimi, "Television and Nationalism," has shown of Japan, where television was first shown in the streets in the 1950s, and Pertierra and Turner, *Locating Television*, argue more generally, the Anglo-American Western model of privatized domestic viewing, although it has certainly dominated the accounts of television in television studies, does not encompass global television viewing.

Pertierra and Turner instead propose the increased necessity of specifying "zones of consumption" when discussing television at both general and particular levels.

6. The news that Apple, in the context of falling iPhone revenues, has been in talks with Time Warner revealed the comparative health of Time Warner, which has retained its back catalog, in contrast with other "content providers" that "eagerly sold reruns to streaming services, not realising viewers might be more content to watch the old library than to keep up with the new shows." Sam Thielman, "iPhone Sales Start to Falter," *Guardian*, 28 May 2016, 25. Thielman is reporting on stories that first appeared in the *New York Post* and were confirmed by Matthew Garrahan and James Fontanella-Khan in the *Financial Times*, 26 May 2016.

7. McCarthy's *Ambient Television* enumerates the many sites outside the U.S. home—such as the tavern or the barber's—in or at which television is viewed. One of the reasons that her research is so significant, though, is precisely because it punctures assumptions about the place of television. My point is not that television was only a domestic medium in the twentieth century, but that television is assumed and imaged as such. In countries such as Brazil and Japan, as documented in the work of Leal, "Popular Taste and the Erudite Repertoire"; Tufte, *Living with the Rubbish Queen*; and Yoshimi, "Television and Nationalism," television has always had a more public presence.

8. On television and the differential modernities of Britain, France, the United States, and Japan, see Hartley, *Uses of Television*, 92–111; Ross, *Fast Cars, Clean Bodies*; Spigel, *Make Room for TV*; Yoshimi, "'Made in Japan.'" On television and modernity more globally, see Morley, *Media, Modernity and Technology*, 275–310; Pertierra and Turner, *Locating Television*, 108–23.

9. Spigel, *Welcome to the Dreamhouse*, 31–59; Silverstone, *Visions of Suburbia*; Morley, *Home Territories*, 128–48.

10. Indicatively, see Charney and Schwartz, *Cinema and the Invention of Modern Life*; Donald, *Imagining the Modern City*; Friedberg, *Window Shopping*; Highmore, *Cityscapes*; Mennel, *Cities and Cinema*; Nead, *The Haunted Gallery*; Stewart, *Migrating to the Movies*.

11. There is an extensive literature here, but the originary texts are: Baudelaire, "The Painter of Modern Life"; Benjamin, "The Flâneur"; Benjamin, *The Arcades Project*. See also the essays collected in Tester, *The Flâneur*, and Donald's discussion of this figure in city/cinema scholarship, "Talking the Talk, Walking the Walk." Solnit summarizes the debate pithily: "What exactly a flâneur is has never been satisfactorily defined, but among all the versions of the flâneur as everything from a primeval slacker to a silent poet, one thing re-

mains constant: the image of an observant and solitary man strolling about Paris" (*Wanderlust*, 198).

12. The problem of the flâneuse is discussed in Wolff, "The Invisible Flaneuse"; Pollock, "Modernity and the Spaces of Femininity" in her *Vision and Difference*; Wilson, "The Invisible Flaneur"; Wilson, *The Sphinx in the City*; Ryan, "Women, Modernity and the City"; Friedberg, *Window Shopping*; Nord, *Walking the Victorian Streets*; Gleber, *The Art of Taking a Walk*; Solnit, "Walking after Midnight" in her *Wanderlust*.

13. Bowlby, *Just Looking*; Friedberg, *Window Shopping*.

14. *Sex and the City* ran for six seasons from 1998 to 2004. Susan Seidelman, who had depicted Madonna as a flâneuse figure in *Desperately Seeking Susan*, directed several first-season episodes, including the opening one. Full production details and episode guide can be found in Smith, *Manhattan Dating Game*, and on the HBO website.

15. Jermyn, *Sex and the City*, 80–81. On flânerie and *Sex and the City*, see also Richards, "*Sex and the City*"; Akass and McCabe, *Reading "Sex and the City"*; Arthurs, "*Sex and the City* and Consumer Culture." Haggins and Lotz give a shrewd account of the evolution of the series within the HBO network identity in "Comedy Overview," 164. The Brooklyn-set HBO drama *Girls* (2012–17), which includes occasional location material—often single iconic New York shots—has not attracted discussion of the city in the way that *Sex and the City* did, but both have been subject to criticism for the class and ethnic privilege of their heroines. See, for example, essays in Silva and Mendes, "HBO's *Girls*," such as DeCarvalho, "Hannah and Her Entitled Sisters," and Nash and Grant, "Twenty-Something *Girls* v. Thirty-Something *Sex and the City* Women."

16. While she discusses literature, not film or television, Marcus (in her *Apartment Stories*) is one of a small number of scholars who directly address home and the city together. Wojcik's suggestive notion in *The Apartment Plot*, which is concerned mainly with U.S. film 1945–75, does succeed in reconfiguring an understanding of the inside and outside of the city. She is particularly attentive to the role of Manhattan and the potential for a single lifestyle in apartment plots, and also has some interesting observations about television and the apartment plot. Billingham's 2000 book *Sensing the City through Television* analyzed five city dramas, including the San Francisco of *Tales of the City*, the London of *Holding On*, and the Manchester of *Queer as Folk*, but is more concerned with questions of identity.

17. Taunton, *Fictions of the City*, 2.

18. On the cultural status of television, see Brunsdon, *Screen Tastes*, 105–64; Boddy, "The Place of Television Studies"; Brunsdon and Gray, "The Place

of Television Studies"; Brunsdon, "Is Television Studies History?"; Newman and Levine, *Legitimating Television*; Gray and Lotz, *Television Studies*.

19. Polan explicitly addresses some of these transitions, and their discursive construction, in his "Cable Watching," as do Newman and Levine in *Legitimating Television*. There is an extensive literature on quality television, including most germanely McCabe and Akass, *Quality TV*; Anderson, "Producing an Aristocracy of Culture in American Television"; Kackman, "Flow Favorites."

20. "Editorial," *Cineaste*, 1.

21. Television scholars have been alert to the implications of these moves, as the titles of essays by Mills, "What Does It Mean to Call Television 'Cinematic'?," and Jaramillo, "Rescuing Television from 'the Cinematic,'" suggest.

22. See Brunsdon, "The Attractions of the Cinematic City," on the contours of the discussion of the cinematic city.

23. McQuire, *The Media City*, provides a sophisticated combination of media in this chronology, moving through Marville's photographs of nineteenth-century Paris (pre- and post-Hausmannization) and city symphonies, right through to CCTV and the digital home. McQuire does include television, and its aesthetics of liveness, in his discussion of the media city and "relational space," but his concern is with the broadcasting of private life, his preferred text *Big Brother*. See also Krajina, *Negotiating the Mediated City*; and Georgiou, *Media and the City*.

24. For example, the work of Robert C. Allen in his investigation of moviegoing in North Carolina, "Going to the Show," docsouth.unc.edu (see also his "Getting to 'Going to the Show'"), and the AHRC-funded Cinematic Geographies of Battersea project led by François Penz (cinematicbattersea.blogspot .co.uk).

25. The work of Mittell in particular has been associated with "complex television," which he has elaborated in relation to *The Wire* in *Complex TV* and its earlier online iterations. Scholarship on *Treme* such as that in the themed issue of *Television and New Media* 13, no. 3 (2012), particularly Helen Parmett's work, has contributed very interestingly to understanding the media ecologies of television cities.

26. Newcomb, "*Cagney and Lacey*," 403.

27. See Wheatley's exposition in *Spectacular Television*, 7.

28. A point that is exemplified by the pioneering 2009 University College Dublin conference Television and the City, organized by Diane Negra and Liam Kennedy, in which six of the twenty-seven papers concerned *The Wire*, with two on *Sex and the City*.

29. Since the decline of the networks, the headquarters of TV companies, those other home spaces of television, have attracted interesting scholarship on the institutional architecture of television. See Spigel, *TV by Design*, 68–143; Ericson and Reigert, *Media Houses*.

30. Augé, *Non-places*.

31. Anderson, *Imagined Communities*, 32–36.

32. Curtin, "Media Capitals."

33. See the discussion in Pines, "Black Cops and Black Villains in Film and TV Crime Fiction"; on equal opportunities, see Brunsdon, "Structure of Anxiety."

34. The Brighton setting of this show also enabled the plausible employment of out gay police. While this book was in production, it was announced that *Cuffs* would not be renewed.

35. In addition to discussion of particular detectives, and urban and modern sensibilities in scholarship such as Worpole, *Dockers and Detectives*, and Moretti, "Clues," in *Signs Taken for Wonders*, this has long included curiosity about real settings for detective fiction, such as Jakubowski, *Following the Detectives*.

36. Jermyn, "Silk Blouses and Fedoras," examines the journalistic obsession with the blouses and, in a sophisticated, self-reflexive article, challenges the entertainment of the sexual sadism of this critically lauded show.

37. In a particular version of the television tourism discussed by Couldry in *The Place of Media Power*, Belfast gossip maintained in 2014 that this was a room number which has been booked up ever since.

38. The persistence of the dead woman in relation to feminism is suggestively discussed by Dillman, *Women and Death in Film, Television and News*.

39. Scholarship such as Nichols-Pethick, *TV Cops*; Piper, *The TV Detective*; Turnbull, *The TV Crime Drama*; and McElroy, *Cops on the Box*, explores some of the innovations and repetitions of this flourishing genre.

40. Bhabha, "Introduction."

41. Ellis, *Visible Fictions*, 5. On the nationalness of television, see Caughie, "Playing at Being an American"; Morley, *Home Territories*, 149–70. On the continuing salience of the category of the national in the analysis of television, see Turner, "Television and the Nation"; and Pertierra and Turner, *Locating Television*, chapter 2.

42. For example, a critical article by Larry Elliott about current economic policy in a national newspaper in 2014 was headed, "Del Boynomics—When Work and Tax Doesn't Add Up," *Guardian*, 11 August 2014, while the BBC called a 2014 documentary series "following the nation's wheeler-dealers" *Del Boys and Dealers* (1 May–11 June 2014). I live quite near a grocery store called

Only Food and Sauces, which declares its commercial empire as "New York, Paris, Cubbington."

43. Turner, "Television and the Nation"; Pertierra and Turner, *Locating Television*, chapter 2.

44. John Sullivan, the writer and creator of the program, observed, "I got the New York—Paris—Peckham idea on the side of the van from a packet of Dunhill cigarettes except theirs says London—Paris—New York. Del would have seen it and been slightly in awe of it and therefore impressed and stuck it on his van." Sullivan quoted in Clark, *"Only Fools and Horses,"* 201.

45. For an account of what might be at stake in Peckham as a location, see Stanton, "Peckham Tales." In the twenty-first century, Peckham is one of the fastest gentrifying areas of London as its historical poverty has kept property prices comparatively low.

46. See Brunsdon, *London in Cinema*, for further discussion of cinematic London.

47. Curtin, "Media Capitals," points to their historical ebb and flow by considering Los Angeles, Chicago, and Hong Kong. London is clearly, within his terms, a media capital, but it is also, in the terms of this book, a television city. In the British context, the changing situation of Manchester and Belfast is of interest, while in an international context, Mexico City and Bombay would reward attention.

48. The contours of this scholarship are outlined by Phillips and Vincendeau in their book on Paris and the cinema, *Beyond the Flâneur*.

49. On *Cagney and Lacey*, see D'Acci's exemplary study, *Defining Women*.

50. The Simenon Estate entered into new production agreements in the twenty-first century to make a series of British ITV (Independent Television) television films aimed at the international market starring Rowan Atkinson as Maigret. Filmed partly in Hungary, the first two of these, *Maigret Sets a Trap* (2016) and *Maigret's Dead Man* (2016), were judged sufficiently successful for further films to be contracted.

51. See notes to chapter 3 for references to scholarship on *The Wire*.

52. Wright, *On Living in an Old Country*.

Chapter 1. The Modernity of Maigret's Paris

Epigraph source: Audience Research Report, 21 November 1960, p. 1, BBC Written Archives Centre, Caversham (henceforth, WAC), T5/2, 167/1.

Note on archive sources for this chapter: The BBC Written Archives Centre holds more than seventy bulky files on the 1960s *Maigret*. There are individual files for each episode, and groups of files called, for example, "Maigret: General" and "Maigret: Legal." The series are also discussed in a range of other BBC files and sets of minutes. Most files hold a mixture of material including memos, letters, invoices, shooting scripts, location plans, and committee discussion of programs. Dating is inconsistent: for example, shooting schedules may include dates but are almost never themselves dated. Sometimes it is possible to deduce roughly when something was written, although often I am reduced to n.d. (no date). Internal BBC memos, many of which survive only as carbon copies (all this material is pre-computer), characteristically use the abbreviations of BBC posts for sender and addressee (see n. 15 below). All of these posts are normally capitalized within BBC correspondence if they are spelled out—for example, Maud Vidal was the Television Secretary of the BBC in Paris. If these posts are associated with television (still very much the new medium for the BBC), they include the abbreviation "Tel." at the end. BBC (and British) usage refers to a television "series" to mean what U.S. usage calls a season (there is thus no differentiation between series and season), and this usage has been retained here. The BBC in this period also refers to most television drama as "plays."

1. One source for the notion of a dérive comes from Debord, "Theory of the Dérive," which is available in McDonough, *The Situationists and the City*. See also, on walking in Paris, Solnit, "Paris, or Botanizing on the Asphalt," in *Wanderlust*, 196–213. Merlin Coverley's *Psychogeography* provides a balanced account of a rather intense field and key references.

2. Produced by Andrew Osborn, with Rupert Davies as Maigret, the four BBC series ran between 1960 and 1963.

3. Cobb argues that the 1930s dominate the sensibility of the detective, which still has something of the peasant, a first-generation émigré from the country-side: "Simenon is right to have made so much of the girl with the fibre suitcase as she nervously feels her way through a Paris terminal. He is a novelist of loneliness and alienation, of the process of urbanisation in individual terms" ("Maigret's Paris," 183).

4. Maigret has a still-active fan constituency, and details of the television productions can be found in Haining, *The Complete Maigret*; Willemen, "Maigret," 216–17; Kosmicki, "Les Maigret, de Jean Richard à Bruno Cremer," 96–105; Forshaw, "Georges Simenon and Maigret's Paris," 160–69.

5. Vincendeau, "Maigret pour toujours?," 89–100.

6. Cited in Vincendeau, "Maigret pour toujours?," 94 (my translation).

7. Norman Rutherford, BBC press release, week 4, 1960, WAC, T5/2, 166/1.

8. Mme. Simenon, letter to Heather Dean (BBC Copyright Dept), 26 September 1956, WAC, RCONT1, Georges Simenon Copyright 1956 62, File 1.

9. Mme. Simenon, letter to Heather Dean, 26 May 1958, WAC, RCONT1, Georges Simenon Copyright 1956–62, File 1.

10. Mme. Simenon, letter to Heather Dean, 1 November 1956, WAC, RCONT1, Georges Simenon Copyright 1956–62, File 1.

11. Heather Dean, letter to Mme. Simenon, 13 November 1956, WAC, RCONT1, Georges Simenon Copyright 1956–62, File 1. The BBC pays £19,900 for twenty-six stories for ten years from 31 August 1959, with an option of £5,450 for a further thirteen stories. "Physical ownership" reverts to the author (WAC, R22/495/1). The manifest popularity of the series further strengthens Mme. Simenon's position when it comes to negotiating the fourth and final series, and in 1962, Simenon's fee rises by a further 25 percent, putting him into "the highest prestige category of authors." The extreme complexity of the contractual situation only emerges in the negotiation for the fourth series when it transpires that Winwell Productions, one of the signatories, has been misrepresenting its own position to both the BBC and the Simenons. Ronald Waldman, letter to BBC legal adviser, "'Maigret': Simenon and Winwell Productions Ltd.," 30 March 1962, WAC, R22/495/1, Legal Maigret.

12. It was initially agreed that there should be 500 man hours per episode (all calculations at the BBC used the term "man hours"). Episode 1 came in at 750 hours. John Mair (Senior Planning Assistant), memo to A.H.D. Tel. (Assistant Head of Drama, Television), 11 May 1960, WAC, T5/2, 166/5. These calculations are separate from actor rehearsal time, which was ten days for each play (WAC, T5/2, 166/1).

13. As with the Simenon stories, Maigret's investigations are not all confined to Paris in the BBC series, but Maigret always remains a Parisian detective, and it is with his Paris that I am concerned.

14. Ronald Waldman, memo to H.D. Tel. (Head of Drama, Television), "Maigret Series," 13 September 1960, WAC, T5/2, 166/1.

15. Michael Barry, memo to Ronald Waldman, 31 July 1961 (copied to C.P. Tel, H.P.P. Tel., H.S.D. Tel., A.H.D. Tel., and producer Andrew Osborn), WAC, TV/2, 166/5, Maigret General.

16. A sense of the distinction of the BBC product from U.S. television pervades the regular, careful, institutional discussion of individual scripts and programs in a way that supports Elke Weissman's argument about the imbrication of British and U.S. television with each other throughout the twentieth century (*Transnational Television Drama*, 3). For example, Gerard Glaister's detailed notes on the script for "Maigret Sets a Trap" include, "I think that somehow we have lost the character of Maigret here and in the subsequent interrogation scenes. Possibly because they are not fully enough developed;

so that at times Maigret begins to sound like a beetle-browed New York cop on a murder investigation." Memo, Glaister to Andrew Osborn, "Maigret Sets a Trap," 9 June 1961, WAC, T5/2, 204/1.

17. Jacobs, "Selling the Medium."

18. WAC, R44/1, 092/1, Pamphlets, Maigret, n.d., c. 1960.

19. Main sales of the programs, as recorded in 1965, were to Australia, Canada, New Zealand, and Rhodesia. There were also substantial receipts from Barbados, Bermuda, Liberia, Malta, Pakistan, Singapore, and Trinidad. Given the list of territories above, the additional sales revenue from "Commonwealth" is slightly mysterious. "Maigret, Statement as at 31st March, 1965 (Amended)," WAC R22/495/1, Legal Maigret.

20. The BBC standard tape was 405 lines, which was not used internationally, so programs had to be converted to 525 or 625 lines for overseas sales. There was lengthy discussion in April 1960 about formats, with the basic plan to use live recording combined with film inserts. The demands of the international market ("it cannot be emphasised too heavily that this must be the choice of the customer and not the BBC") informed the decision to record in "standards converted-videotape, 35mm and 16mm telerecording" (Ronald Waldman, letter to Dennis Scuse [Senior Planning Officer], "Maigret Recording Requirements," 26 April 1960, WAC, T5/2, 166/5). The logistics of this decision were difficult for both planning and program making, as the producer notes: "Production would continue to use every effort to record in the studio exact parallels between Tape and 35mm. The difficulties of producing two products at one and the same time was stated, i.e. a product that was capable of being shown both with and without six commercial inserts, and the difficulties of cutting into tape necessary retakes was discussed" (Andrew Osborn, memo to Peter Tyrrell, "Maigret Recordings," 20 October 1960, WAC, T5/2, 166/1).

21. See Caughie, *Television Drama*, 54.

22. Andrew Osborn, "Maigret, Notes for Directors," n.d., WAC, T5/2, 166/1, Maigret General.

23. Vincent Tilsley, memo to H.S.D. Tel. (Head of Script Department, Television), 9 November 1960, WAC, T5/2, 166/1.

24. Non-Parisian episodes, such as "The Flemish Shop" (tx. 5 November 1963), sometimes involve proportionately more location filming. The research details in a letter from Terence Williams to Robin Scott about barges, canals, and locks for "The Crime at Lock 14" (*Le Charretier de la Providence*) form an early 1960s historical record of French waterways (22 November 1960, WAC, T5/2, 166/1).

25. The titles were filmed against the wall of Shoreditch Public Library in East London (shooting script "Maigret Titles," n.d., WAC, T5/2, 166/1, Maigret General).

26. The *Maigret* theme was composed by Ron Grainer. Many British viewers of the original series have spontaneously hummed this tune to me when they have learned of my research, which, given they would have watched it fifty years ago, suggests that it was indeed memorable.

27. Audience Research Report, week 42, 1963, VR/63/589, in WAC, T5/2, 212/1 (Maigret no. 42, "The Lost Life"). Audience share given in this report was 23 percent, comfortably higher than ITV's 17 percent for the slot.

28. The ferocious copyright conditions agreed with the Simenons, which meant, for example, that physical copies of the programs had to be returned to them, have kept the Davies Maigrets mainly out of circulation. Many of the programs are documented in off-screen photographs by John Cura, records that are themselves subject to copyright uncertainty (and therefore could not be reproduced here). There are, for example, sixty-eight individual images from just one program, "The Trap" (WAC, T5/2, 204/1), from transmission on 10 December 1962. On Cura's pioneering photographs of British television programs, see Wallace, "John Cura."

29. Maud Vidal (Television Secretary in BBC Paris Office), cable to Vanessa Virgo (secretary to producer Andrew Osmond), 4 May 1960, WAC, T5/2, 164/1, Maigret Filming.

30. Shooting script, "The Trap," n.d., WAC, T5/2, 204/1 ("Trap, The").

31. "Scenery Requirements," 6 March 1961, WAC, T5/2, 185/1 ("Winning Ticket, The," Maigret no. 14).

32. Vanessa Virgo, letter to Maud Vidal, 13 June 1960, WAC, T5/2, 166/1.

33. Vanessa Virgo, letter to Maud Vidal, 20 June 1960, WAC, T5/2, 166/1. The correspondence refers to the "company Gauloises-Gitanes," although these are the brand names for cigarettes produced by the state tobacco company SEITA. This usage indicates the production's slightly awkward relation to French culture, discussed further in n. 48 in this chapter on French language use.

34. Eric Tayler, memo, 21 June 1960, WAC, T5/2, 171/1. This is a recurrent topic throughout the production, with each usage noted, as in Ron Travers, 13 September 1962 memo, "Real Beer in the Studio," to the property master, Terry Williams, which reads, "Please may we have permission to use nine bottles of real continental beer in the studio" (WAC, T5/2, 204/1, "The Trap").

35. Andrew Osborn, memo to Eric Tayler and Gerry Glaister, 23 December 1960, WAC, T5/2, 166/1.

36. N.d., WAC, T5/2, 185/1, "The Winning Ticket."

37. N.d., WAC, T5/2, 185/1, "The Winning Ticket." The productions are referred to as plays in all the BBC material of the time.

38. N.d., WAC, T5/2, 185/1, "The Winning Ticket."

39. When this set was re-created for "Maigret at Bay," the one-off revival in 1969, the French production secretary declared that the calendar she was sending was "the only one left in Paris" (Christine Debat, Paris Office, to Ann Kirch, BBC, 24 July 1968, WAC, T5/1, 629/1).

40. "Maigret at Bay," review, *The Times*, 10 February 1969.

41. This view was filmed for the second episode and subsequently reused. "Boulevard Richard Lenoir: LS, MLS," "Locations," WAC, T5/2, 171/1 (Maigret, "Unscheduled Departure"). Maigret lives in Boulevard Richard-Lenoir throughout the BBC series, although in some of the books, Maigret lives in Place de Vosges (where Simenon also lived).

42. No such confidence is displayed by the producers of the latest Maigret adaptation. In "Maigret's Dead Man" (tx. 25 December 2016, Maigret Productions/Ealing Studios for ITV), the dish is translated unceremoniously as "creamed cod" and is shown onscreen looking like a boil-in-the-bag piece of fish in cream sauce.

43. Barry Norman, "Review: *Maigret at Bay* (Play of the Month)," *Daily Mail*, 10 February 1969, n.p., WAC, T5/1, 629/1.

44. Ronald Waldman, memo to H.D. Tel., 13 September 1960, WAC, T5/2, 166/1.

45. Synopsis, "Murder in Montmartre," 23 November 1961, WAC, T5/2, 167/1.

46. Film 2nd Schedule, "Murder in Montmartre," n.d., WAC, T5/2, 167/1.

47. Prop list, "Murder in Montmartre," n.d., WAC, T5/2, 167/1. Some of this material was also reused later in other episodes.

48. Ginette Vincendeau has pointed out to me that normal French usage would be "Nus," even though the "nus" in question are women. The technical grammatical correctness of the sign in the titles, as opposed to its conformity to common usage, can be seen as an instance of the awkwardness of some of the engagements with French culture in this production, also exemplified by the formulation "Gauloises-Gitanes," as opposed to the name of the state tobacco company, SEITA, and the general absence of accents in the BBC files (although it should be remembered that French accents were near impossible to include with British typewriter keyboards in the 1960s).

49. "Maigret au Picratt's," Antenne 2, 1985.

50. "Maigret and the Night Club Dancer," *Maigret* Granada, episode 2.1, written by Douglas Livingstone, directed by John Strickland, tx. 14 March 1993.

51. Prop requisition form, 9, "Maison Harris Set," 10 June 1960, WAC, T5/2, 171/1, Maigret—"Unscheduled Departure."

52. Memo from General Manager, Television Enterprises (Ronald Waldman), to E. A. C. Bostock, "Maigret," 16 July 1962, WAC, R22/495/1, Legal Maigret. See also n. 11.

53. Most of the images of the Palais de Justice in this episode were achieved by using models, and there was some difficulty with achieving the lighting effects required at the end ("Maigret's Little Joke," shooting script, n.d., WAC, T5/2, 213/1). There is a full set of photographs by John Cura from transmission on 24 December 1963 held in this program file.

54. Filmed in Ville-Franche and the Corniche, 18–19 September 1963 ("Maigret's Little Joke," shooting script, n.d., WAC, T5/2, 213/1).

55. An attribution that follows the primary authorial credit, "Maigret at Bay by Georges Simenon," *Radio Times*, 8–14 February 1969, 12.

56. Jules Dassin's *Rififi* (1955) has a celebrated real-time robbery sequence set in a jeweler's.

57. Locations list, n.d., main filming 4–9 August 1968, WAC, T5/1, 629/1 ("Maigret at Bay").

58. A. P. W. Makepeace, memo, "Studio Times," 31 July 1986, WAC, T5/1, 629/1 ("Maigret at Bay").

59. Review, *Daily Telegraph*, 11 February 1969, n.p., WAC, T5/1, 629/1 ("Maigret at Bay").

60. MacMurraugh-Kavanagh, "'Drama' into 'News.'"

61. Review of "Maigret at Bay," *The Times*, 10 February 1969, n.p., WAC T5/1, 629/1.

62. See, for example, Christine Geraghty on the European woman in "The Woman Between"; and Harper and Porter on nudity, sex, and social change in their *British Cinema of the 1950s*, 237–40.

63. George Dixon, at the end of each episode of the long-running British police series *Dixon of Dock Green*, always gave a direct-to-camera little moral to sign off. *Z Cars*, the innovative police series that was first broadcast almost simultaneously with *Maigret*, was set in New Town (Kirby, near Liverpool) and had a rather less comfortably patriarchal police force.

64. Roland Barthes's famous essay on the Citroën DS (first published in 1957), identifies the car as "a superlative object," an example of the mid-twentieth-century equivalence between cars and cathedrals: "The New Citroen," *Mythologies*, 88. The very distinctive design of this car would signify Frenchness in the mid-twentieth century.

65. For example, "The Trap: Location Breakdown," which includes twenty-two separate locations, lists nineteen shots with either "extras" or "NIL" in the "Artists" column (n.d., c. 1962, WAC, T5/2, 204/1, Maigret, "Trap, The").

66. "Filming Schedule France," August 1962, WAC, T5/2, 204/1 (Maigret, "Trap, The").

67. M. Olliver, letter to C.P. Tel, RTF, quoted by Noble L. Wilson (BBC Paris representative), memo to H.P.P. Tel, 12 October 1962, WAC, T5/2, 166/2, Maigret General, File 1.

68. "Filming Schedule France," August 1962, WAC, T5/2, 204/1 (Maigret, "Trap, The").

69. Haining, *The Complete Maigret*, 94–103.

70. Cobb, "Maigret's Paris," 182.

71. The Cremer version, as Vincendeau notes, is redeemed through a convincing and charismatic central performance, while the Gambon-Granada version, although impaired by British thespianism in the lead role, at least has gravitas and seriality over the Rowan Atkinson vehicle, which has been envisaged as single films. This, with a performance that does not shake off Mr. Bean, has the effect of making Maigret seem rather stupid as there is no serial repetition of his understanding and skills, although following the broadcast of the third film, *Night at the Crossroads* (tx. 16 April 2017, ITV), one critic observed that "Maigret was almost good this time around" (Euan Ferguson, TV Reviews, *Observer*, 23 April 2017, 26).

72. O'Sullivan, "Television Memories and Cultures of Viewing," 161.

73. David Hare evokes the association between sex and French films in the 1960s: "Our time was spent in the Continentale in Kemp Town [Brighton] watching Jeanne Moreau movies—the best was one in which you could see her right breast in the bath" (*The Blue Touch Paper*, 66).

74. The opening lines in full are: "Sexual intercourse began / In nineteen sixty-three / (Which was rather later for me) / Between the end of the Chatterley ban / And the Beatles' first LP." But popular memory elides the line about the lateness. Larkin, "Annus Mirabilus," in *Collected Poems*, 167.

75. Sandbrook, *Never Had It So Good*; Sandbrook, *White Heat*; see also Davenport-Hines, *An English Affair*; Hall, "Reformism and the Legislation of Consent"; Mort, *Capital Affairs*; Bray, *1965*.

76. Elizabeth David's influential books on Mediterranean food had been published throughout the previous decade (*A Book of Mediterranean Food*, 1950; *French Country Cooking*, 1951; *French Provincial Cooking*, 1960) and were available in paperback by the end of the decade.

77. Habitat, an interiors shop, was first opened in 1964. See Highmore, "Feeling It."

78. Nic Pillai, expert on all matters *Maigret*, has pointed out to me that these black-and-white images may be structured through the horizontal stripes of the red, white, and blue of the French tricolor flag. Color television was

introduced in Britain in 1967, so these images would have been broadcast as black and white.

Chapter 2. Living-Room London

1. British commercial television is organized on a regional basis with different companies holding franchises for a fixed term. Thames shared the lucrative London franchise with London Weekend Television between 1968 and 1991, when Thames lost to Carlton Television. For a detailed discussion of the fluctuating regions of British commercial television, see Johnson and Turnock, ITV Cultures.

2. Andrew Wiseman's Television Room hosts a description of the history and constitutive elements of the Thames logo, "The Thames Logo Parade," rev. 1 March 2017, http://625.uk.com/tv_logos/thames.htm.

3. Hilmes, Network Nations, and Weissmann, Transnational Television Drama, give some idea of these complexities in relation to U.S. and U.K. television cultures.

4. There are lively media cultures in Glasgow (Scotland) and Cardiff (Wales), with key productions such as Doctor Who made in the latter, and continuing investment in Belfast (Northern Ireland), but London remains the U.K. media center. This was so much the case, particularly since the 2004 closure of BBC Pebble Mill in Birmingham, that in 2012 the BBC undertook an enforced move of much production to Salford (outside Manchester) to counter accusations of London-centricity in a publicly funded broadcaster. In some ways this move has functioned to display the London-centricity of British culture, as key news and current affairs programs have to remain in London for proximity to political culture.

5. There was a consistent strategy of devolution through regions and nations in the latter part of the twentieth century, so that, for example, TV licenses are handled in Bristol, while motor vehicle licensing is based in Cardiff, but there remains, despite devolution and privatization, an irreducible core to the London-based Civil Service.

6. BBC External Services (under various titles) were historically funded directly by government through the Foreign Office. This arrangement ceased only in 2014 when a license fee settlement seen as unsympathetic to the BBC included the transfer of this budgetary responsibility to the BBC.

7. John Reith, "Memorandum of Information on the Scope and Conduct of the Broadcasting Service," 1925, cited by Scannell and Cardiff, A Social History of British Broadcasting, 7.

8. See Geppert, *Fleeting Cities*, 134–78, for an analysis of the British Empire Exhibition.

9. Mansell, *Let Truth Be Told*.

10. Anonymous editor cited by Reigert, "The End of the Iconic Home of Empire," 68.

11. The association of London with news is further complicated by the history of the international television news agencies, with two of the most significant located in London. As Chris Paterson has demonstrated, this means that most international news image packages used by international broadcasters actually originate in London (Paterson, *The International News Agencies*).

12. Paddy Scannell gives one of the best accounts of British public service broadcasting (which is philosophically and institutionally quite distinct from U.S. PBS channels) in "Public Service Broadcasting," 45–62.

13. It has been twenty-first-century popular historians, as distinct in their politics as Joe Moran and Dominic Sandbrook, in a series of histories of postwar Britain, who have begun to address the cultural centrality of television to twentieth-century Britain. See Moran, *Armchair Nation*; Sandbrook, *Never Had It So Good*; and Sandbrook, *White Heat*.

14. Caughie, *Television Drama*.

15. Melvyn Bragg, reflecting on the 1975 Edinburgh Television Festival, observed of the early days of television, "We thought television could change society for the better and bring people outside the various tight circles of British culture into the ring" (Maggie Brown, "40 Years of MacTaggart: One Speech with a Track Record of Changing the TV Industry," *Guardian*, 24 August 2015).

16. See, for example, Garnett, "Contexts," 16–29; and interviews in Bakewell and Garnham, *The New Priesthood*.

17. Mercer, "General Introduction," 1.

18. Kleinecke-Bates, *Victorians on Screen*.

19. Jakubowski, *Following the Detectives*, 217–18.

20. Sir John Summerson estimates that 73,000 new structures were built in London in the 1860s alone. See Summerson, *The London Building World of the 1860s*. See also Schwarzbach, *Dickens and the City*; Tambling, *Going Astray*; Schlicke, *The Oxford Companion to Charles Dickens*, 348–65.

21. There is an extensive literature on adaptation in general. See, for an outline of its contours, Elliott, *Rethinking the Novel/Film Debate*; Geraghty, *Now a Major Motion Picture*; Cardwell, *Adaptation Revisited*.

22. And not just for the British viewer; as Tom O'Regan observes, "British television is simultaneously praised and derided internationally" ("The International Circulation of British TV," 317).

23. A sense of the quantity and international span of Dickens adaptations can be gained from Pointer, *Charles Dickens on the Screen*; and Carnell, "Dickens Composed." Grahame Smith provides a succinct summary of Dickens and British television in "Television Adaptations of Charles Dickens," 565.

24. Christine Geraghty provides a detailed account of Dickens television debates and rhetorics in her analysis of the production and publicity for the BBC 2005 *Bleak House*. See Geraghty, *"Bleak House,"* 13–15, for a discussion of this rhetoric.

25. The debate over the "Dickensian aspect" of *The Wire* demonstrates the complexity of Dickensian television, as the melodramatic associations of Dickens's work jostle with their campaigning and canonical status. See Klein, "'The Dickensian Aspect'"; Williams, *On "The Wire,"* 116–19, 122–31; Simon, Interview.

26. Samuel, *Theatres of Memory*, 401–25.

27. Demonstrated and illustrated by Michael Eaton and Adrian Wootton in their BBC4 film made for the Dickens centenary, *Dickens on Film* (tx. 10 January 2012).

28. Samuel, *Theatres of Memory*, 402.

29. Richards, *Films and British National Identity*, 345.

30. *Our Mutual Friend*, adapted by Freda Lingstrom, directed by Eric Tayler, and produced by Douglas Allen. Broadcast at 9:00 on Friday evenings (including Christmas Eve), when it competed with the drama slot ITV *Playhouse*, which gained 38 percent of the audience, as opposed to the BBC's 13 percent.

31. BBC, WAC, *Our Mutual Friend*, ep. 12, T5/2, 293/1, Audience Research Report, VR/59/51, 23 January, ep. 12, 1.

32. Continuity announcement preceding the first episode of *Our Mutual Friend* (tx. 9 March 1998). Broadcast copy preserved in University of Warwick Moving Image Collection.

33. *Our Mutual Friend* was first published in serial form in 1864–65.

34. Dickens, *Our Mutual Friend*, 3.

35. Dickens, *Our Mutual Friend*, 3–4. *Our Mutual Friend* (BBC, 1976), dramatized in seven fifty-minute episodes by Julia Jones and Donald Churchill. *Our Mutual Friend* (BBC, 1998), dramatized by Sandy Welch in four ninety-minute episodes.

36. WAC, *Our Mutual Friend*, T5/2, 286/1, Audience Research Report on first episode, VR/58/610, 2.

37. Helen Wheatley explores the spaces of studio drama in 1970s British television in "Rooms within Rooms," 143–58.

38. The section heading cites Raphael Samuel's designation of the widely praised 1987 adaptation of *Little Dorrit* (dir. Christine Edzard) as "Dockland

Dickens" because it was during the 1980s that the docks on the Isle of Dogs were converted into the new London financial center of Docklands. The term "Docklands" thus embodies the shift, during the 1980s, from the import and export of raw materials and manufactured goods to the dealing in financial goods and services. Samuel, *Theatres of Memory*, 401–12.

39. John Rentoul, "Intensely Relaxed about People Getting Filthy Rich," *The Independent Blogs*, accessed 24 August 2015, www.blogs.independent.co.uk /2013/02/14. Rentoul dates Peter Mandelson's first version of this comment to 23 October 1998.

40. Orr, "Traducing Realisms."

41. Newland, "Global Markets and a Market Place," 72–85. See also chapter 6 of Brunsdon, *London in Cinema*, on these transformations.

42. Geraghty, *Women and Soap Opera*, 147.

43. White, *London in the Twentieth Century*, 131.

44. Pines, *Black and White in Colour*; Malik, *Representing Black Britain*; Givanni, *Remote Control*; Bourne, *Black in the British Frame*. See also Barry, "Black Mythologies"; and *The Black and White Media Show* (BBC, 1989).

45. Newton, *Paving the Empire Road*; Schaffer, *The Vision of a Nation*. One of the complications of British television history is the emphasis on the BBC produced by its exceptional archives.

46. The calypso, which commented satirically on the news, was written by Bernard Levin (a prominent right-wing satirist) and was a feature of *Tonight* from its inception in 1957.

47. Schwarz, "Reveries of Race."

48. Newton, *Paving the Empire Road*, 103–83; Schaffer, *The Vision of a Nation*, 76–83; Brebber, "'Till Death Us Do Part."

49. Gilroy, "C4—Bridgehead or Bantustan?"

50. Malik, *Representing Black Britain*, 35–56; Newton, *Paving the Empire Road*, 51–102.

51. Hall, "Black and White in Television," 20.

52. Stuart Hall, response to heckler in a public meeting in 1978, reedited into John Akomfrah's film *The Stuart Hall Project* (U.K., 2013); Kobena Mercer uses the same phrase in *Welcome to the Jungle*, 7.

53. *This Week*, "The Negro Next Door" (1965), featured Desmond Wilcox interviewing people in Leeds and is discussed by Malik, *Representing Black Britain*, 41–43. Darrell M. Newton refers to the way the BBC "cautiously structured the television persona of the West Indian immigrant/African-Caribbean as a new neighbour" (*Paving the Empire Road*, 239).

54. Turnock, *Television and Consumer Culture*, 107–40.

55. Hall, "Black and White in Television," 18.

56. Schaffer, *The Vision of a Nation*, 181.

57. Malik, *Representing Black Britain*, 91–107.

58. For full production details and discussion of the program's significance, see Malik, "*Desmond's.*"

59. Pines, *Black and White in Colour*, 184.

60. Gareth Stanton, from whom I have borrowed the title of this section, contextualizes both *Desmond's* and *Only Fools and Horses* in his discussion of Peckham, and particularly Rye Lane. See Stanton, "Peckham Tales."

61. On this figure within London history, see White, *London in the Twentieth Century*, 244–56.

62. Peckham features heavily in associated material such as Sullivan, "*Only Fools and Horses*," vols. 1 and 2. The tower-block exteriors for *Only Fools and Horses* were filmed in Bristol. For a longer discussion of *Only Fools and Horses*, see Brunsdon, "The Cinematic and the Televisual City."

63. The name Mandela House involves a characteristic joke that implicitly juxtaposes the literal domestication of antiracist policies within the public sphere of local government with the less politically correct opinions of many inhabitants of social housing (such as Del).

64. The 1948 arrival of the *Empire Windrush* in Tilbury symbolizes the inaugural moment of postwar West Indian immigration. As many have pointed out, there has been a black presence in Britain for many centuries. See Fryer, *Staying Power*; Phillips and Phillips, *Windrush*.

65. Hurvin Anderson, "Reporting Back," IKON Gallery, Birmingham, 25 September–10 November 2013. The continuing vibrancy of this cultural space can be seen in the film *The Fade* [trailer], YouTube, 17 October 2012, http://www.youtube.com/watch?v=m_hFC8tl644.

66. Chambers, "Double Consciousness," 72.

67. Pines, *Black and White in Colour*, 184.

68. Liarou, "British Television's Lost New Wave Moment," discusses the small number of single-author television plays by black dramatists in the 1950s and 1960s within the context of a broader discussion of television plays about an ethnically and socially extended working class.

69. Malik, *Representing Black Britain*, 56–78, gives a shrewd account of some of the politics and development in multicultural programming in the late 1970s to mid-1990s.

70. Lenny Henry, "I Have a—Dream—Screen," BAFTA Television Lecture 2014, accessed 18 August 2014, http://guru.bafta.org/lenny-henry-bafta-television-lecture-watch-live.

71. Michael Wearing, the executive producer of *Holding On*, who was also responsible for Peter Flannery's epic of postwar Britain, *Our Friends in the*

North (BBC, 1996), which told the longitudinal story of postwar Britain from a non-London starting point, is a significant enabling figure here, embodying premarket, public service, radical contemporary drama BBC values. See Eaton, *"Our Friends in the North."* Wearing also produced the 1998 version of *Our Mutual Friend* discussed earlier in the chapter.

72. Billingham cites Marchant observing, in an interview, that "Blair's conservatism is a manifestation of that Thatcherite revolution" (*Sensing the City through Television*, 60).

73. Claire to Brenda in the final episode when she is trying to persuade her not to return to her husband in the north of England: "We both know it can be dicey here, but you can make your own luck." Brenda's husband responds, "You want her to live like you, by the skin of your teeth."

74. Hewett, "Essentially English," discusses BBC production and export strategies for the 1965–68 BBC series, which contrast interestingly with those for both *Sherlock* and *Maigret*.

75. For example, the prime-time 2016 New Year's Day schedule on BBC1 was all set in the nineteenth century, with the twenty-part Tony Jordan Dickens mash-up, *Dickensian*, followed by a nineteenth-century-set *Sherlock* episode, "The Abominable Bride."

76. See Hills, *"Sherlock,"* for discussion of the constraints on the updated *Sherlock* that led, on 1 January 2016, to a very arch nineteenth-century episode ("The Abominable Bride").

77. Granada Television: *The Adventures of Sherlock Holmes*, 1984–85; *The Return of Sherlock Holmes*, 1986–88; *The Casebook of Sherlock Holmes*, 1991; *The Memoirs of Sherlock Holmes*, 1993. A full account of the production can be found in Haining, *The Television Sherlock Holmes*. Other television versions of Sherlock Holmes are listed in Haining, "The Television Super-Sleuth."

78. Cited in Haining, *The Television Sherlock Holmes*, 119.

79. Newman, "Holmes, Sherlock," 173.

80. The first two series (2012–13) were Tiger Aspect / Look Out Point productions for the BBC. The third series (2014) was produced by Tiger Aspect / Look Out Point in association with BBC Worldwide and Amazon Prime, with continuing support from the Irish Film Board and BBC America.

81. Brunsdon, *London in Cinema*. See also Newland, *The Cultural Construction of London's East End*.

82. "Series One: Set Sketches and Pictures Comparison," *Ripper Street*, BBC Two, accessed 11 November 2013, http://www.bbc.co.uk/programmes/galleries/p015g1md.

83. BBC America, accessed 11 November 2013, http://www.bbcamerica.com/ripper-street/photos.

84. Nick Goundry, "BBC's *Ripper Street* to Double Dublin for Period London with Irish Film Board Help," The Location Guide, 7 February 2012, http://www.thelocationguide.com/2012/02/bbc%E2%80%99s-ripper-street-to-double-dublin-for-period-london-with-irish-film-board-help/.

85. Christine Geraghty summarizes this discussion in *"Bleak House,"* 32–35.

86. Richard Warlow, *"Ripper Street*: Policing the Meanest Streets Imaginable," *Love TV* (blog), 4 January 2013, http://www.bbc.co.uk/blogs/tv/entries/eef12a66-0328-3082-964d-ea3d83a28835.

87. Elke Weissman, in "Troubled by Violence," makes a spirited case for *Ripper Street* as a drama of troubled masculinity with a useful elucidation of its post-*Deadwood* generic affiliations with the Western. See also Meldrum, "Yesterday's Women."

88. Jan Moir, "Who Decided to Make the BBC's Sunday Night Period Drama an Anti-women Orgy of Gore?," *DailyMail.com*, 7 January 2013, http://www.dailymail.co.uk/debate/article-2258723/Ripper-Street-Who-decided-make-BBCs-Sunday-night-period-drama-anti-women-orgy-gore.html; Grace Dent, "Sperm Deposits, Wombs in Ribbons and Ripped-Out Fallopian Tubes . . . Who Enjoys This?," *Independent (Radar)*, 5 January 2013, 5; Jake Kanter, "Ripper Street Draws Nearly 90 Complaints," *Broadcast*, 3 January 2013, http://www.broadcastnow.co.uk/ripper-street-draws-nearly-90-complaints/5050299.article. This article, after the launch of the series, reports an audience of 6,090,000 (23.6 percent), with seventy-nine complaints to the BBC and nine to Ofcom.

89. Drew Gray in Matthews-Jones, "Ripper Street Reflections."

90. Warlow, *"Ripper Street."*

91. The narratives, personae, and settings of *Whitechapel* (ITV, 2009–13), created and mainly written by Ben Court and Caroline Ip, exemplify the twenty-first-century mash-up East End. Commencing with homage to Jack the Ripper, the four series went on to incorporate the Kray twins, horror in the London Underground, and a range of gruesome and ingenious murders, becoming more gothic/horror inflected as it progressed.

92. *Call the Midwife* was so successful that a special was commissioned as the centerpiece of the BBC1 Christmas Day schedule (7:30 P.M., 25 December 2015).

93. "Call the Midwife Delivers Bumper Ratings for BBC1: Sunday-Night Drama Is a Bigger Hit than Sherlock with Nearly 9m Viewers," *Radio Times*, 23 January 2012, http://www.radiotimes.com/news/2012-01-23/call-the-midwife-delivers-bumper-ratings-for-bbc1.

94. Chatham Docks are now a maritime museum, the Historic Dockyard Chatham, which advertises its availability for filming. See www.thedockyard.co.uk.

95. Tincknell, "Dowagers, Debs, Nuns, and Babies." Fitzgerald, "Taking a Pregnant Pause," carefully traces the journalistic reception of *Call the Midwife* and assesses its politics and modes of nostalgia differently.

96. In 2013, the BBC announced that *Call the Midwife* had joined *Sherlock* and *Top Gear* with sales to more than one hundred territories. "How the BBC Exports to the World," *Ariel*, 1 March 2013, http://www.bbc.co.uk/ariel /21617735.

97. Boym, *The Future of Nostalgia*. Boym is mainly concerned with the former USSR, and I am not proposing direct parallels with postwar Britain, nor that *Call the Midwife* is a text of radical critique. But its nostalgia is more complex than critics assume.

98. *Top Boy* (Channel 4, 2011–12) deals with the drug trade on an East London council estate. The four-episode *Run* (Channel 4, 2013) originated as an online drama, and features characters interlinked by devices such as stolen mobile phones, criminal subcultures, and illegal immigration rackets. The six-part *River* (BBC, 2015) also offered the extracivic world of illegal immigration as (invisibly) constitutive of contemporary London.

99. Mark Fisher provides a nuanced discussion of the disappearance of the future in other popular culture of the twenty-first century, notably music, in *Ghosts of My Life*, 1–47.

100. Ellis, "Scheduling." Within the contested terrain of attitudes to public service broadcasting, I take it as proven that the market will not provide certain types of programming.

101. The high-end programs are exported as produced, while the other programming is exported as formats for national customizing. Helen Wheatley discusses the modalities of television and spectacle in *Spectacular Television*.

102. Dorling, *All That Is Solid*, 176–90. John Lanchester's 2012 novel about the London housing market, *Capital*, was adapted by the BBC as a three-part series in 2015. Commenting on the changes in the ten years since he had begun work on the novel, Lanchester argues that the social division created by the bubble of London property market has been exacerbated since the financial crash. John Lanchester, "Peak London," *Guardian Review*, 21 November 2015.

103. Cited in Sarah Neville and John Burn-Murdoch, "High Earners Face London Lockout," *Financial Times FT Weekend*, 22–23 February 2014. See also Hamnett, *Unequal City*. As the makers of a BBC television series about London observe of a street on the edge of Notting Hill: "a process that is slowly but relentlessly expelling a population of working-class Londoners from the centre of the city. Public housing no longer exists in anything like the form it once did—and there is nowhere else for these people to go but

further and further from the heart of London. Portland Road is merely one more neighbourhood where this process of population transfer has taken place—but it represents the apotheosis of this syndrome. What happens to a neighbourhood that becomes a social monoculture, hidden behind security gates and protected by security systems? What form does its future take? And how do such examples affect the London of the future?" Bullman, Hegarty, and Hill, *The Secret History of Our Streets*, 288–89.

104. The planned move of the U.S. Embassy to the south bank is emblematic here, and the accompanying development of the former (nonresidential) Nine Elms site to provide gated, luxury accommodation that will include a "pool in the sky."

105. Poor doors are separate entrances in upmarket developments such as 1 Commercial Street, in which rich owners are sheltered from any interaction with less wealthy tenants. Hilary Osborne, "Poor Doors: The Segregation of London's Inner-City Flat Dwellers," *Guardian*, 25 July 2014.

Chapter 3. Portable Cities: Baltimore

1. Wright, "Baltimore," discusses the decision to prosecute six police officers in the alleged murder of Freddie Gray.

2. Although scholarship on media events tends not to work with concepts of genre (or indeed consider riots), it is in some ways closest to what these analyses would require. On media events, see Dayan and Katz, *Media Events*; Couldry, Hepp, and Krotz, *Media Events in a Global Age*.

3. As David Simon commented on these events at the time, there were clear opportunities to bring together the world of the news with the world of *The Wire*. See, for example, David Simon, "Baltimore," *The Audacity of Despair* (blog), 27 April 2015, http://davidsimon.com/baltimore/. His commentary was itself picked up as newsworthy, for example, NBC News, "'The Wire' Creator David Simon Pleads for Peace in Baltimore," 28 April 2015, http://www.nbcnews.com/storyline/baltimore-unrest/wire-creator-david-simon-pleads-peace-baltimore-n349546.

4. *Frank's Place*, the 1987–88 New Orleans–set show analyzed by Herman Gray in *Watching Race*, 113–29, has proved a significant comparison point for later scholarship inspired by *Treme* such as Parmett, "Space, Place and New Orleans"; and Gray's own "Recovered, Reinvented, Reimagined."

5. Chaddha and Wilson, "'Way Down in the Hole,'" 166; Ault, "'You Can Help Yourself,'" 388; Mittell, *Complex TV*; Jameson, "Realism and Utopia in *The Wire*"; Williams, On "*The Wire*."

6. The Reginald F. Lewis Museum of Maryland African American History and Culture provides three galleries documenting different aspects of enslavement, but the city visitor centers have a rather more upbeat emphasis.

7. Baltimore, Where Maps, 2013.

8. Academic books include Vint, *"The Wire"*; Potter and Marshall, *"The Wire"*; Kennedy and Shapiro, *"The Wire"*; Williams, *On "The Wire"*; Corkin, *Connecting "The Wire."* Special journal issues include *darkmatter: in the ruins of imperial culture*, May 2009; *Criticism* 52, nos. 3–4 (2010); *Critical Inquiry* 38, no. 1 (2011). "*The Wire* as Social Science Fiction?," a two-day conference organized by the ESRC Centre for Research on Socio-Cultural Change at Leeds Town Hall (U.K.), 26–27 November 2009, exemplified the interdisciplinary academic interest.

9. This is available on a range of sites, such as The Poke (http://www.the-poke.co.uk) and Nerve (http://www.nerve.com), but it is not clear where it originated.

10. Busfield, "Foreword," 1. The *Guardian* is the left-liberal newspaper in Britain, and *The Wire* was widely regarded as a "guardianista" TV show.

11. Caughie, "Mourning Television"; Spigel and Olsson, *Television after TV*.

12. Toscano and Kinkle, "Baltimore as World and Representation."

13. For a thoughtful account of DVD television viewing, see Polan, *"The Sopranos,"* 19–31.

14. Kompare, "Publishing Flow," 337. For an early discussion of the possibilities here, in a timely collection, see Walters, "Repeat Viewings." For a discussion of the DVD and fan cultures, see Klinger, *Beyond the Multiplex*; Hills, "From the Box in the Corner to the Box Set on the Shelf."

15. Clive James, "Once upon a Time in America," *Guardian Weekend*, 6 August 2016, 40 (extract from *Play All*).

16. For example, the DVD of the pioneering British series *Prime Suspect* (1991), which was originally broadcast in Britain over two nights with commercial breaks, reedits the programs to make one rather long and very oddly structured feature-length film. For a detailed discussion of the transformations television can undergo as it is released on DVD, see Moseley, "It's a Wild Country."

17. Kompare, "Publishing Flow," 352.

18. Even if what is revealed is the extent to which national television is penetrated by multinational companies.

19. Turner, "Television and the Nation," 55.

20. See, for example, responses to Lotz's "Rethinking Meaning Making": Jonathan Gray heads his response "Binge TV"; Jason Mittell refers to "binging

on DVD" (both 23 September 2006, *Flow*, http://www.flowjournal.org/2006
/09/rethinking-meaning-making-watching-serial-tv-on-dvd/).

21. See Mills, "What Does It Mean to Call Television 'Cinematic'?"; Jaramillo, "Rescuing Television from the 'the Cinematic'"; Newman and Levine, *Legitimating Television*.

22. Stella Bruzzi uses the notion of men's cinema to shift discussion from questions of representation to aesthetics (*Men's Cinema*); there is not an exact parallel, as these television shows are very explicitly about the drama of masculinity. The already noted difficulty about the status of *Sex and the City* as quality television exemplifies the point.

23. *Collins Dictionary* nominated *binge-watch* as 2015 word of the year. Alison Flood, "The Week in Books," *Guardian Review*, 7 November 2015.

24. There is an important generic heritage here. It is primarily soap opera to which viewers were seen as addicted, and this is the association from which much quality television is most often cleansed. Newman and Levine, in *Legitimating Television*, have been scrupulous in tracing historical genealogies for serial fiction on television that include reference to soap opera and soap opera scholarship. For a contrasted view that is nevertheless attentive to soap opera scholarship, see Mittell, *Complex TV*, 234–40.

25. Monica Langley, "How Steve Ballmer Became a Rookie Basketball Mogul," *Wall Street Journal*, 25 August 2014.

26. Adam Sherwin, "Steve Ballmer Recovers from Losing Microsoft Job by Binge-Watching 100 Episodes of The Good Wife," *Independent*, 26 August 2014.

27. Turnbull, *The TV Crime Drama*, 66–67, 94–95.

28. Martin, *Difficult Men*; Vest, *"The Wire," "Deadwood," "Homicide" and "NYPD Blue."*

29. Simon, *Homicide*; Simon and Burns, *The Corner*.

30. Williams, "Ethnographic Imaginary."

31. Exemplifying some of these changes is the confusing matter of the transfer to DVD, and the way in which this eliminates "the noise" of television. *Homicide*, as first broadcast in the United States, was never very secure in either its recommission or its scheduling, and the first season consisted of nine episodes, the second only four. While U.S. DVD releases seem to retain this distinction between the first and second (very short) season, in the U.K., the first and second are amalgamated, which then changes the season numbers for subsequent seasons, so that the British DVD purchaser buys a six- (not seven-) season box set. Although I have worked from British releases, I have retained the U.S. numbering. The British DVD release thus smooths out the insecurity of the original broadcast scheduling and commissioning.

32. Williams, "A Lecture on Realism."

33. Lavik, "Forward to the Past," 84. Lavik demonstrates his analysis in convincing detail in his video essay, "Style in *The Wire*," Vimeo, accessed 28 April 2014, https://www.vimeo.com/39768998.

34. Martin, *Difficult Men*, 142, discusses the transition between the equally "constructed realities" of *The Wire* and *Multiple Maniacs*.

35. Kraig Greff, "Fell's Point Out of Time: Vince Peranio Interview, February 11, 2004," http://fellspoint.us/images/fpoot_transcripts/Vince_Peranio _021104.pdf. Peranio is variously credited across Baltimore set work, usually as either art director or production designer.

36. Corbin's discussion of the way in which *Boyz n the Hood* (1991) and *Menace II Society* (1993) shift the "allegorical center of urban crisis" from New York to Los Angeles is germane here (*Cinematic Geographies and Multicultural Spectatorship*, 154). In my argument, Baltimore then becomes the next locus for the "authenticity of black culture" to be displayed for the tourist gaze.

37. Nichols-Pethick, *TV Cops*, 76.

38. Bruce Goldfarb, "Vincent Peranio: Giving Props to Baltimore," Welcome to Baltimore, Hon!, 6 June 2010, http://welcometobaltimorehon.com /vincent-peranio-giving-props-to-baltimore/.

39. Goldfarb, "Vincent Peranio."

40. Greff, "Fell's Point Out of Time."

41. Goldfarb, "Vincent Peranio."

42. Bignell, "The Police Series," 31.

43. See Michael Z. Newman's 2008 discussion of the erection of the statue *The Bronz Fonz* in Milwaukee in relation to ethnicity and normal American towns ("The Bronze Fonz").

44. The question of what kinds of multiple murders get classified as serial killing becomes an explicit concern in seasons 4 and 5 of *The Wire* in the comparison between Marlo's enforcement and McNulty's fictional serial killer.

45. Olson, *Baltimore*, 367–68.

46. Heller's celebratory analysis of *Hairspray* makes an interesting case about the film's contribution to popular memory about Baltimore in narratives of civil rights.

47. Lipsitz, *How Racism Takes Place*.

48. Haggins, "*Homicide*," 17. Haggins points out that the casting strategies of the show "diversified" the majority-white squad room from the book (17).

49. See Mascaro, "Shades of Black on *Homicide: Life on the Street*," for discussion of the range of black characters in *Homicide*.

50. Fields discusses the particularity of Baltimore's situation and demographics, describing it as "the metropolis of a border state, more closely integrated with the world of free labor than of slaves, [which] occupied just such a margin" (*Slavery and Freedom on the Middle Ground*, 57).

51. Greff, "Fell's Point Out of Time."

52. Piper, *The TV Detective*.

53. Cited in Nichols-Pethick, *TV Cops*, 80.

54. Nichols-Pethick, "*Homicide: Life on the Street*," 1122. Nichols-Pethick discusses space, community, and the use of music in some detail in *TV Cops*, 103–26.

55. Nichols-Pethick, "*Homicide: Life on the Street*," 1122.

56. "#85 *The Wire*," *Stuff White People Like* (blog), 9 March 2008, https://stuffwhitepeoplelike.com/2008/03/page/3/. See also some of the discussion cited in Walters, "*The Wire* for Tourists?"

57. Turnbull, *The TV Crime Drama*; on *The Wire* as genre, see also Gibb and Sabin, "Who Loves Ya, David Simon?"

58. For critical aesthetic analysis of the 2014 release of the wide-screen version of *The Wire*, see Callaghan, "Wider Still and Wider."

59. Lavik, "Style in *The Wire*"; also Lavik, "Forward to the Past." This invitation to make a "referential reading" is taken up by Stanley Corkin in *Connecting "The Wire*," 5, where he discusses it as a reading strategy.

60. Lavik, "Forward to the Past," 79.

61. The significance of utopian elements is discussed in Jameson, "Realism and Utopia in *The Wire*."

62. This was argued elegantly in Zborowski, "The Rhetoric of *The Wire*."

63. Linda Williams, in *On "The Wire*," has argued that *The Wire* should be considered as melodrama. Her theorization of melodrama sees it as the significant cultural mode of Western modernity, rather than in its more popular form as the degraded second term in the binary realism/melodrama. Melodrama is all about moral legibility in this argument. Thus the melodramatic mode is not opposed to realist coding and, in this case, provides a framework through which the realist presentation of particular lives can be made meaningful. She argues that melodrama, contrary to popular prejudice, does not specify a style but does contain within it the recognition that things should be other than they are. This enables her to incorporate Jameson's identification of *The Wire*'s utopian elements with Lavik's analysis of its stylistic realism as part of her argument that *The Wire* both looks real and is melodrama.

64. See Creeber, *Serial Television*, for discussion of most of these shows as long-form drama.

65. In addition to the claims about melodrama by Linda Williams, *On "The Wire,"* Polan's analysis of *The Sopranos* as a work of popular modernism is pertinent. *The Wire,* although it may have some of the borrowings from modernist European art cinema that Polan identifies as constituting this mode in television, lacks the focus on the interiority and existential crises of the central protagonist that is defining in modernist art cinemas.

66. "Seriality," "quality," and "narration" are the key terms here: Jason Mittell has used *The Wire* as a key text in his exposition of "narrative complexity," while it also features in the expanding discussion of "vast narratives" and the changing modes of television production associated with HBO. Mittell, "All in the Game"; also Jason Mittell, "The Wire and the Serial Procedural: An Essay in Progress," *Just TV* (blog), 22 May 2007, http://justtv.wordpress.com/2007/05/22/the-wire-and-the-serial-procedural. Frank Kelleter organizes *Wire* writing in a different typology in *"The Wire* and Its Readers."

67. Corkin gives the most extended and contextualized analysis of *The Wire*'s engagement with the real in a book published as this book was being copyedited (*Connecting "The Wire"*).

68. Chaddha and Wilson, "'Way Down in the Hole.'"

69. For example, Harvey is cited in three of the essays in Kennedy and Stephen, *"The Wire"*; Kennedy and Shapiro, "Tales of the Neoliberal City"; Kraniauskas, "Elasticity of Demand"; and Carroll, "Policing the Borders of White Masculinity," as well as in Penfold-Mounce, Beer, and Burrows, *"The Wire* as Social Science-Fiction." Corkin too refers to Harvey, but does so within a discussion of his own method more generally. Corkin, *Connecting "The Wire,"* 14–18.

70. Harvey, *Spaces of Hope*, 133.

71. Harvey, *Spaces of Hope*, 181.

72. Harvey, *The Urban Experience*, 48–51.

73. Vint, *"The Wire"*; Clandfield, "'We Ain't Got No Yard.'"

74. Fields, *Slavery and Freedom on the Middle Ground.*

75. It is noticeable that Didier Fassin's fastidiously detailed ethnography of urban policing in Paris invokes the rhythm of *The Wire* in the preface to the English edition, *Enforcing Order*, xii.

76. Although much of the first season drama is set in West Baltimore, it was shot in East Baltimore, so although it is location shooting, the location is not quite playing itself.

77. Cited in Gadi Dechter, "Wish You Weren't Here," *City Paper* (Baltimore), 24 May 2006, http://www.citypaper.com/news/thewire/bcpnews-wish-you-werent-here-20150520-story.html.

78. Peranio himself collaborated on a guided tour for the Baltimore *City Paper* in 2006 (see Dechter, "Wish You Weren't Here"). For other tour guides, see "Walking The Wire?," Trip Advisor, 9 October 2011, https://www.tripadvisor.co.uk/ShowTopic-g60811-i165-k4870485-Walking_The_Wire-Baltimore_Maryland.html; "The Wire Tour," Wikitravel, accessed 13 August 2013, http://wikitravel.org/en/The_Wire_Tour; "Baltimore: *The Wire* Locations, Part Two," A.V. Club, 13 July 2011, http://www.avclub.com/articles/baltimore-the-wire-locationsopart-two,57347/; Bruce Goldfarb, "The Wire: A Streetview Tour," Welcome to Baltimore, Hon!, accessed 13 August 2013, http://welcometobaltimorehon.com/the-wire-a-streeTView-tour; "Wired: Touring the Mean Streets of Baltimore," accessed 13 August 2013, travel.uk.msn.com/aventure-travel/touring-the-mean-streetsof-baltimore; Andy Lynes, "Close to *The Wire* on the Mean Streets of Baltimore," *Independent*, 20 July 2008.

79. Williams, On *"The Wire,"* 114, and see n. 63 above; Bramall and Pitcher, "Policing the Crisis," 88.

80. Lavik, "Forward to the Past," 79.

81. "*The Wire* can thus be read as a 'realist' fantasy: it doesn't describe an ideal world . . . but rather it depicts an ideal knowledge of, or orientation to, the world." Bramall and Pitcher, "Policing the Crisis," 88.

82. Lipsitz, *How Racism Takes Place*, 95–113.

83. Ault discusses Namond's narrative thread in some detail as part of her argument discussed below in "'You Can Help Yourself,'" 395–98.

84. Ault, "'You Can Help Yourself,'" 387.

85. Ault, "'You Can Help Yourself,'" 398.

86. Ault, "'You Can Help Yourself,'" 391.

87. Amy Holdworth provides a differently inflected reading of this sequence in *Television, Memory and Nostalgia*, 60–63.

88. "Natural police" is the highest term of professional approbation that can be offered by fellow officers within the world of the drama.

89. Brunsdon, "The Attractions of the Cinematic City."

90. Michael Curtin in discussion at Brunsdon seminar, "The Attractions of the Cinematic City," University of California, Santa Barbara, 14 April 2011.

91. On teaching *The Wire*, see "Harvard Class on *The Wire*," *New York Post*, 2 November 2009. The course was taught by W. J. Wilson. See Chaddha and Wilson, "'Way Down in the Hole.'" Other discussions of teaching the show include Jason Mittell, "Teaching The Wire," *Just TV* (blog), 6 February 2009, https://justtv.wordpress.com/2009/02/06; Drake Bennett, "This Will Be on the Midterm. You Feel Me?," *Slate*, 24 March 2010, http://www.slate.com

/articles/arts/culturebox/2010/03/this_will_be_on_the_midterm_you_feel _me.html.

92. Peranio contributed the giant lobster that attacks Divine in *Multiple Maniacs* (1970).

93. Zukin, *Loft Living*.

94. Greff, "Fell's Point Out of Time."

95. See Mayer, "Yeah You Rite: The *Treme* Issue."

Bibliography

Akass, Kim, and Janet McCabe, eds. *Reading "Sex and the City."* London: I. B. Tauris, 2004.

Allen, Robert C. "Getting to 'Going to the Show.'" In *Locating the Moving Image: New Approaches to Film and Place*, edited by Julia Hallam and Les Roberts, 31–43. Bloomington: Indiana University Press, 2014.

Alvarez, Rafael. *"The Wire": Truth Be Told.* Edinburgh: Canongate, 2009.

Anderson, Benedict. *Imagined Communities*, 2nd ed. London: Verso, 1991.

Anderson, Christopher. "Producing an Aristocracy of Culture in American Television." In Edgerton and Jones, *The Essential HBO Reader*, 23–41.

Arthurs, Jane. "*Sex and the City* and Consumer Culture." *Feminist Media Studies* 3, no. 1 (2003): 83–98.

Augé, Marc. *Non-places: Introduction to an Anthropology of Super-modernity.* Translated by John Howe. London: Verso, 1995.

Ault, Elizabeth. "'You Can Help Yourself / but Don't Take Too Much': African American Motherhood in *The Wire.*" *Television and New Media* 14, no. 5 (2002): 386–401.

Bakewell, Joan, and Nicholas Garnham. *The New Priesthood: British Television Today.* London: Allen Lane, 1970.

Banet-Weiser, Sarah, Cynthia Chris, and Anthony Freitas, eds. *Cable Visions: Television beyond Broadcasting.* New York: New York University Press, 2007.

Barry, Angela. "Black Mythologies: Representation of Black People on British Television." In *The Black and White Media Book*, edited by John Twitchin, 83–102. Stoke-on-Trent: Trentham, 1988.

Barthes, Roland. *Mythologies.* Translated by Annette Lavers. St. Albans: Paladin, 1973.

Baudelaire, Charles. "The Painter of Modern Life." In *The Painter of Modern Life and Other Essays*, translated by Jonathan Mayne, 1–41. London: Phaidon, 1964.

Benjamin, Walter. *The Arcades Project*. Translated by Howard Eiland and Kevin McLaughlin. Cambridge, MA: Harvard University Press, 1999.

Benjamin, Walter. "The Flâneur." In *Charles Baudelaire: A Lyric Poet in the Era of High Capitalism*, translated by Harry Zohn, 35–66. London: Verso, 1983.

Bhabha, Homi K. "Introduction: Narrating the Nation." In *Nation and Narration*, edited by Homi K. Bhabha, 1–7. London: Routledge, 1990.

Bignell, Jonathan. "The Police Series." In *Close-Up 03*, edited by John Gibbs and Doug Pye, 1–66. London: Wallflower, 2009.

Billingham, Peter. *Sensing the City through Television*. Bristol: Intellect, 2000.

Boddy, William, ed. "The Place of Television Studies." *Cinema Journal* 45, no. 1 (2006): 79–117.

Bodroghkozy, Aniko. "'Is This What You Mean by Color TV?': Race, Gender, and Contested Meanings in NBC's Julia." In *Private Screenings: Television and the Female Consumer*, edited by Lynn Spigel and Denise Mann, 143–68. Minneapolis: University of Minnesota Press, 1992.

Bourne, Stephen. *Black in the British Frame: Black People in British Film and Television, 1896–1996*. London: Cassell, 1998.

Bowlby, Rachel. *Just Looking: Consumer Culture in Dreiser, Gissing and Zola*. New York: Methuen, 1985.

Boym, Svetlana. *The Future of Nostalgia*. New York: Basic Books, 2001.

Bramall, Rebecca, and Dan Pitcher. "Policing the Crisis, or Why We Love *The Wire*." *International Journal of Cultural Studies* 16, no. 1 (2013): 83–97.

Bray, Christopher. *1965: The Year Modern Britain Was Born*. London: Simon and Schuster, 2014.

Brebber, Brett. "*Till Death Us Do Part*: Political Satire and Social Realism in the 1960s and 1970s." *Historical Journal of Film, Radio and Television* 34, no. 2 (2014): 253–74.

Brunsdon, Charlotte. "The Attractions of the Cinematic City." *Screen* 53, no. 3 (2012): 209–27.

Brunsdon, Charlotte. "The Cinematic and the Televisual City: South London Revisited." In *Cinematic Urban Geographies*, edited by François Penz and Richard Koeck, 223–43. New York: Palgrave Macmillan, 2017.

Brunsdon, Charlotte. "Introduction." *Cinema Journal* 47, no. 3 (2008): 122–27.

Brunsdon, Charlotte. "Is Television Studies History?" *Cinema Journal* 47, no. 3 (2008): 127–37.

Brunsdon, Charlotte. *London in Cinema: The Cinematic City since 1945*. London: BFI, 2007.

Brunsdon, Charlotte. *Screen Tastes: Soap Opera to Satellite Dishes.* London: Routledge, 1997.

Brunsdon, Charlotte. "Structure of Anxiety: Recent British Television Crime Fiction." *Screen* 39, no. 3 (1998): 223–43.

Brunsdon, Charlotte, and Ann Gray, eds. "The Place of Television Studies: The View from the Midlands." *Cinema Journal* 47, no. 3 (2008): 122–66.

Bruzzi, Stella. *Men's Cinema: Masculinity and Mise-en-Scène in Hollywood.* Edinburgh: Edinburgh University Press, 2013.

Bullman, Joseph, Neil Hegarty, and Brian Hill. *The Secret History of Our Streets.* London: BBC / Random House, 2013.

Busfield, Steve. "Foreword." In *"The Wire" Re-up: The Guardian Guide to the Greatest TV Show Ever Made*, edited by Steve Busfield and Paul Owen, 1–3. London: GuardianBooks, 2009.

Callaghan, Daniel. "Wider Still and Wider: The New Version of *The Wire*." *Critical Studies in Television Online*, 9 January 2015, http://cstonline.tv /wider-still-and-wider-the-new-version-of-the-wire.

Cardwell, Sarah. *Adaptation Revisited: Television and the Classic Novel.* Manchester: Manchester University Press, 2002.

Cardwell, Sarah. "Is Quality Television Any Good? Generic Distinctions, Evaluations and the Troubling Matter of Critical Judgement." In McCabe and Akass, *Quality TV*, 19–34.

Carnell, Kate. "Dickens Composed: Film and Television Adaptations 1897–2001." In *Dickens on Screen*, edited by John Glavin, 201–16. Cambridge: Cambridge University Press, 2003.

Carroll, Hamilton. "Policing the Borders of White Masculinity: Labor, Whiteness, and the Neoliberal City in *The Wire*." In Kennedy and Shapiro, *"The Wire*," 262–82.

Caughie, John. "Mourning Television: The Other Screen." *Screen* 51, no. 4 (2010): 410–21.

Caughie, John. "Playing at Being an American." In *Logics of Television*, edited by Patricia Mellencamp, 44–58. Bloomington: Indiana University Press / BFI, 1990.

Caughie, John. *Television Drama: Realism, Modernism and British Culture.* Oxford: Clarendon, 2000.

Chaddha, Anmol, and William Julius Wilson. "'Way Down in the Hole': Systemic Urban Inequality and *The Wire*." *Critical Inquiry* 38, no. 1 (2011): 164–88.

Chambers, Eddie. "Double Consciousness." In *Hurvin Anderson: Reporting Back*, edited by Stuart Tulloch and Jonathan Watkins, 71–77. Birmingham: Ikon Gallery, 2013.

Charney, Leo, and Vanessa R. Schwartz, eds. *Cinema and the Invention of Modern Life.* Berkeley: University of California Press, 1995.

Clandfield, Peter. "'We Ain't Got No Yard': Crime, Development, and Urban Environment." In Potter and Marshall, *"The Wire,"* 37–49.

Clark, Steve. *"Only Fools and Horses": The Official Inside Story.* Droxford: Splendid, 2011.

Cobb, Richard. "Maigret's Paris." In *Tour de France*, 179–84. London: Duckworth, 1976.

Corbin, Amy Lynn. *Cinematic Geographies and Multicultural Spectatorship in America.* Houndmills: Palgrave Macmillan, 2015.

Corkin, Stanley. *Connecting "The Wire": Race, Space, and Postindustrial Baltimore.* Austin: University of Texas Press, 2017.

Couldry, Nick. *The Place of Media Power: Pilgrims and Witnesses of the Media Age.* London: Routledge, 2000.

Couldry, Nick, Andreas Hepp, and Frederick Krotz, eds. *Media Events in a Global Age.* London: Routledge, 2010.

Couldry, Nick, and Anna McCarthy, eds. *Mediaspace: Place, Scale and Culture in a Media Age.* London: Routledge, 2004.

Coverley, Merlin. *Psychogeography.* Harpenden: Pocket Essentials, 2006.

Creeber, Glen. *Serial Television: Big Drama on the Small Screen.* London: BFI, 2004.

Curtin, Michael. "Media Capitals: Cultural Geographies of Global TV." In *Television after TV: Essays on a Medium in Transition*, edited by Lynn Spigel and Jan Olsson, 270–302. Durham, NC: Duke University Press, 2004.

D'Acci, Julie. *Defining Women: Television and the Case of "Cagney and Lacey."* Chapel Hill: University of North Carolina Press, 1994.

Davenport-Hines, Richard. *An English Affair: Sex, Class and Power in the Age of Profumo.* London: William Collins, 2013.

Dayan, Daniel, and Elihu Katz. *Media Events: The Live Broadcasting of History.* Cambridge, MA: Harvard University Press, 1992.

Debord, Guy. "Theory of the Dérive" [1956]. In *The Situationists and the City*, edited by T. McDonough, 77–85. London: Verso, 2009.

DeCarvalho, Lauren J. "Hannah and Her Entitled Sisters: (Post)feminism, (Post)recession, and *Girls.*" *Feminist Media Studies* 12, no. 2 (May 2003): 367–70.

Dejmanee, Tisha. "Consumption in the City: The Turn to Interiority in Contemporary Postfeminist Television." *European Journal of Cultural Studies* 19, no. 1 (2016): 119–33.

Dickens, Charles. *Our Mutual Friend.* 1864. Reprint, Oxford: Oxford University Press, 1989.

Dillman, Joanne Clarke. *Women and Death in Film, Television and News: Dead but Not Gone.* Basingstoke: Palgrave Macmillan, 2014.

Donald, James. *Imagining the Modern City.* London: Athlone, 1999.

Donald, James. "Talking the Talk, Walking the Walk." *Screen* 40, no. 3 (1999): 295–303.

Dorling, Danny. *All That Is Solid: The Great Housing Disaster.* London: Allen Lane, 2014.

Eaton, Michael. *"Our Friends in the North."* London: BFI, 2005.

Edgerton, Gary R., and Jeffrey P. Jones, eds. *The Essential HBO Reader.* Lexington: University Press of Kentucky, 2009.

"Editorial." *Cineaste* 39, no. 4 (2014): 1.

Elliott, Kamilla. *Rethinking the Novel/Film Debate.* Cambridge: Cambridge University Press 2003.

Ellis, John. "Scheduling: The Last Creative Act on Television?" *Media Culture and Society* 22, no. 1 (2000): 25–38.

Ellis, John. *Visible Fictions.* London: Routledge, 1992.

Ericson, Staffan, and Kristina Reigert, eds. *Media Houses: Architecture, Media, and the Production of Centrality.* New York: Peter Lang, 2010.

Fassin, Didier. *Enforcing Order: An Ethnography of Urban Policing.* Cambridge: Polity, 2013.

Feuer, Jane. "HBO and the Concept of Quality TV." In McCabe and Akass, *Quality TV,* 145–57.

Fields, Barbara Jean. *Slavery and Freedom on the Middle Ground. Maryland during the Nineteenth Century.* New Haven, CT: Yale University Press, 1985.

Fisher, Mark. *Ghosts of My Life: Writings on Depression, Hauntology and Lost Futures.* Alresford: Zero, 2014.

FitzGerald, Louise. "Taking a Pregnant Pause: Interrogating the Feminist Potential of *Call the Midwife.*" In Leggott and Teddeo, *Upstairs and Downstairs,* 249–61.

Forshaw, Barry. "Georges Simenon and Maigret's Paris." In *Following the Detectives,* edited by Maxim Jakubski, 160–69. London: New Holland, 2010.

Friedberg, Anne. *Window Shopping: Cinema and the Postmodern.* Berkeley: University of California Press, 1993.

Fryer, Peter. *Staying Power: The History of Black People in Britain.* London: Pluto, 1984.

Garnett, Tony. "Contexts." In *British Television Drama,* edited by Jonathan Bignell and Stephen Lacey, 16–29. Houndmills: Palgrave Macmillan, 2014.

Georgiou, Myria. *Media and the City.* Cambridge: Polity, 2013.

Geppert, Alexander. *Fleeting Cities: Imperial Expositions in Fin-de-Siècle Europe.* Basingstoke: Palgrave, 2010.

Geraghty, Christine. *"Bleak House."* London: BFI / Palgrave Macmillan, 2012.

Geraghty, Christine. *Now a Major Motion Picture: Film Adaptations of Literature and Drama.* Lanham, MD: Rowman and Littlefield, 2008.

Geraghty, Christine. "The Woman Between: The European Woman in Post-war British Cinema." *European Journal of Cultural Studies* 2, no. 2 (1999): 147–62.

Geraghty, Christine. *Women and Soap Opera.* Cambridge: Polity, 1990.

Gibb, Jane, and Roger Sabin. "Who Loves Ya, David Simon?" *darkmatter*, 29 May 2009, www.darkmatter101.org/site/2009/05/29/who-loves-ya-david-simon/.

Gilligan, Paula. "'Harsh Realism': Gender, Reality Television, and the Politics of the 'Sink' Housing Estate in Austerity Britain." *Television and New Media* 14, no. 3 (2012): 244–60.

Gilroy, Paul. "C4—Bridgehead or Bantustan?" *Screen* 24, no. 4 (1983): 130–36.

Givanni, June, ed. *Remote Control: Dilemmas of Black Intervention in British Film and TV.* London: BFI, 1995.

Gleber, Anke. *The Art of Taking a Walk: Flanerie, Literature, and Film in Weimar Culture.* Princeton, NJ: Princeton University Press, 1999.

Gray, Herman. "Recovered, Reinvented, Reimagined: *Treme*, Television Studies and Writing New Orleans." *Television and New Media* 13, no. 3 (2012): 268–78.

Gray, Herman. *Watching Race: Television and the Struggle for "Blackness."* Minneapolis: University of Minnesota Press, 1995.

Gray, Jonathan, and Amanda D. Lotz. *Television Studies.* Cambridge: Polity, 2012.

Haggins, Bambi. "*Homicide*: Realism!" In *How to Watch Television*, edited by Ethan Thompson and Jason Mittell, 13–21. New York: New York University Press, 2013.

Haggins, Bambi, and Amanda D. Lotz. "Comedy Overview: At Home on the Cutting Edge." In Edgerton and Jones, *The Essential HBO Reader*, 151–71.

Haining, Peter. *The Complete Maigret.* London: Boxtree, 1994.

Haining, Peter. *The Television Sherlock Holmes.* London: Virgin, 1994.

Haining, Peter. "The Television Super-Sleuth." In *A Sherlock Holmes Compendium*, edited by Peter Haining, 270–81. London: Warner, 1994.

Hall, Stuart. "Black and White in Television." In *Remote Control: Dilemmas of Black Intervention in British Film and TV*, edited by June Givanni, 13–28. London: BFI, 1995.

Hall, Stuart. "Reformism and the Legislation of Consent." In *Permissiveness and Control: The Fate of the Sixties Legislation*, edited by National Deviancy Conference, 1–43. London: Macmillan, 1980.

Hallam, Julia, and Les Roberts, eds. *Locating the Moving Image: New Approaches to Film and Place.* Bloomington: Indiana University Press, 2014.

Hamnett, Chris. *Unequal City: London in the Global Arena.* London: Routledge, 2003.

Hardy, Phil, ed. *The BFI Companion to Crime.* London: Cassell / BFI, 1997.

Hare, David. *The Blue Touch Paper: A Memoir.* London: Faber and Faber, 2015.

Harper, Sue, and Vincent Porter. *British Cinema of the 1950s: The Decline of Deference.* Oxford: Oxford University Press, 2003.

Hartley, John. *Uses of Television.* London: Routledge, 1999.

Harvey, David. *Spaces of Hope.* Edinburgh: Edinburgh University Press, 2000.

Harvey, David. *The Urban Experience.* Athens: University of Georgia Press, 2009.

Heller, Dana. *Hairspray.* Chichester: Wiley-Blackwell, 2011.

Hewett, Richard. "Essentially English: Sherlock Holmes at the BBC." *Journal of British Cinema and Television* 13, no. 1 (2016): 1–18.

Highmore, Ben. *Cityscapes: Cultural Readings in the Material and Symbolic City.* Houndmills: Palgrave Macmillan, 2005.

Highmore, Ben. "Feeling It: Habitat, Taste and the New Middle Class in 1970s Britain." *New Formations* 88 (Spring 2016): 105–22.

Hills, Matt. "From the Box in the Corner to the Box Set on the Shelf." *New Review of Film and Television Studies* 5, no. 1 (2007): 41–60.

Hills, Matt. *"Sherlock": Detecting Quality TV.* London: I. B. Tauris, 2018.

Hilmes, Michele. *Network Nations: A Transnational History of British and American Broadcasting.* London: Routledge, 2011.

Holdworth, Amy. *Television, Memory and Nostalgia.* Houndmills: Palgrave Macmillan, 2011.

Jacobs, Jason. "Selling the Medium: A Brief History of the BBC's Commercial Arm." *CST Online,* 27 April 2012. cstonline.net.

Jacobs, Jason, and Stephen Peacock, eds. *Television Aesthetics and Style.* London: Bloomsbury, 2013.

Jakobson, Roman. "On Realism in Art." In *Readings in Russian Poetics,* edited by Ladislav Matejska and Krystyna Pomorska, 38–46. Cambridge, MA: MIT Press, 1971.

Jakubowski, Maxim, ed. *Following the Detectives: Real Locations in Crime Fiction.* London: New Holland, 2010.

James, Clive. *Play All.* New Haven, CT: Yale University Press, 2016.

Jameson, Fredric. "Realism and Utopia in *The Wire.*" *Criticism* 52, nos. 3–4 (2010): 359–72.

Jaramillo, Deborah. "Rescuing Television from 'the Cinematic': The Perils of Dismissing Television Style." In Jacobs and Peacock, *Television Aesthetics and Style,* 67–76.

Jermyn, Deborah. *Sex and the City*. Detroit: Wayne State University Press, 2009.

Jermyn, Deborah. "Silk Blouses and Fedoras: The Female Detective, Contemporary TV Crime Drama and the Predicaments of Postfeminism." *Crime, Media, Culture*, 3 February 2016. doi: 10.1177/1741659015626578.

Johnson, Catherine, and Rob Turnock, eds. *ITV Cultures: Independent Television over Fifty Years*. Maidenhead: Open University Press, 2005.

Kackman, Michael. "Flow Favorites: Quality Television, Melodrama, and Cultural Complexity." *Flow*, 25 March 2010, https://www.flowjournal.org/2010/03/flow-favorites-quality-television-melodrama-and-cultural-complexity-michael-kackman-university-of-texas-austin/.

Kelleter, Frank. "*The Wire* and Its Readers." In Kennedy and Shapiro, "*The Wire*," 33–70.

Kennedy, Liam. *Race and Urban Space in Contemporary American Culture*. Edinburgh: Edinburgh University Press, 2000.

Kennedy, Liam, and Stephen Shapiro. "Tales of the Neoliberal City: *The Wire*'s Boundary Lines." In Kennedy and Shapiro, "*The Wire*," 147–69.

Kennedy, Liam, and Stephen Shapiro, eds. "*The Wire*": *Race, Class, and Genre*. Ann Arbor: University of Michigan Press, 2012.

Kinder, Marsha. "Re-wiring Baltimore: The Emotive Power of Systemics, Seriality, and the City." *Film Quarterly* 62, no. 2 (2008–9): 50–57.

Klein, Amanda Ann. "'The Dickensian Aspect': Melodrama, Viewer Engagement, and the Socially Conscious Text." In Potter and Marshall, "*The Wire*," 177–89.

Kleinecke-Bates, Iris. *Victorians on Screen: The Nineteenth Century on British Television, 1994–2005*. Basingstoke: Palgrave Macmillan, 2014.

Klinger, Barbara. *Beyond the Multiplex*. Berkeley: University of California Press, 2006.

Kompare, Derek. "Publishing Flow: DVD Box Sets and the Reconception of Television." *Television and New Media* 7, no. 4 (2006): 335–60.

Kosmicki, Anne-Marie. "Les Maigret, de Jean Richard à Bruno Cremer." "Littérature et television," *CinémAction*, no. 79 (1996): 96–105.

Krajina, Zlatan. *Negotiating the Mediated City: Everyday Encounters with Public Screens*. London: Routledge, 2014.

Kraniauskas, John. "Elasticity of Demand: Reflections on *The Wire*." In Kennedy and Shapiro, "*The Wire*," 170–94.

Lanchester, John. *Capital*. London: Faber and Faber, 2012.

Larkin, Philip. *Collected Poems*. London: Marvell / Faber and Faber, 1988.

Lavik, Erlend. "Forward to the Past: The Strange Case of *The Wire*." In *Relocating Television: Television in the Digital Context*, edited by Jostein Gripsrud, 76–87. London: Routledge, 2011.

Leal, Ondina Fachel. "Popular Taste and the Erudite Repertoire: The Place and Space of Television in Brazil." *Cultural Studies* 4, no. 1 (1990): 19–29.

Leggott, James, and Julie Anne Teddeo, eds. *Upstairs and Downstairs: British Costume Drama Television from "The Forsyte Saga" to "Downton Abbey."* Lanham, MD: Rowman and Littlefield, 2015.

Liarou, Eleni. "British Television's Lost New Wave Moment: Single Drama and Race." *Journal of British Cinema and Television* 9, no. 4 (2012): 612–27.

Lipsitz, George. *How Racism Takes Place.* Philadelphia: Temple University Press, 2011.

Lotz, Amanda. "Rethinking Meaning Making: Watching Serial TV on DVD." *Flow* 4, no. 12 (2006), http://www.flowjournal.org/2006/09/rethinking-meaning-making-watching-serial-tv-on-dvd/.

Lotz, Amanda. *The Television Will Be Revolutionized.* New York: New York University Press, 2007.

MacMurraugh-Kavanagh, Madeleine. "'Drama' into 'News': Strategies of Intervention in 'The Wednesday Play.'" *Screen* 38, no. 3 (1997): 247–59.

Malik, Sarita. "*Desmond's.*" In Newcomb, *Encyclopedia of Television*, 2nd ed., vol. 2, 689–90.

Malik, Sarita. *Representing Black Britain: Black and Asian Images on Television.* London: Sage, 2002.

Mansell, Gerard. *Let Truth Be Told: 50 Years of BBC External Broadcasting.* London: Weidenfeld and Nicolson, 1982.

Marcus, Sharon. *Apartment Stories: City and Home in Nineteenth-Century Paris and London.* Berkeley: University of California Press, 1999.

Martin, Brett. *Difficult Men: Behind the Scenes of a Creative Revolution: From "The Sopranos" and "The Wire" to "Mad Men" and "Breaking Bad."* London: Faber and Faber, 2013.

Mascaro, Thomas A. "Shades of Black on *Homicide: Life on the Street*: Progress in the Portrayals of African-American Men." *Journal of Popular Film and Television* 32, no. 1 (2004): 10–19.

Matthews-Jones, Lucinda. "Ripper Street Reflections." *Journal of Victorian Culture Online*, 2 March 2013, http://blogs.tandf.co.uk/jvc/2013/03/02/ripper-street-reflections/.

Mayer, Vicki. "Yeah You Rite: The *Treme* Issue." *Television and New Media* 13, no. 3 (2012): 191–92.

McCabe, Janet, and Kim Akass, eds. *Quality TV: Contemporary American Television and Beyond.* London: I. B. Tauris, 2007.

McCann, Graham. *"Only Fools and Horses": The Story of Britain's Favourite Comedy.* Edinburgh: Canongate, 2011.

McCarthy, Anna. *Ambient Television.* Durham, NC: Duke University Press, 2001.

McElroy, Ruth, ed. *Cops on the Box: Contemporary British TV Crime Drama.* Farnham: Ashgate, 2017.

McQuire, Scott. *The Media City: Media, Architecture and Urban Space.* London: Sage, 2008.

Meldrum, Claire. "Yesterday's Women: The Female Presence in Neo-Victorian Television Detective Programs." *Journal of Popular Film and Television* 43, no. 4 (2015): 201–11.

Mennel, Barbara. *Cities and Cinema.* Abingdon: Routledge, 2008.

Mercer, Kobena. "General Introduction." In *The Colour Black: Black Images in British Television,* edited by Therese Daniels and Jane Gerson, 1–12. London: BFI, 1989.

Mercer, Kobena. *Welcome to the Jungle.* London: Routledge, 1994.

Mills, Brett. "What Does It Mean to Call Television 'Cinematic'?" In Jacobs and Peacock, *Television Aesthetics and Style,* 57–66.

Mittell, Jason. "All in the Game: *The Wire,* Serial Storytelling, and Procedural Logic." In *Third Person: Authoring and Exploring Vast Narratives,* edited by Pat Harrigan and Noah Wardrup-Fruin, 429–38. Cambridge, MA: MIT Press, 2009.

Mittell, Jason. *Complex TV: The Poetics of Contemporary Television Storytelling.* New York: New York University Press, 2015.

Moran, Joe. *Armchair Nation: An Intimate History of Britain in Front of the TV.* London: Profile, 2013.

Moretti, Franco. *Signs Taken for Wonders.* London: Verso, 1983.

Morley, David. *Home Territories: Media, Mobility and Identity.* London: Routledge, 2000.

Morley, David. *Media, Modernity and Technology.* London: Routledge, 2007.

Mort, Frank. *Capital Affairs: London and the Making of the Permissive Society.* New Haven, CT: Yale University Press, 2010.

Moseley, Rachel. "'It's a Wild Country. Wild . . . Passionate . . . Strange': *Poldark* and the Place-Image of Cornwall." *Visual Culture in Britain* 14, no. 2 (2013): 218–37.

Nash, Meredith, and Ruby Grant. "Twenty-Something *Girls* v. Thirty-Something *Sex and the City* Women." *Feminist Media Studies* 15, no. 6 (2005): 976–91.

Nead, Lynda. *The Haunted Gallery: Painting, Photography Film c. 1900.* New Haven, CT: Yale University Press, 2007.

Nelson, Robin. "Quality TV Drama: Estimations and Influences through Time and Space." In McCabe and Akass, *Quality TV,* 38–51.

Newcomb, Horace. *"Cagney and Lacey."* In Newcomb, *Encyclopedia of Television*, 2nd ed., vol. 1, 400–404.

Newcomb, Horace, ed. *Encyclopedia of Television.* 2nd ed. 4 vols. New York: Fitzroy Dearborn, 2004.

Newland, Paul. *The Cultural Construction of London's East End.* Amsterdam: Rodopi, 2008.

Newland, Paul. "Global Markets and a Market Place: Reading *EastEnders* as the Anti-Docklands." *Journal of British Cinema and Television* 5, no. 1 (2008): 72–85.

Newman, Kim. "Holmes, Sherlock." In Hardy, *The BFI Companion to Crime*, 167–73.

Newman, Michael Z. "The Bronze Fonz: Public Art/Popular Culture in Milwaukee, Wisconsin." *Flow Favorites*, 31 October 2008, https://flowjournal.org /2008/10/the-bronze-fonz-public-artpopular-culture-in-milwaukee -wisconsin-michael-newman-university-of-wisonsin-milwaukee/.

Newman, Michael Z., and Elana Levine. *Legitimating Television: Media Convergence and Cultural Status.* New York: Routledge, 2012.

Newton, Darrell M. *Paving the Empire Road: BBC Television and Black Britons.* Manchester: Manchester University Press, 2011.

Nichols-Pethick, Jonathan. *"Homicide: Life on the Street."* In Newcomb, *Encyclopedia of Television*, 2nd ed., vol. 2, 1122–25.

Nichols-Pethick, Jonathan. *TV Cops: The Contemporary American Television Police Drama.* New York: Routledge, 2012.

Nord, Deborah Epstein. *Walking the Victorian Streets: Women, Representation and the City.* Ithaca, NY: Cornell University Press, 1995.

Nygaard, Taylor. "Girls Just Want to Be 'Quality': HBO, Lena Dunham, and *Girls'* Conflicting Brand Identity." *Feminist Media Studies* 12, no. 2 (May 2003): 370–74.

Olson, Sherry H. *Baltimore.* Baltimore, MD: Johns Hopkins University Press, 1980.

O'Regan, Tom. "The International Circulation of British TV." In *British Television: A Reader*, edited by Edward Buscombe, 303–21. Oxford: Oxford University Press, 2000.

Orr, John. "Traducing Realisms: *Naked* and *Nil by Mouth."* *Journal of Popular British Cinema*, no. 5 (2002): 104–13.

O'Sullivan, Tim. "Television Memories and Cultures of Viewing, 1950–65." In *Popular Television in Britain*, edited by John Corner, 159–81. London: BFI, 1991.

Parmett, Helen Morgan. "Media as a Spatial Practice: *Treme* and the Production of the Media Neighbourhood." *Continuum: Journal of Media and Cultural Studies* 28, no. 3 (2014): 286–99.

Parmett, Helen Morgan. "Space, Place and New Orleans on Television: From *Frank's Place* to *Treme*." *Television and New Media* 13, no. 3 (2012): 193–212.

Paterson, Chris. *The International News Agencies: The World from London.* New York: Peter Lang, 2011.

Penfold-Mounce, Ruth, David Beer, and Roger Burrows. "*The Wire* as Social Science-Fiction?" *Sociology* 45, no. 1 (2011): 152–67.

Pertierra, Anna Cristina, and Graeme Turner. *Locating Television: Zones of Consumption.* London: Routledge, 2013.

Phillips, Alastair, and Ginette Vincendeau, eds. *Beyond the Flâneur: Paris in the Cinema.* London: BFI / Palgrave Macmillan, forthcoming.

Phillips, Mike, and Trevor Phillips. *Windrush: The Irresistible Rise of Multiracial Britain.* London: HarperCollins, 1998.

Pines, Jim, ed. *Black and White in Colour: Black People in British Television.* London: BFI, 1992.

Pines, Jim. "Black Cops and Black Villains in Film and TV Crime Fiction." In *Crime and the Media*, edited by David Kidd-Hewitt and Richard Osborne, 67–77. London: Pluto, 1995.

Piper, Helen. *The TV Detective: Voices of Dissent in Contemporary Television.* London: I. B. Tauris, 2015.

Pointer, Michael. *Charles Dickens on the Screen: The Film, Television, and Video Adaptations.* Lanham, MD: Scarecrow, 1996.

Polan, Dana. "Cable Watching: HBO, *The Sopranos*, and the Discourses of Distinction." In *Cable Visions: Television beyond Broadcasting*, edited by Sarah Banet-Weiser, Cynthia Chris, and Anthony Freitas, 261–83. New York: New York University Press, 2007.

Polan, Dana. "*The Sopranos*." Durham, NC: Duke University Press, 2009.

Pollock, Griselda. *Vision and Difference.* London: Routledge, 1988.

Potter, Tiffany, and C. W. Marshall, eds. "*The Wire*": *Urban Decay and American Television.* New York: Continuum, 2009.

Reigert, Kristina. "The End of the Iconic Home of Empire: Pondering the Move of the BBC World Service from Bush House." In *Media Houses: Architecture, Media, and the Production of Centrality*, edited by Staffan Ericson and Kristina Reigert, 59–80. New York: Peter Lang, 2010.

Richards, Helen. "*Sex and the City*: A Visible *Flâneuse* for the Post-modern Era?" *Continuum* 7, no. 2 (2003): 147–57.

Richards, Jeffrey. *Films and British National Identity: From Dickens to "Dad's Army."* Manchester: Manchester University Press, 1997.

Ross, Kristin. *Fast Cars, Clean Bodies: Decolonisation and the Re-ordering of French Culture.* Cambridge, MA: MIT Press, 1995.

Ryan, Jenny. "Women, Modernity and the City." *Theory, Culture and Society* 11, no. 4 (1994): 35–63.

Samuel, Raphael. *Theatres of Memory.* London: Verso, 1994.

Sandbrook, Dominic. *Never Had It So Good: A History of Britain from Suez to the Beatles.* London: Abacus, 2005.

Sandbrook, Dominic. *White Heat: A History of Britain in the Swinging Sixties.* London: Abacus, 2006.

Scannell, Paddy. "Public Service Broadcasting: The History of a Concept." In *British Television: A Reader*, edited by Edward Buscombe, 45–62. Oxford: Oxford University Press, 2000.

Scannell, Paddy, and David Cardiff. *A Social History of British Broadcasting.* Oxford: Blackwell, 1991.

Schaffer, Gavin. *The Vision of a Nation: Making Multiculturalism on British Television, 1960–80.* Basingstoke: Palgrave Macmillan, 2014.

Schlicke, Paul, ed. *The Oxford Companion to Charles Dickens.* Oxford: Oxford University Press, 2011.

Schwarz, Bill. "Reveries of Race: The Closing of the Imperial Moment." In *Moments of Modernity*, edited by Becky Conekin, Frank Mort, and Chris Waters, 189–207. London: Rivers Oram, 1999.

Schwarzbach, F. S. *Dickens and the City.* London: Athlone, 1979.

Silva, Kumarini, and Kaitlynn Mendes, ed. "HBO's *Girls*." *Feminist Media Studies* 12, no. 2 (May 2003): 355–74.

Silverstone, Roger, ed. *Visions of Suburbia.* London: Routledge, 1997.

Simon, David. *Homicide: A Year on the Killing Streets.* Boston: Houghton Mifflin, 1991.

Simon, David. Interview by Jesse Pearson. *Vice*, 1 December 2009, www.vice .com/read/david-simon-280-v16n12.

Simon, David, and Ed Burns. *The Corner: A Year in the Life of an Inner-City Neighborhood.* New York: Broadway, 1997.

Simon, Ron. "*Sex and the City*." In Edgerton and Jones, *The Essential HBO Reader*, 193–203.

Simon, Sherry. *Translating Montreal: Episodes in the Life of a Divided City.* Montreal: McGill-Queen's University Press, 2006.

Smith, Graham. "Television Adaptations of Charles Dickens." In *The Oxford Companion to Charles Dickens*, edited by Paul Schlicke, 565. Oxford: Oxford University Press, 2011.

Smith, Jim. *Manhattan Dating Game: An Unofficial and Unauthorised Guide to Every Episode of "Sex and the City."* London: Virgin, 2004.

Sohn, Amy. *"Sex and the City": Kiss and Tell.* New York: Pocket, 2004.

Solnit, Rebecca. *Wanderlust: A History of Walking.* London: Verso, 2002.

Spigel, Lynn. *Make Room for TV*. Chicago: University of Chicago Press, 1992.

Spigel, Lynn. *TV by Design*. Chicago: University of Chicago Press, 2008.

Spigel, Lynn. *Welcome to the Dreamhouse*. Durham, NC: Duke University Press, 2001.

Spigel, Lynn, and Jan Olsson, eds. *Television after TV: Essays on a Medium in Transition*. Durham, NC: Duke University Press, 2004.

Stanton, Gareth. "Peckham Tales: Mass Observation and the Modalities of Community." In *Media and Cultural Theory*, edited by James Curran and David Morley, 100–114. Abingdon: Routledge, 2006.

Stewart, Jacqueline. *Migrating to the Movies: Cinema and Black Urban Modernity*. Berkeley: University of California Press, 2005.

Sullivan, John. *"Only Fools and Horses": The Bible of Peckham*. 2 vols. London: BBC Worldwide, 1999–2000.

Summerson, John. *The London Building World of the 1860s*. London: Thames and Hudson, 1973.

Tambling, Jeremy. *Going Astray: Dickens and London*. London: Pearson, 2009.

Taunton, Matthew. *Fictions of the City: Class, Culture and Mass Housing in London and Paris*. Basingstoke: Palgrave Macmillan, 2009.

Tester, Keith. *The Flâneur*. London: Routledge, 1994.

Tincknell, Estella. "Dowagers, Debs, Nuns, and Babies: The Policies of Nostalgia and the Older Woman in the British Sunday Night Television Serial." *Journal of British Cinema and Television* 10, no. 4 (2013): 769–84.

Toscano, Alberto, and Jeff Kinkle. "Baltimore as World and Representation: Cognitive Mapping and Capitalism in *The Wire*." *Dossier*, no. 8 (2009), http://dossierjournal.com/read/theory.baltimore-as-world-and-representation-cognitive-mapping-and-capitalism-in-the-wire/.

Tufte, Thomas. *Living with the Rubbish Queen: Telenovelas, Culture and Modernity in Brazil*. Luton: University of Luton Press, 2000.

Turnbull, Sue. *The TV Crime Drama*. Edinburgh: Edinburgh University Press, 2014.

Turner, Graeme. "Television and the Nation: Does This Matter Any More?" In *Television Studies after TV: Understanding Television in the Post-broadcast Era*, edited by Graeme Turner and Jinna Tay, 55–64. London: Routledge, 2009.

Turner, Graeme, and Jinna Tay, ed. *Television Studies after TV: Understanding Television in the Post-broadcast Era*. London: Routledge, 2009.

Turnock, Rob. *Television and Consumer Culture*. London: I. B. Tauris, 2007.

Vest, Jason P. *"The Wire," "Deadwood," "Homicide" and "NYPD Blue": Violence Is Power*. Santa Barbara, CA: Praeger, 2011.

Vincendeau, Ginette. "Maigret pour toujours?" In *Policiers et criminals: Un genre populaire européen sur grand et petit écrans*, edited by Raphaëlle Moine, Brigitte Rollet, and Geneviève Sellier, 89–100. Paris: L'Harmattan, 2009.

Vint, Sherryl. *"The Wire."* Detroit: Wayne State University Press, 2013.

Wallace, Richard. "John Cura: Pioneer of the Television Archive." *Journal of British Cinema and Television* 13, no. 1 (2016): 99–120.

Walters, Ben. *"The Wire* for Tourists?" *Film Quarterly* 62, no. 2 (2008): 64–65.

Walters, James. "Repeat Viewings: Television Analysis in the DVD Age." In *Film and Television after DVD*, edited by James Bennett and Tom Brown, 63–80. New York: Routledge, 2008.

Weissmann, Elke. *Transnational Television Drama: Special Relations and Mutual Influence between the US and UK*. Basingstoke: Palgrave Macmillan, 2012.

Weissmann, Elke. "Troubled by Violence: Transnational Complexity and the Critique of Masculinity in *Ripper Street*." In Leggott and Teddeo, *Upstairs and Downstairs*, 275–86.

Wheatley, Helen. "Rooms within Rooms: *Upstairs Downstairs* and the Studio Costume Drama of the 1970s." In *ITV Cultures: Independent Television over Fifty Years*, edited by Catherine Johnson and Rob Turnock, 143–58. Maidenhead: Open University Press, 2005.

Wheatley, Helen. *Spectacular Television: Exploring Televisual Pleasure*. London: I. B. Tauris, 2016.

White, Jerry. *London in the Twentieth Century: A City and Its People*. London: Viking, 2001.

Willemen, Paul. "Maigret." In Hardy, *The BFI Companion to Crime*, 216–17.

Williams, Linda. "Ethnographic Imaginary: The Genesis and Genius of *The Wire*." *Critical Inquiry* 38, no. 1 (2011): 208–26.

Williams, Linda. *On "The Wire."* Durham, NC: Duke University Press, 2014.

Williams, Raymond. "A Lecture on Realism." *Screen* 18, no. 1 (1977): 61–74.

Wilson, Elizabeth. "The Invisible Flâneur." *New Left Review*, no. 191 (1992): 90–110.

Wilson, Elizabeth. *The Sphinx in the City*. London: Virago, 1991.

Wojcik, Pamela Robertson. *The Apartment Plot: Urban Living in American Film and Popular Culture, 1945 to 1975*. Durham, NC: Duke University Press, 2010.

Wolff, Janet. "The Invisible Flaneuse: Women and the Literature of Modernity." *Theory, Culture, and Society* 2, no. 3 (1985): 37–46.

Wolff, Janet. *Resident Alien: Feminist Cultural Criticism*. Cambridge: Polity, 1995.

Worpole, Ken. *Dockers and Detectives.* London: Verso, 1983.

Wright, Patrick. *On Living in an Old Country: The National Past in Contemporary Britain.* London: Verso, 1985.

Wright, Steven H. "Baltimore: What Hasn't Changed." *New York Review of Books,* 9 June 2015, http://www.nybooks.com/daily/2015/06/09.

Yoshimi, Shunya. "'Made in Japan': The Cultural Politics of 'Home Electrification' in Postwar Japan." *Media Culture and Society* 21, no. 2 (1999): 149–71.

Yoshimi, Shunya. "Television and Nationalism: Historical Change in the National Domestic TV Formation of Postwar Japan." *European Journal of Cultural Studies* 6, no. 4 (2003): 459–87.

Zborowski, James. "The Rhetoric of *The Wire.*" *Movie: A Journal of Film Criticism,* no. 1 (2010): 1–6.

Zukin, Sharon. *Loft Living: Culture and Capital in Urban Change.* Baltimore, MD: Johns Hopkins University Press, 1982.

Index

Note: Page numbers in italics refer to images.

documentary: British programs, 72, 88–89; style or look, 135, 139
domesticity: of the sitcom, 89; of the television medium, 21, 88, 124
Dorling, Danny, 114, 185n102
dramas, 34, 90, 149; everyday life, 85, 113; London-set, 73, 97–100, 112; of masculinity, 7; serial, 2, 85, 117, 124. *See also* crime drama; melodrama
drug trade: in *The Corner*, 140–42, 144; in *The Wire*, 146–48, 150, 152
Dutton, Charles S., 140
DVD box sets, 122–23, 188n31

EastEnders, 73, 97; ethnic diversity of, 86–87; history and setting, 85–86, 104
editing techniques: *The Corner*, 139; *Homicide*, 135–36; *The Wire*, 147–48
Elba, Idris, 12
Elliot, Larry, 169n42
Ellis, John, 15
Empire Road, 97
Empire Windrush (ship), 87, 92, 93, 182n64
Engrenages, 25
ethnicity. *See* race relations
everyday life: of detectives in crime series, 133; domestic sphere of, 6; in London, 98–100; in Paris, 27, 34; sense of future in, 112; television as a medium for, 74, 84, 85; of young black men, 95, 97

Fall, The, 13–14, 169n36
Fassin, Didier, 191n75
female characters, 13–14, 85, 106–7, 111

femininity, 13–14, 124
feminism, 169n38
Fields, Barbara Jean, 190n50
Fisher, Mark, 185n99
flâneur/flâneuse, 4–6, 25, 85, 142, 167n14; definition, 166n11
Flynn, Jerome, 106
Fontana, Tom, 135–36
Fox, 114
franchises, television, 67, 69, 178n1
Frank's Place, 186n4
French culture, 41, 44, 49, 56, 62
French language, 36, *38–39*, 174n33
Frenchness, 176n64; of BBC's *Maigret* sets, 20, 26, 32, 36, 42, 56; of Davies as Maigret, 62
Friedberg, Anne, 5
future, sense of, 112–13, 185n99

Game of Thrones, 13
Gandolfini, James, 124
genres, 11–12, 72
Geraghty, Christine, 86, 180n24
Gilroy, Paul, 88
Girls, 167n15
Glaister, Gerard, 172n16
Good Wife, The, 125–26
Granada Television, 85; Sherlock Holmes series, 103, 183n77. See also *Maigret* (Gambon)
Grant, Cy, 88
Graves, Rupert, 103
Gray, Freddie, 116, 186n1
Griffiths, Peter, 89–90
Guardian, 120, 187n10
Gunsmoke, 30

Habitat shops, 62, 177n77
Haggins, Bambi, 131, 167n15, 189n48

140, 142; property/housing, 114, 185n102; Thames Television, 67; U.S., 30, 105, 106

Martin, Brett, 124, 126

masculinity: dramas of, 7, 124, 188n22; flâneur's, 4–5; of police fiction, 157–58; in *The Wire*, 156

McCarthy, Anna, 166n7

McCullum, Julito, 157

McQuire, Scott, 7, 168n23

media capitals, 11, 13, 170n47

media city, 2, 7, 168n23

media cultures, 178n4

medium, television: banality of, 74; changing historical forms of, 3; contributions to decolonization, 21, 87, 88; cultural status of, 6, 76; Dickens and, 75–76; as a domestic medium, 15, 88; everyday life stories and, 84, 85, 163; hybridity of, 9, 65; influence on British culture, 72–73; modernity and, 60, 69; new neighbors discourse and, 90; as a new/old medium, 73, 113; old London and, 21, 74; quality television and, 123

melodrama, 126, 149, 158, 190n63, 191n65

Menace II Society (1993), 189n36

Mercer, Kobena, 73, 86, 181n52

Miami Vice, 126, 129

Mittell, Jason, 168n25, 187n20, 191n66

mobility: of female characters, 5; flâneur's, 4, 142; social, 72; of television, 2; urban, 13–14

modernity, 190n63, 191n65; in Britain, 21, 59–60, 62, 64, 69; cinema/city and, 4, 6, 19; excitement and terror of, 75; icons of domestic,

115; London landmarks, 68–69; Paris, 19, 20, 24, 26; suburban, 4; urban, 9

monarchy, 70

money, 81–83

Moran, Joe, 179n13

Moran, Pat, 128, 162

Morrissey, David, 97

multiculturalism: in London, 87; moments in British programs, 86, 97, 182n69

Munroe, Carmen, 92, 93

Naked City, 19, 126, 147

nation/nation-state, television and, 15–16, 122–23, 169n42

naturalism, 127, 144–45, 157

NBC, 138

neoliberalism, 125, 150

Newcomb, Horace, 8

New Labour government (Blair), 83, 98

Newman, Kim, 103

Newman, Michael, 188n24, 189n43

new neighbors, notion of, 21, 73, 87–90, 181n53

news: Baltimore broadcasts, 116, 186n3; BBC London broadcasts, 70, 71, 72, 73; television studios, 9–10, 10

Newton, Darrell M., 87, 88, 181n53

New York, 5, 19, 126, 129–30, 165n3, 167n15

Nichols-Pethick, Jonathan, 129, 136, 138, 190n54

Norman, Barry, 43

Northern Ireland, 13, 178n4

nostalgia, 74, 102, 112, 185n97

realism, 127, 147, 190n63
Reith, John, 70
Richard, Jean. See *Maigret* (Richard)
Richards, Jeffery, 76–77
Ripper Street, 73, 102, 184nn87–88;
audience knowledge, 107, 108–9;
cast and characters, 106–7;
forensic procedures, 108–9;
production and marketing, 104–5,
183n80; progressive vision, 112;
version of London, 105, 108
River, 185n98
River Thames: in *EastEnders* credits,
85, 86; as a London landmark, 65,
67; *Our Mutual Friend*, 78, 79, 80,
80–81; transformation of south
bank, 114, 186n104
Rothenburg, Adam, 106
Run, 84, 185n98

Samuel, Raphael, 76, 83, 180n38
Sandbrook, Dominic, 62, 179n13
Scannell, Paddy, 179n12
Schaffer, Gavin, 87, 88, 90
Schreiber, Pablo, 159
Schwarz, Bill, 88
Secor, Kyle, 132
Seidelman, Susan, 5, 167n14
serial narratives, 149
series/seasons, definition, 165n1
sex: attractions in Paris, 43–44, *44*,
45, 48–50; in European art cinema, 60, 177n73; in 1960s Britain,
62; in *Ripper Street*, 106
Sex and the City, 168n28; location
shots, 1, 165n3, 167n15; series duration, 167n14; title sequence, 5
Sherlock (2010 series), 74, 183nn74–
76, 185n96; location shots and
pace, 103–4, 105; title sequence,

65, *66*, 67–69; twenty-first-century
setting, 102
Sherlock Holmes. *See* Holmes, Sherlock (fictional character)
Short Cuts (1993), 98
Simenon, Georges, 27, 43, 171n3,
174n28; Estate, 170n50; *Inspector
Maigret* novels, 20, 55–56; relations with the BBC, 28–29
Simenon, Mme. (wife of Georges),
28, 31, 172n11
Simon, David, 124, 128, 186n3; writer
for *Homicide*, 126–27
sitcom, 12, 117, 163; burden of representation in, 94–95, 97; classic
settings, 91; new neighbors aspect
of, 89–90; "racial," 90
sixties decade, 62
slavery, 119, 190n50
soap operas, 15, 85, 123, 135, 163,
188n24
Solnit, Rebecca, 166n11
Sopranos, The, 7, 100, 122, 123–24,
149, 191n65
soundtracks, 32, 45, 85, 92
space: in *The Corner*, 142–44, *145*,
146; domestic, 51, 91; generic, 37,
158–59; place, 22; and power, 132;
public, 3, 94, 132; as socially constructed, 143–44, 149; television, 9
Stanton, Gareth, 182n60
storytelling, 12, 23, 99, 117, 149, 163;
serial, 23, 117
Sullivan, John, 91, 165n1, 170n44,
182n62
Summerson, Sir John, 179n20

Taunton, Matthew, 6
Tayler, Eric, 36, 174n34
television, etymology, 3